Mystical Journey

Books by William Johnston

The Mysticism of "The Cloud of Unknowing"
The Still Point
Christian Zen
Silent Music
The Inner Eye of Love
The Mirror Mind
The Wounded Stag
Being in Love
Letters to Friends
Mystical Theology
"Arise My Love": Mysticism for a New Era

Translations

Silence by Shusaku Endo
The Bells of Nagasaki by Takashi Nagai

Mystical Journey

An Autobiography

William Johnston

ORBIS BOOKS

Maryknoll, New York 10545

Founded in 1970, Orbis Books endeavors to publish works that enlighten the mind, nourish the spirit, and challenge the conscience. The publishing arm of the Maryknoll Fathers and Brothers, Orbis seeks to explore the global dimensions of the Christian faith and mission, to invite dialogue with diverse cultures and religious traditions, and to serve the cause of reconciliation and peace. The books published reflect the views of their authors and do not represent the official position of the Maryknoll Society. To learn more about Maryknoll and Orbis Books, please visit our website at www.maryknoll.org.

Library of Congress Cataloging-in-Publication Data

Johnston, William, 1925–
    Mystical Journey : an autobiography / William Johnston.
        p.   cm.
    Includes index.
    ISBN-13: 978-1-57075-675-7 (pbk.)
    1. Johnston, William, 1925– 2. Jesuits—Biography. 3. Mysticism—
Catholic Church. I. Title
    BX4705.J64A3 2006
    271'.5302—dc22
                                                                            2006009468

For Alexander William Johnston
with
Great Expectations

Contents

Preface..ix

1. The Black North 1

2. Across the Sea 9

3. War 17

4. Back to Belfast 22

5. The Pious Novice 29

6. The Jesuit Marriage 34

7. To Dublin 41

8. The Bog 48

9. The Lure of Asia 56

10. Japan 63

11. The Shack 70

12. More Theology...77

13. Enlightenment in Rome...84

14. The Search in Brussels 91

15. The Search in Asia 98

16. The Mystery of Endo..105

17. Dialogue with Zen..113

18. California, Here I Come! 121

19. Zen and Mysticism..129

20. Knocked into Conversion 137

21. Greene and Lonergan 144

22. The Coincidence of Opposites..151

23. Oxford and All That 159

24. To the Philippines..166

25. Serpent Power or Inner Fire? 173

26. The Song of Songs 179

27. O Guiding Night!..187

28. Toward an Asian Spirituality 194

29. The Struggle in the Cloud..201

30. The Mystical Way..206

31. From Ego to Self..215

Acknowledgments 221

Index 223

Preface

I WAS BORN in the midst of terror.

Yes, I emerged from my mother's womb in Belfast, Northern Ireland in 1925, at a time when Protestants and Catholics were fighting like cats and dogs. Protestants, with the help of the British army, were determined to maintain their ascendancy. Catholics with equal vigor were determined to fight for freedom and for their religion. My parents were in the Catholic camp, and the old IRA was in my blood. The institutional church, it is true, did not openly support violence, but bishops and priests and sisters quietly understood how the Catholics felt. Quite often they just said nothing.

While I was still a small boy, my family moved to Liverpool, and although my education was English and my speech was awfully, awfully English, I was Irish Catholic to the marrow of my bones. The war broke out, bringing terror from German planes, and we Johnstons sat around the wireless, as we called it in those days, listening to Winston Churchill ruthlessly advocating slaughter and demanding unconditional surrender.

When I came to Japan in 1951, things were different. The Japanese had suffered from two atomic bombs and felt it was their mission to warn the world that such conflagrations must never occur again. The cry "No more Hiroshimas! No more Nagasakis!" echoed throughout the country from Sapporo in the north to Kagoshima in the south and on to Okinawa. The atmosphere of the country was strongly pro-peace. I could even say that "Peace" was the religion of Japan.

Decades later came the nuclear crisis and terrorism raised its ugly head throughout the world. Thinking people began to say that the only way to peace was through the religions. Islam, Buddhism, Christianity, Judaism, and Hinduism were still powerful influences. Could they cooperate and save today's civilization from destruction? In 1986 the charismatic Pope John

Paul II invited religious leaders from all over the world to pray together for peace at Assisi. This was a turning point in the history of humanity.

When I came to Japan there was little talk of interreligious dialogue. Our sole aim was to convert Japan to Catholicism. However, one missionary had recognized the wonderful culture of Buddhism. The German Jesuit Hugo Lassalle, who became a Japanese citizen and took the name Enomiya (meaning "temple of love"), practiced Zen as a Christian and eventually taught Zen for Christians throughout the world. Lassalle saw that the Western spirituality he had learned, all in the upper levels of the conscious mind, paid little attention to the deeper unconscious. Only mystics like Meister Eckhart, the anonymous author of the *Cloud of Unknowing*, and St. John of the Cross had delved deeply into the unconscious to which Zen quickly led the meditator. And so Lassalle devoted himself unhesitatingly to the practice of Zen.

I myself was deeply interested in mysticism and was practicing contemplative prayer that I had learned from *The Cloud of Unknowing* and St. John of the Cross. Though I did not follow Lassalle literally, I saw that he was part of a tradition that included great men like Dom Bede Griffiths in India and Thomas Merton in the United States. I wanted to be part of that tradition.

Then in 2005 the Swiss theologian Hans Küng came to Tokyo to receive the Niwano Peace Prize from a Buddhist sect for his teaching of a *global ethics*. I had already been asking myself if we could teach a *global meditation* based on the Assisi meeting of Pope John Paul II, who had said that the exigencies of peace "transcend all religions." And I still ask myself if we can develop the pope's thought in such a way that people throughout the world—with or without religion—will be willing to sit together in silence, faithful to their own beliefs but united in a great love for peace and for the earth. This is part of my message in this book.

And so I moved from my Belfast bigotry to advocating a global meditation that calls for cooperation and communion between religions of the world. Yet I must honestly confess that purification of the unconscious comes slowly. I still need release from the anger and religious prejudice of my childhood. I see that this will come only from the deep conversion of heart that all religions speak of: "Blessed are the peacemakers, for they shall be called the children of God."

1
The Black North

AN INDIAN FRIEND ONCE TOLD ME that if he ever came to write his autobiography he would call it "My Cup Overflows." Alas, my friend Tony died tragically in a bus crash and his autobiography never saw the light. Much as I would like to follow his example and make my autobiography a hymn of praise, I cannot do that while my story remains in Ireland. I must turn my eyes toward Asia where I see the rise of a new, mystical Christianity that, in dialogue with Asian spirituality, will wonderfully serve the world.

But first let me reflect on my early days in Northern Ireland.

I was born in Belfast in 1925. I learned that James Craig, later known as Lord Craigavon, prime minister of the Stormont Parliament, called his government a Protestant government for a Protestant people. His successor Basil Brooke boasted that he didn't have a Catholic around his place because Catholics were 90 percent disloyal. There was some truth in this. The northern six counties—"the black north" they were called—were divided into Protestant districts and Catholic districts. The Protestant ascendancy held the money, the property, and the good jobs, while the Catholic minority were hewers of wood and drawers of water. "Croppy, lie down" was the slogan of the Stormont Government.

I was born in the Falls Road, the heart of the IRA district. My parents had lived in another area that was too dangerous for Catholics, and so they swapped houses with a Protestant gentleman who lived in the Falls and wanted to get out. This was in 1921 when the violence was at its height. When the Protestant gentleman got out, my parents with their two babies moved in.

When I was born, things had simmered down and even the Falls was relatively peaceful. But I heard stories, terrible and frightening stories,

My parents, William Johnston and Winnie Clearkin, on their wedding day in Belfast, 1918.

of the cruelty and violence of the so-called troubles.

My parents, like almost all the Catholics in the Falls, supported the rebellion against the British and sometimes gave shelter to IRA gunmen. My mother was proud that Hugh McKelvey, a prominent IRA leader, had spent a night in our house. Not surprisingly, we were raided by the military and the police. My mother told us of how she once said in exasperation, "What are you looking for?" And the Scottish commander replied: "Guns, Madam, guns! We know there are guns around; but we can't find them." My mother belonged to the women's division of the IRA, known by its Gaelic name, *Cumman na mBan*, and when the soldiers came banging on the door she would drop her incriminating badge into a bowl of cream before letting the intruders in.

There was also a good deal of laughter and fun. Between our house and that of the family next door, whose name was Close, there was a secret door so that, even when there was a curfew, the families could play cards. "Leo Close was a great mathematician," my father used to say. Sometimes when the soldiers came and it was not safe for the men to remain in the house, they would creep into the neighboring little garden that was used for making headstones for graves. One time my father found himself sitting under a headstone that read: "Sacred to the Memory of William Johnston."

Then there was the story of my mother's brother Phonsie—our Uncle Phonsie—a true blue, an admirer of the Union Jack, who had spent his life as a doctor working in British colonies in Africa. Unknowingly he carried guns across Belfast with his golf clubs.

And guns there were. Close to our house was a big Protestant cemetery. One time the rowdy "Protestant crowd" returning through the Catholic area to their homes began to sing a famous anti-papal song, "O Dolly's Braes," and to dance in the street:

> The song we'll sing
> Is kick the pope
> Right over Dolly's Braes.

My father was standing at the window looking out. Three shots rang out; and three of the dancers fell dead on the street. The sudden change of mood in the crowd was awesome as they fled back to their home in the Shankhill Road.

At the center of the conflict was hatred for the pope. The Protestants shouted, "To hell with the pope!" The Catholics sang about "the panting heart of Rome" and "God bless our pope, the great, the good."

The two big houses still stand at the bottom of the Whiterock Road and terrible scenes of violence were to continue, even at the end of the twentieth century. In my time there was a broken window at the top of our house, the glass having been shattered by a bullet. My mother refused to have it fixed. She wanted it to remain as a memory of what the British had done in our country.

BUT LET ME GET BACK to our family.

I was the youngest of four boys. After my mother had given birth to three sons, she was hoping for a girl. Years later she told me how, when she got the news about me, she clenched her fists in bed and said, "Another boy!" But this initial rejection quickly changed to love, and I was thoroughly spoiled. I had a peaches-and-cream complexion and red curls which, after they were cut, my mother kept in a box. "I would love to paint that child," said James Craig, a famous artist.

At the age of two and a half, however, I got diphtheria ("dip" it was called) and Dr. Robb saved my life by putting a tube into my throat. One of my earliest memories is of jumping up and down in the taxi going home and everyone laughing.

My mother's family was quite traditional. Her father, Thomas Clearkin—"Pa" she called him—was born to a well-to-do farming family in County Monaghan. It was said that if one of the boys went out to milk the cows he would end up in America. Pa, however, went to the little town of

Larne where he became the principal of the Technical School, a wonder for a papist. He married Mary MacErlean from Cushendun and they had seven children. The two boys became doctors and all five girls became teachers. The Clearkins, my poor father's family thought, were awful snobs.

My mother, Winnie Clearkin, was very intelligent. She earned a degree in mathematics from Queen's University at a time when women were supposed to wash the dishes. But at heart she was literary rather than mathematical. She loved Wordsworth and the romantic poets and she had a flair for writing. She was also musical and loved Beethoven.

At the teachers' Training College in the Falls Road, run by the Dominican sisters, my mother got in with a group of pious yet nationalistic girls. And it was there that she joined the women's division of the IRA. She was crazy about her Pa. "He was a great man," she often said.

My father's family, the Johnstons, were more plebeian. Born in Leeson Street at the bottom of the Falls Road, my father was the youngest of a large family, two of whom died in the Battle of Jutland in World War I. A poor boy, my father first sold newspapers and then worked his way up, eventually earning university degrees in commerce and in law. In addition he was an athlete who ran the mile.

My father was literary also. He loved to read us Rudyard Kipling's *The Jungle Book*, and he was forever quoting *Hamlet*. Getting up from a siesta he would say: "I will arise and go now, and take a cup of tea." But deep down he was a workingman and he always voted for the British Labor Party.

ONCE MY FATHER'S ELDEST SISTER, my Aunt Mary, said to me: "Your great, great grandfather was a bigoted Orangeman." I innocently mentioned this to my mother who said hastily, "Don't tell that to anyone!" Then she drew herself up and said proudly, "*I* am completely Irish." Like all the Irish, she was descended from kings. In her case the kings were the Four Masters, great writers whose name was something like Cleary. Her cousin was a Jesuit historian, John McErlean, who traced his family back to the Scottish Highlands, claiming that it had originated in Ireland.

Later my brother Kevin studied the Johnston history and found to his embarrassment that the original Johnstons might have been Scottish soldiers who had come to Ireland to drive the natives to hell or to Connaught. Then one of these soldiers fell in love with a papist colleen; and that was that.

Brought up in a violently Republican atmosphere, my loyalist name was always an embarrassment. My brothers were Thomas after Pa; Kevin

The Johnston boys, Tom, Kevin, Eamon, and baby Billy.

after Kevin Barry; and Eamon after De Valera. But I was William Johnston! Was I named after William of Orange who crossed the Boyne? When I, the fourth boy, was born, it seems that my father said definitively, "This one will be called after me. William and no second name." His father was William and the name was widespread in his family.

Much later a Jesuit teacher in Liverpool laughed at me and said, "A weak-kneed lowlander." I never forgot that. And my Jesuit master of novices was at first astonished at the arrival of this Protestant novice from the North. "Your cousin John McErlean was a Catholic," he mused. Others asked if my father was a Catholic.

If only my name had been Patrick O'Connell or Michael O'Rourke!

Only decades later did I become proud of my ecumenical blood and ashamed of the IRA atrocities. I began to see sterling qualities in the Scots Presbyterians, qualities that the Catholics needed. The Scots Presbyterians were efficient, hardworking, honest, and sincere, compared with the easy-going, soft-spoken, devious southerners with their blarney. Let me here make a brief digression.

Visiting busy and bustling Hong Kong before its return to mainland China in 1997, I asked a Spanish friend, "Why is Hong Kong so efficient and prosperous while Macau is a mess? "That's easy," he said. "The British were Protestants and the Portuguese were Catholics."

He said a mouthful there.

WHAT BROUGHT MY PARENTS TOGETHER was music and literature. My mother first met my father when she heard him sing in the choir of St. Paul's church. "Who is that fellow who sings so beautifully?" my mother had asked. They fell very much in love—though they fought a lot, it seems—and after marriage they toured Ireland, my father singing Irish songs in his rich baritone voice and my mother playing the piano.

At home we had sing-songs with my father singing *Annie Laurie, Love Thee, Dearest,* and *Eileen Alana.* After singing his solo, my father would wave his hand as conductor and we would all sing the chorus: "Soon I'll be back to the colleen I adore...." At the end, my father would sigh, "My singing days are over."

Yet there was a Freudian tension in the family between the Johnstons and the Clearkins, and I was on the Clearkin side. I can recall—I must have been two or three years of age—furiously pushing aside my father's grisly chin and shouting, "Go away, Daddy. I want Mummy." This became a standard joke in the family, but I suspect that my father was deeply hurt. Again, I can remember crying in the dark, with only a little red light shining, until my mother came to console me. At another time, I had a dream that I will never forget: a slim man, dressed in black with a top hat and a walking stick, bounced cheerfully into my room when I was in bed. I screamed with fear and my mother came to embrace and console me.

On holidays we often visited Cushendun and went out on boats with the fisherman whom we called "John o' the Rocks." "The boat'll fall. The boat'll fall," I used to scream. At other times my father, when he was still young and vigorous, would pick us up in his arms and run into the stormy sea. I can remember screaming with fear.

For schooling I went first to the kindergarten of the Dominican Convent in the Falls Road. Here my mother had many friends both among the laity and the nuns. I remember particularly a Sister Mary Pius whom my mother and her sister called "Pie." As a boarding girl my mother thought of becoming a nun and loved to kneel in the chapel at night before the red sanctuary lamp and the Blessed Sacrament, watching the nuns come in and out. Besides being a member of the IRA, my mother was a member of the Third Order of St. Dominic. She was buried in the Dominican religious habit.

After marriage she got a part-time job, teaching in the Dominican school. One time, at some celebration, the bishop asked, "Who is that woman?" (My mother claimed that he knew her well and was putting on an act.) And when he was told that she was Mrs. Johnston he said "Mrs.? She should be at home taking care of her children." And my mother was fired.

But Winnie Clearkin was something of a feminist before her time; and she got a job at the Methodist College. She was a born teacher and wherever she went and however busy she was, she always found a teaching job.

BUT THE IRISH WAR! Was it a religious war? This is a question I have been asked again and again in Japan where the fighting between Irish Catholics and Protestants is a major scandal.

I have sometimes said that it was not a religious war but a war between the local Irish and the invaders from England and Scotland. But deep down I know that it was also a hangover from the old religious wars in Europe. "Remember 1690!" when the Protestant William of Orange defeated the Catholic James II at the Battle of the Boyne. And even further back Oliver Cromwell had quoted the Bible, "The Lord hath delivered them into our hands," when he descended with his Roundheads to slaughter the Catholics of Drogheda. And then there were the penal days and the Mass rock, and "No Pope Here" and "Home Rule is Rome Rule."

My family supported the rebellion. And we took it for granted that it was a just war, even when we did not use that terminology. Although the church condemned the violence, the priests, particularly the Franciscans, always found an excuse to absolve the gunmen. I recall my father showing me a picture of an Irish soldier in a green uniform sitting in a prison cell, his rosary dangling from his hands. And underneath were the words: "Blessed are they who suffer persecution for the sake of justice, for theirs is the kingdom of heaven." It was dangerous to have that picture around during the so-called troubles.

Was this, then, a war of the poor against the rich, of the persecuted against the persecutors? Was it a just war? Even after I read and loved Mahatma Gandhi, Martin Luther King, and the Dalai Lama, I maintained a grain of sympathy with the IRA, no matter what awful atrocities they committed. "Scratch the surface of the Johnstons and you'll find the IRA," said a nephew of mine somewhat cynically.

Although this is an autobiography, I cannot help skipping a few decades ahead to speak about my conversion to total non-violence. This is an important issue about which I will speak at greater length. Here let me refer simply to my indebtedness to three women.

The first is the Nobel Peace Prize winner Mairead Corrigan Maguire whom I met in Tokyo at the time of the Gulf War. Born in Belfast and horrified by state violence and injustice, she had asked a priest if it was right to take a gun and to fight. "Pray about it, Mairead," the priest had said. So she went to church and sat down before the crucifix. Quite clearly there came to her the message of Jesus, "Love one another. Love your enemy. Thou shalt not kill. Do good to those who hate you." And then she understood what Christianity is all about.

Two things struck me about the non-violence of Mairead. The first was that it was *active*. She became the organizer of massive peace demonstrations all over Ireland. The second thing was that it was deeply religious. It was the outcome of a mystical experience before the cross. Enough is enough! No more war!

The second woman was Dr. Priscilla Elworthy, director of the Oxford Research Group, who visited Tokyo in 2003. Traveling to Baghdad before the war she brought back a detailed proposal for peace, which went to Tony Blair, the British media, and the United States. Yet no one published it except *The Guardian* and the Quakers in the United Kingdom. Herself a Quaker, Dr. Priscilla is open to all religions; she sees a world-wide uprising of people questioning the very validity of war. A worthy recipient indeed of the Niwano Buddhist Peace Prize.

The third woman was my mother. As time went on she grew out of her narrow nationalism and became more and more cosmopolitan. Finally, she became radically pacifist. When she was old I heard her bitterly criticize the IRA for its cruel bombing in Britain. "But didn't my mother tell me of the atrocities of the British soldiers who smashed into our house on the Falls Road?" I asked.

She just smiled.

2

Across the Sea

WHEN THE IRISH FREE STATE was set up in 1921, my father, being a civil servant, had the option of getting a job in Dublin. This, however, he refused. He had a wife and two children, a growing family, and this new Irish State, he thought, had no future. So he decided to stay with John Bull. I'm not sure that my mother ever forgave him for this. She had a great love for Dublin and she saw her friends go south, get the good jobs, and forget about their suffering compatriots in the North.

After some years, when he already had four children, my father was transferred to Holyhead in North Wales. It sounded like a God-forsaken hole and my father sat up at night composing letters to the civil service commissioners asking to remain in Belfast, but it was all to no avail. And so, in 1932, when I was seven years of age, we moved to North Wales.

I sometimes wonder at the wisdom of Divine Providence. Had we stayed in Belfast, how different my life would have been—and how much poorer! As it was, we settled down rather quickly in the UK. While remaining Irish to the core, I soon spoke with an English accent and found English friends.

I still recall the glorious scenery of Holyhead with the so-called mail boat coming into the harbor. The breakwater, instead of protecting the harbor, stretched out in the wrong direction into the sea. The architect, we were told, committed suicide when he realized the awful mistake he had made.

One incident stands out in my memory. Eamon de Valera, president of the Irish Republic, was passing through Holyhead on his way to London. As he got off the mail boat, the Welsh crowd were shouting, "Boo . . . boo . . !" My mother, who loved Dev and had brought her children to the boat to greet him, ran forward and shouted, "Up Dev! Up Dev!"

My mother's friends were astonished at this outbreak of Irish nationalism. Dev, it should be noted, was an excellent mathematician, a brilliant politician, and a deeply religious person. A leader of the Irish rebellion of 1916, he escaped the British death penalty only because he was an American citizen, born in New York of a Spanish father and an Irish mother. Instead of being put to death, he was put in prison where he served the Catholic Mass every morning.

WE SPENT JUST ONE YEAR in Wales, and a wonderful year it was. The summer was magnificent and large numbers of relatives, both Johnston and Clearkin, came to visit us and to swim at the beautiful beaches of North Wales. I recall how we all walked arm in arm to Triarder Bay singing, "My bonnie lies over the ocean, My bonnie lies over the sea . . . ." We also saw Conway Castle and LLandudno and other places that I cannot now remember.

But the problem was school. Eamon and I attended the Catholic elementary school and we were altar boys. Kevin, who was older, went to the Protestant college that we called by the strange name "Cubbie." Tom remained in Belfast and went to St. Malachy's College. My parents by all means wanted a Catholic education for their children, so my father applied to the civil service for Liverpool and there we went.

LIVERPOOL QUICKLY BECAME a second home for Eamon and myself, and we sang, "Take me back to dear old Liverpool. Knock me off the car at Norris Green . . . ." Our family settled into a Catholic Irish ghetto at Aigburth and the priests from St. Charles Church visited us regularly to play cards and to have fun. When Tom and Dad played bridge against the priests, Dad would say it was the church against the state. There were also in the neighborhood Franciscans and Benedictines.

Yet the atmosphere was English. My mother was astonished when a priest in his homily said that we are all like Nelson, putting the telescope to our blind eye. And when my cousin Yvonne came to stay with us (she was a cousin on the Johnston side and I was very jealous of her and persecuted her), she refused to go into the Franciscan church because the Union Jack was floating over it. "That's a Protestant church," she said.

As for my mother, she looked down on the bustling Lancashire crowd "with the industrial revolution written all over their faces." Strange to say, my father adapted most easily to England. One time, while on holiday in Ireland, the adults, including a Republican friend, were discussing Irish unity. "What would you say to a united Ireland under England?" asked my father. The republican friend blessed himself hurriedly and said: "Jesus, Mary, and Joseph!"

Tom, Kevin, and Eamon went to the Jesuit college, Saint Francis Xavier's, popularly known as S.F.X., while I, the baby, went to St. Charles elementary school run by a a tyrannical Irish nun called Mother Monica. She faithfully kept the British externals and on "Empire Day" we all gave glory to the glorious Empire, marching around the yard singing, "What is the meaning of Empire Day?" The meaning, of course, was that "our heroes bold in the days of old" had done wonderful things that were never to be forgotten.

In school we had to report on whether we had been to confession on Saturday and to Mass on Sunday. And God help anyone who missed Sunday Mass! We also learned by heart the Westminster catechism and were able to chime off all the answers. How much religious experience was in this I do not know.

I myself learned to pray with a little red prayer book called *Close to Jesus*. For me, this Jesus was the Eucharist. I was fascinated by the mystery of the tabernacle in which Jesus was really present. Later I came to understand the words written on the altar cloth: *Magister adest et vocat te* (The Master is here and calls for you) and I loved to pray. One Christmas my mother gave me a present of *Merry in God* by Charles Doyle. This was a life of the holy Irish Jesuit Willie Doyle written by his brother who was also a Jesuit. Willie Doyle, in some strange way, recited thousands of holy ejaculations every day. I did not quite understand this, but I saw that this man was deeply in love with Jesus. A chaplain in the first World War, he was killed instantly by a shell.

Later, as a novice, I read the definitive life of Willie Doyle by Alfred O'Rahilly. This was impressive. But the Jesuit superior general was not impressed—Willie Doyle once plunged naked into a bed of nettles as a manifestation of his love of God—and the canonization process was duly crushed. Much later I came to read Bernard Lonergan about "being in love with God" and how one's being becomes being-in-love. This impressed me a lot and I came to see Willie Doyle as an example of one whose being was being-in-love. His influence on me was very great.

While my brothers went to S.F.X. on Saturday mornings, there were no Saturday classes at my elementary school. And so at that time I used to crawl into my mother's bed and listen to her stories about George Bernard Shaw, William Butler Yeats, and other great writers. In fact, most of my education came from my mother. She taught me how to play the piano. She introduced me to Dickens. How I loved *David Copperfield*, with Dora and Little Emily and Steerforth! And then the romantic poets Wordsworth and Keats and Shelley! I lived in my own world, somehow aloof from the other members of the family.

One time, as a small boy, I was cycling thoughtlessly and was hit by an oncoming bike. "You fool!" shouted the other cyclist. When I was picked up I had a big gash in my leg, and blood streaming out. I still remember how my mother took me in her arms and ran around distracted and crying. The injury was not in fact serious, and Dr. Reynolds fixed it up with five stitches. But I stayed home from school, and my mother took me to the cinema to see *Lost Horizon* with Ronald Colman. This made a big impression, especially when the beautiful Tibetan girl flees from Shangri-La with her lover and overnight becomes an old, old, dead woman. "Look at her face! Look at her face!" screams the young lover, and the camera focuses in on the aged, wrinkled face that had been so startlingly beautiful. The distraught lover runs out and we hear the pistol shot that brings his life to an end.

I still like to watch *Lost Horizon* on video. It is always inspiring.

My parents were not happy when we children went to the movies. Mum was nervous about nudity and sex. Dad agreed that most pictures (the word "movie" was still American and not used in Britain) were semi-pornography and he was worried about "the germs and one thing and another in those overcrowded cinemas." One time a little fellow came up to my father begging for "a tanner to go to the pictures." My father was appalled. "A tanner to go to the pictures? If there's another word out of you, I'll hand you over to the police."

Yet we boys all loved the pictures. My favorite star was the romantic Errol Flynn. How I loved *The Charge of the Light Brigade*. And then there was Clark Gable, the king of Hollywood, and Deanna Durbin in *A Hundred Men and a Girl*. All these stars I admired and loved. Was I an incurable romantic?

I GOT A SCHOLARSHIP to Saint Francis Xavier's and joined my brothers. They were called "Johno's" and I was "young Johno." There was some bullying in the school, but Eamon always saved me. "You leave my young brother alone."

The rector of the college was Father Tommy Roberts who subsequently became archbishop of Bombay and, after handing over his position to a local Indian, distinguished himself by opposing Pope Paul VI's encyclical against contraception. He was a cheerful, lovable little man who bounced onto the stage on the first day and proclaimed a holiday. After that we scarcely met him.

An outstanding teacher and educator was the tall, thin prefect of studies, Father Joe Woodlock. Joey, as we called him, taught Latin and Greek and religion. He was a humanist with a remarkable love for Homer and Virgil. He also had a telescope on the roof and could talk eloquently about the Milky Way. And he loved fishing.

In Latin class Joey emphasized "clear thinking." I believe I caught something of his message: people say my writing is clear and simple. Joey also taught translation from Latin to English, telling us to read and re-read and re-read the text without writing a word, until the thought of the writer was in our mind. This again influenced me many decades later when I translated Shusaku Endo's *Chinmoku* (in English, *Silence*) from the Japanese. People say the translation is pretty good. And it is.

In one religion class Joey read the gospel. And this was inspiring. Joey knew the Roman Empire and could bring to life not only Jesus but also

My class at St. Francis Xavier Jesuit College in Liverpool in 1939.
Father Joe Woodlock is at the center. Sitting at the end of the second row is
Bill Johnston, known as Johno.

Pilate and Herod and the rest. But his other religion class was a dull and drab repetition of the orthodox doctrine of the Council of Trent. And he spouted out the traditional doctrine on sexuality, which we dutifully wrote down in our notebooks. What about prayer?

Much later, when I became a priest and came into contact with other religions, I began to quote the gospel passage where the disciples say to Jesus, "Lord, teach us to pray as John taught his disciples." I then would say that Buddhists and Hindus teach meditation, Moslems teach prayer, and we teach catechism.

Perhaps this was not a completely fair criticism of S.F.X., because the Sodality of Our Lady taught us to say the rosary and we all filed into the church for Mass during which we sang the Our Father. Nevertheless, I think that quite a few boys went through the system without learning any prayer. And perhaps this is one explanation for the subsequent crash within the Catholic Church.

ANOTHER TEACHER WHO INFLUENCED ME taught history. Dr. Grace (we called him "Putty") knew all the Johnstons and when this young redhead appeared Putty said, "One of them?" And then he answered his own question: "No, you are not a Johnston. I'll call you Smith."

Putty had a fantastic grasp of history, but it was all English history. Continental Europe scarcely existed. Much less did Asia. And so we wrote glowing essays about scoundrels like Francis Drake and Walter Raleigh and the defeat of the Spanish Armada. All to the glory of England. Yet I came to love history, and when I returned to Ireland I got first place in history in the state examination.

Putty was one hundred percent English and he loved to make jokes— sometimes cruel jokes—about Ireland. "Saints and scholars!" he once said. "'Pubs and gangsters' would be better."

My mother told me not to laugh at his jokes and I (unfortunately, I believe) obeyed her. While all the Liverpool Irish boys (with names like Ryan, Connolly, Geoghegan) roared with laughter, I put on a tragic face; and Putty would point at me in glee. I was marked as an Irishman.

The awful and cruel thing about S.F.X. was the punishment. One was not punished on the spot. The teacher handed out a bill which the unfortunate student carried to the president of the college and then to the room where a young, energetic Jesuit scholastic was waiting, wielding a savage strap called a "ferula." The very sound of the thing was frightening. For quite small offences one received nine or twelve lashes, and for more serious things one could receive twice-nine or even twice-twelve.

I recall that one boy just couldn't take it. After receiving six or nine he would run around howling, with a number of jeering kids running after him. Subsequently he went out of his mind and wrote in an essay that the Pilgrim fathers went to America in the good ship Lollipop. This was a huge joke. I never heard that anyone apologized for this appalling insult to human dignity. Only Joey Woodlock, who himself never ordered ferulas, said in our house in Aigbuth: "I wish I had known about this."

Yet these Jesuit scholastics who wielded the fierce ferula were not savage. They were nice young fellows who visited our home and sang Gilbert and Sullivan. My mother loved them. Was it Jesuit obedience that induced them to practice those hideous acts? More likely there is a Freudian explanation. Young, vigorous, and celibate, the scholastics unconsciously found in the use of the ferula an outlet for their repressed energy. It is significant that this cruel punishment was inflicted only by young, celibate Jesuits, never by laypersons or by priests. Today there would be a court case.

WE ENJOYED MERSEYSIDE. Going by ferry to the Wallesey swimming pool and to New Brighton was fun. And we cycled to Chester to see the beautiful cathedral and we went to Wigan.

During the summer we always returned home to Northern Ireland. Pa still lived in Larne and we rented a bungalow so as to visit him every day. Uncle Phonsie had a fund of fascinating stories about men and animals in Africa. A brilliant doctor, he had discovered a new disease. "As if there were not enough diseases in the world without him finding another," my father commented.

"Wherever the Union Jack is flying the Catholic Church is free," Phonsie used to say. But the Union Jack flying in Larne had little to do with freedom. At night we could hear the frightening sound of the orange drums. And during the day we saw parades of Orangemen with blue suits, bowler hats, and orange sashes. "No surrender! No surrender! No surrender!" All this meant that we did not have much contact with the local people in Larne.

Aunt Mary's house in the district of Glenravel was different. There we met the locals. Mary Johnston, my father's eldest sister, had married Billy McDermott, the schoolmaster in the little town of Martinstown and they had a big family. I vaguely recall Uncle Bill, a big bald man, laughing as he lifted me up to the ceiling. He liked his wee jar of whisky. Alas, he died when I was still very young.

We mixed with the people. Eamon and I helped Hugh Kerr drive his cart to the creamery to get the milk, and we cut turf in the bog. In the evening we went to the parties in the homes to sing and dance. But in all this Eamon was more important than I. He was a Johnston and I was a Clearkin. Aunt Mary quickly saw that I was a spoiled child—"treated like a god!"

Martinstown was a Catholic town, though in the evenings we sometimes saw the infamous "B-specials"—an all-Protestant, pro-unionist police force—parading along the lane, with rifles slung over their shoulders. But Aunt Mary paid little attention to them. She always carried her rosary and at night she would say, "God, give us all the light of heaven, for it's hard to see in the dark." And on Sunday she would always make that long walk to the church for Mass and to meet the people. The church was a central place in Martinstown.

From Glenravel, Scotland was close. The speech of the people was like that of the Scots. A few miles down the road from Glenariff we had a magnificent view of the Irish Sea and the Scottish coast. "If you can see the Scottish coast, it's going to rain. If you cannot see the Scottish coast, it's already raining."

"The blue hills of Antrim I see in my dreams."

BACK IN LIVERPOOL my mother would ask: "What are we going to do if there is a war? What are our plans?" And my father would answer confidently: "There will be no war. There would be a revolution in this country if there was a war."

But he was wrong. We listened to our battered old radio (we called it a "wireless") telling us that Hitler had invaded Austria. Then he invaded Czechoslovakia. And, on September 1, 1939, he invaded Poland.

3
War

THE OUTBREAK OF THE WAR was a time of great stress for my parents. It became clear that they had different ways of thinking about everything—about money, about the education of their children, and about the future. Only on religion were they in total agreement. My father used to say: "There are enough things to fight about without fighting about religion." Yet the Johnstons and the Clearkins did come from different worlds.

My father was basically a working-class man. A civil servant, he was determined that Tom and Kevin would follow in his footsteps. Kevin even complained he had had no choice about his future. His father simply presented him with the application form for the civil service examination and said: "Sign this. If anything should happen to me, you will have to look after your mother." Tom's future was decided in the same way. And so my brothers, at the age of sixteen, left Saint Francis Xavier's and joined the civil service in London.

My mother, on the other hand, was highly educated. She never lost her interest in literature and poetry or her love for music. And she was determined that her sons would excel in mathematics or literature or science and become great. When the school reports from S.F.X. showed that they were lazy or not studying, my mother raised Cain, while my father quietly smoked his pipe or went out to work in the garden. Her Pa, whom she adored, hearing that the two sixteen-year-old boys were leaving school, gave her a hundred pounds (a lot of money in those days) and said: "Give them a good education, Winnie."

Furthermore, the IRA was still in my mother's blood. "England's hour of need is Ireland's opportunity." No son of hers would wear a British uniform and fight for the traditional enemy. I recall how Tom and my mother and I sat in Switzer's cafe in Dublin and drafted Tom's letter of resignation to the civil service. Tom then studied at the university in Dublin and became a volunteer in the Regiment of Pearse (named after the heroic Patrick Pearse who was executed by the British in 1916) in the Irish army.

Kevin, however, had his own mind. He remained in Liverpool and, with a few Irish friends, joined the British navy the day before he was due to be drafted. The next five years were painful for my mother. Remembering that Dad's brothers had died in the Battle of Jutland, she had a nervous fear that this kind of thing might run in families. But Kevin got through the war safely.

Eamon went to St. Malachy's College in Belfast.

And what about Billy?

I was just fourteen, with all the adolescent, emotional, and sexual problems of that age. I was like the Liverpool Irish boy Liam in the movie with that title. Liam (the Irish for William) pores through picture books with morbid curiosity and finally stumbles into the bathroom where his mother, stark naked, has just emerged from the bath. She screams. Liam rushes out and, overcome with scruples, goes to confession to an understanding priest who readily absolves him.

I was Liam, except that I did not find the understanding priest. I was overcome with scruples.

My father was in Liverpool at this time and my mother thought of keeping me in Ireland and sending me to one of the prestigious Jesuit colleges: Clongowes or Belvedere. She was willing to work for the money. We even visited Belvedere and talked to the Jesuit principal. But we were not impressed, and finally the decision was made that I would return to S.F.X., which had been relocated from Liverpool to North Wales. In retrospect I see that this was the best decision.

MY MOTHER AND I TRAVELED by the night boat from Dublin to Liverpool. And a terrible night it was. I see it as one of the major transitions in my life.

The boat was camouflaged and prepared for war. After all, there might be German U-Boats in the Irish Sea. I was alarmed. I said to my mother, "Look at the camouflage!" And she answered: "Well, we'll go straight to heaven." I thought I would go straight to hell.

My mother and I shared a cabin, and I was in the upper berth. All night I lay awake, imagining that I heard the German torpedo sizzling through the water to sink the boat and send me to hell. Overcome with terror, I became violently sick and vomited on the floor. My poor mother tried to clean up the mess.

When we arrived in Liverpool, my father was waiting at the docks. Floating high in the sky was the ominous balloon barrage, set to forestall enemy planes. Britain was at war.

AFTER A FEW DAYS I made my way to Rhyl in North Wales, where the college was sharing the buildings of Rhyl County School. Most of my friends were living in billets with Welsh families, but I was chosen to live with a community of students and teachers in a big mansion called Mia Hall.

I cannot say I was happy there. I was a misfit.

For one thing, I was Irish. I had imbibed a lot of pro-German or anti-British feeling in Ireland. I was not prepared to glorify the British Empire and to sing "There'll always be an England and England will be free," nor did I want to pay tribute to the old scoundrel Winston Churchill who, I heard, had been chased out of Belfast with orange peel. I did not (and still do not) like his bloodthirsty talk about unconditional surrender.

One incident brought matters to a head. I was standing by the top table in the refectory and Joey Woodlock, who was superior of the whole works, smilingly said to me in his jolly old English way, "How is Tom?" I answered straight: "Tom is in Ireland."

The atmosphere froze. Tom was in Ireland! He had deserted the cause. He had betrayed Britain. He had run away. Silence descended on the whole refectory. Joey said to me coldly: "You may go!" and I returned humbly to my place.

After that I felt ostracized by everyone, even by the women who did the cooking. One of the Jesuits said to me: "If I was in a country and got all its benefits, I would be willing to fight for it." And a fellow student with an Irish name said to me, "Johno, are you in the IRA?" I was not in the IRA but I did sympathize with two Irishmen, Barnes and McCormack, who had been executed for a bombing incident in Britain. I believed they were innocent.

Now I realize that I was Irish in England, and like so many Irish men and women I was full of anger. I have come to see that the problem of many terrorists, Catholic and Islamic, is anger. And it will be healed only by forgiveness of one's enemies, which is the central teaching of Jesus.

And forgiveness did take place. Joey in a weak moment told me that he had been born in Ireland, in Wexford. "I wonder if you are as Irish as I am," he said. He was a chaplain in the First World War and became more English than the English themselves. When I went to Ireland and entered the Jesuits, we corresponded and became good friends.

But let me return to Rhyl.

I was a misfit not only because I was Irish but also because of my interior life. The summer holidays, culminating in the sleepless night on the boat, had left their mark. After returning from Dublin to Liverpool I went to confession and that gave me deep peace. But the scruples returned. Every time a sexual thought or desire arose in my mind I felt guilty and was afraid to go to Communion. These were "impure thoughts" and receiving Communion without confession would be a sacrilege.

The Jesuit confessors, trained in the traditional theology of the Council of Trent, felt they had to ask questions about sexual sins, without bothering about unimportant things like charity. They would ask, "Did you consent?" and if I said, "No," they would say, "Not sin. Only temptation."

A Dutch student in Mia Hall told me that in a church a few miles away there was an old priest who was "tops." He asked no questions. He simply told one to say a Hail Mary, and that was that. So regularly we walked to this church and got absolution.

But my problem was not solved until much later when I read in a little Catholic pamphlet that unless you are absolutely sure (as you are sure that 2+2=4) that you committed a serious sin, then you can take it for granted that you did not commit a sin. And, when in doubt, go to Communion. This was a modern version of what I later learned in theology as probabilism: a doubtful conscience does not bind. It was a temporary solution, and it gave me peace.

As a Jesuit I learned that Ignatius of Loyola suffered from scruples in the course of his mystical life. In *The Spiritual Exercises* he writes about the person who is anxious, doubting and not doubting that he or she has sinned. This is a temptation of the evil spirit, yet it can have some advantages if it continues for a while. It may purify and cleanse the soul by freeing it from even the appearance of sin. Ignatius quotes St. Gregory: "It is characteristic of a devout soul to see a fault where there is none."

As for my night of fear on the Liverpool boat, I think this also had its advantage. I believe it led me to a new level of consciousness by bringing me face to face with death and ultimate reality. I do not invite such an experience—far from it! But experiences of this kind have come to me several times. And I cannot deny that, while counseling has been a great boon, confrontation with ultimate reality has brought me closer to God, has deepened my creativity, and has helped me to understand other people.

ALL IN ALL, evacuation to the beautiful mountains of Wales from grimy Lime Street in Liverpool was an education for us all. We took part in the cultured Eisteddfod and enjoyed the beautiful Welsh singing. There were no horrible ferulas. And, most important of all, Rhyl County was coeducational, which meant that the S.F.X. boys and their Jesuit teachers had a unique opportunity to socialize with women students.

Yet many Liverpool boys were not happy in billets and their Welsh hosts were not happy either. Moreover, for the first nine months there was no fighting, but only what was called "a phony war," so S.F.X. moved back to its apparently safe quarters in Liverpool. And then the trouble began.

I remember how we sat around our old battered radio at home, listening to the story of the German invasion of Denmark and Norway. Then came the blitzkrieg against Holland and Belgium. The Germans had *stukas*, or dive-bombers, that no one could resist; and France collapsed. The woman next door said to my mother, "Will they [i.e., the British] surrender?" My father said: "If Tom was in Dunkirk I would go out of my mind." Yet we heard Churchill's powerful speeches—"We will never surrender"—and Britain fought on.

This was a difficult time for my family. Tom's resignation from the civil service had embarrassed my father. "Let it go through," he had said when the civil service clerks showed him Tom's letter. But he had also said that if Kevin resigned he would ask to be transferred to Manchester. Still, he kept his sense of humor. Before the war we had asked a fellow to trim the hedge and he caused consternation by cutting the whole thing away. Now my father said: "God be with the days when we had nothing to worry us except the size of the hedge."

My mother was very upset. I think she was going through menopause at that time. She went to Mass and Communion every morning and she said, "God builds the back to bear the burden."

As for myself, I think the time in Wales did me good. I entered a new dimension of awareness in prayer, speaking to God in my own words without any book.

And I prepared for my return to Belfast.

4
Back to Belfast

IN THE SUMMER OF 1940 I moved back to Belfast and remained there until 1943 when I entered the Jesuit novitiate. I got letters from my friends (always with sentences cut out by the censor) telling me of the extensive bombing of Liverpool and the Battle of Britain. One friend, Francis Cullen, whose father was in the navy, wrote that he was looking forward to "getting out there to give Dad a hand." My father wrote that he and Kevin had spent a night in an air raid shelter, with Kevin lying on the concrete and sleeping like a baby through the intense bombing. Then the Germans turned their war machine against Russia, and we listened to the eloquent—Oh so eloquent!—speeches of Winston Churchill.

Belfast was part of the UK, and we too were bombed. One night in particular was very terrible. As the air raid sirens wailed out, we—Mum and Eamon and Uncle Tim and I—gathered under the stairs to escape what might come. As the bombs fell, Mum started praying the rosary and recited the *Memorare* and we all joined in and sang hymns. The windows shook and the furniture was shattered. One huge landmine descended by parachute and demolished the house opposite. I had never been so close to death. Yet this time I was not afraid. I knew I would not die. I had received the sacraments and our prayer beneath the stairs was a real expression of faith.

Now, in the third millennium, the whole thing makes no sense. We lived in a residential area. There were no military targets. Why this useless bombing? And later in the war we heard of the ruthless carpetbombing of the German cities and the cruel destruction of Hiroshima and Nagasaki. Most disturbing of all was the silence of the institutional Catholic Church. Who was listening to the Gospel? "But I say to you, love your enemies, do good to those who hate you, bless those who curse you, pray for those who abuse you."

After the bombing my father came from Liverpool and we moved back to the top of the Falls. Every day I went by bicycle to St. Malachy's College where Eamon already was boarding, having earned for himself the nickname of "Blimey" because of his English accent. Eamon and I loved St. Malachy's. It was more human than Saint Francis Xavier's, and we made many friends. The Belfast novelist Brian Moore, who was a contemporary of Eamon, has bitterly criticized St. Malachy's for its severe punishment. If he had been at S.F.X. he might have sung a different tune.

The general atmosphere in St. Malachy's was pro-German. This was a war between "the haves" and "the have-nots." And at last John Bull was beaten or, as they said in the Irish dialect, "John Bull's bate." At one time, the British government had thought of extending military recruitment to Northern Ireland, but such a massive demonstration was held in the Falls Road that the government had to back down. Again there was talk of taking the railings from the churches for armaments. The Catholic bishop said that if such an attempt were made, he might not be able to restrain his people.

Much later I recall our Latin teacher coming into class and holding up a newspaper with the headline "*Prince of Wales* and *The Repulse* Sunk by Japanese Planes in the Pacific." First-class British ships had gone down. The whole class broke out in applause, clapping their hands and stamping their feet. Yet I was not happy, because Kevin was in the British navy.

At the back of all this was the IRA. In a skirmish at the bottom of the Falls Road a policeman had been shot dead, and a young IRA man, Tommy Williams, was subsequently executed. He is still revered as a martyr in the Falls.

"The Irish broke the British Empire," my father used to say.

CHIEF AMONG OUR FRIENDS was the president of the college. Father John McMullan, known to the students as "Jakie," taught Greek, at which I did very well. Then the English teacher, Bill Conway, who later became the Irish cardinal, got us to write essays in the style of Hillaire Belloc and G. K. Chesterton and Robert Lynd. At this time I also read the novels of A. J. Cronin and the young Graham Greene. Interested in good writing, I read *The Art of Writing* by Arthur Quiller Couch. I loved the adolescent style of Aldous Huxley and roared with laughter at P. G. Wodehouse's Jeeves and Bertie Wooster.

A novel that particularly impressed me was *Come Rack, Come Rope,* by Robert Hugh Benson. This is a romantic story about a young Catholic man and woman in Elizabethan England who are deeply in love, and who sacrifice their erotic love to work together in a celibate way for the preservation of the faith: he becomes a recusant priest, and is racked and killed by Topcliffe—"As thy arms were stretched on the cross, dear Lord." His loved one gives refuge to persecuted priests.

I wanted to imitate this priest—to love a woman deeply and to sacrifice marriage for love of God.

ACADEMICALLY I DID VERY WELL. I got exhibitions and prizes, which gave great joy to my mother. And, in my last year, I sat for a university scholarship to Queen's University. But I flunked. This did not worry me, since I was planning to enter the Jesuits anyhow. Bill Conway had encouraged Jakie to get me into the diocesan seminary. "Oh, the Jesuits have their eyes on that boy," said Jakie. And Bill answered, "They have their claws in him!"

SOCIALLY I WAS A BIT OF A LONER. My mother did not want me to go "up the road" where the young boys and girls gathered to enjoy each other's company. Nor did she like me to go to the Irish dance known as a *caeligh.* I did go once with some friends from St. Malachy's and when I came home that night my mother was sitting in front of her typewriter, grimly looking through her glasses. So that was that.

Though I found some of the local girls very attractive, I could not have a girl friend: that would have been anathema. I did have close boy friends in school, however, and I still treasure the time I spent with the good Jim Keating and the controversial Des Wilson and a host of others.

Yet most of my social life was with my family and with Jakie who drove us around the Glens by car to visit his relatives and to swim in the Irish Sea. Music had an important role in my life. I loved to play the piano, and although I played some Chopin and "The Moonlight Sonata," I preferred to play by ear.

I WAS GREATLY DRAWN TO PRAYER. Every morning I went to Mass (one time my bike was swiped from outside the local church) and I loved to pray in front of the Blessed Sacrament, a practice I have never lost. For Catholic reading I devoured the little pamphlets sold in the porch of the church, being particularly attracted by the writing of Rev. Robert Nash S.J., even though he wrote so much about "holy purity" that he was called "the priest of one sin." But there were other pamphlets about prayer that taught me intimacy with Our Lord. A book that impressed me enormously was the autobiography of Thérèse of Lisieux, which I read again and again. Then I began to think seriously about my vocation.

I spent a few weeks in Dundalk with my Auntie Frank who had been evacuated there with her two babies. Her husband, my Uncle Tim, a big Kerry man, came down on weekends. I recall him sniffing, "You know what they are saying in Belfast?" And he went on:

> Be a woman, not a hen
> Stay at home
> And mind your men.

Frank sniffed back.

There were several beautiful churches in Dundalk and I enjoyed touring around on my bike, seeing them and praying in them. I was growing in friendship with Jesus.

EARLIER I MENTIONED that I was planning to enter the Jesuits. I had first considered this while I was at Saint Francis Xavier, and the thought had never left me. During these years in Belfast the idea of vocation was never far from my mind. Now I went to Dublin and made a retreat with the Jesuit Father Dicky Devane who showed great understanding for my spiritual aspirations as well as for my sexual anxieties and scruples. He arranged for me to go to hiking in the hills with the young Jesuit students who were studying at the university in Dublin.

After this I visited the Jesuit provincial John R. MacMahon, a powerful character whom the young Jesuits nicknamed "The Rock." I had also vaguely thought of the diocesan priesthood and even (in my humility) of becoming a brother. But finally, after the standard interview with four Jesuits, I made the decision to go to the Jesuit novitiate at Portarlington.

Sometimes people have asked me why I entered the Society of Jesus. I am reminded of the Japanese Dominican who was asked: "Why did you, a Japanese, enter the Dominicans?" And he answered: "I have been asking myself that question for the last twenty years."

The fact is that authentic vocation is mysterious. It comes from the true self, from the depths of the unconscious where we are in touch with the Absolute. Perhaps there is no reason for vocation. Perhaps it is an irrational (or shall I say supra-rational?) awakening. Let me explain.

In my study of Asian religions (and also my study of Carl Jung) I have come to see that every person has an ego and a true self. The ego is built up in childhood. The true self, on the other hand, is at first undiscovered or dormant and comes to birth only as one grows up. I believe that, in all the great religions, this true self is born in a semi-mystical experience. The Buddhist enlightenment, for example, comes with the awakening of the true self. Through the practice of meditation or other forms of spiritual experience, the Buddhist discovers more and more who he or she is.

Zen speaks of one's "original face," or one's "original face before one's parents were born." This is not a reference to reincarnation. It refers to the true self divorced from influences of father and mother and early childhood. It is the true self that one discovers in enlightenment. Carl Jung in a brilliant and insightful study saw some resemblance between Zen and his own "individuation."

Now, after studying Asian religions, I found references to this true self in the Bible. Jeremiah hears the words of Yahweh, "Before I formed you in the womb I knew you." Jeremiah is known and loved by God, divorced from any influence, even from his mother's womb. And the voice of Yahweh goes on, "And before you were born I consecrated you." In other words, Jeremiah receives his vocation without any external influence. Perhaps it was so in my case. In searching for my own true self in prayer and in the Gospel, I have asked myself if the voice of God spoke mysteriously in the depths of my being when I decided to become a Jesuit.

I have found the question "Who am I?" running all through the Bible, as when Jesus asks his disciples, "Who do people say that I am?" and "Who do you say that I am?" The fundamental question of biblical theology is "Who is Jesus?" And "Who am I?" is the second question. This question I have asked myself many times in the presence of God.

The ego, of course, is always present. And in my case the influence of my mother was very great. She wanted me to be celibate; she wanted me to be a Jesuit; she wanted me to be a writer. In short, she wanted me to do all the things she could not do because she was a woman. I can well understand priests who wake up at the age of forty and realize that their vocation was their mother's vocation, coming from the ego that was formed in early childhood. And then they feel obliged to ask if their true self wants to jettison celibacy and marry the woman they love.

In my case, however, while the influence of my mother was very great, the root of my vocation goes deeper than my mother. From early childhood I have had a mystical strain that carries me beyond my immediate surroundings to a deeper reality. I have been in touch with my true self. I had a special awakening in that terrible night I have described on the boat from Dublin to Liverpool. At that time, something new was born in me, and I have continued to have spiritual awakenings through similar experiences throughout my life. Even though I have often ignored the rules, I have never thought seriously of leaving the Society. And I believe that this is because my vocation was rooted in my true self.

All this makes me think that Christian moral theology could well be centered on the search for the true self rather than on obedience to the rules. People could be encouraged to find their true self by emptiness or detachment or prayer—by letting go of clinging to created things. This is the way of Meister Eckhart and the mystics. It is the *nada* (nothing) of St. John of the Cross. It is the way of Zen. It is the way of the Gospel. Would not this be more human than obliging people to use the words of the catechism and excommunicating them if they fail to do so?

IN SEPTEMBER 1943 I went with my father to Dublin. We said good-bye and my father gave me his blessing. Then I took the train to Portarlington and a taxi to the Jesuit house in Emo. I gave the taxi driver all my money (it wasn't much anyhow), thinking I would not need money during my noviceship.

My father spent the night in Dublin. Later he told me that he went for a bottle of Guinness with an old friend whose son was a Jesuit. My father said he was sad because his son was entering the Jesuits. "Sad?" asked his friend. "Don't you realize that the Jesuits are the aristocracy of the Catholic Church?"

My father liked that. He often smiled and quoted his friend's remark: "Don't you realize that the Jesuits are the aristocracy of the Catholic Church?"

That was in 1943. Whether or not we were aristocracy, we Jesuits dominated the Catholic Church from Trent to Vatican II. With our vow of special obedience, we were at the right hand of successive popes. Jesuit schools and universities educated thousands in Europe and America. Jesuits were spiritual directors to

With my father in Dublin the day I went to the Jesuit novitiate in 1943.

princes and kings. Jesuits were leaders in moral theology, dogmatic theology, and spiritual theology. The Spiritual Exercises were the spiritual fare of priests and monks and nuns throughout the whole world.

But now, in the third millennium, both the Catholic Church and the world have changed. I wonder about the future of this aristocracy of the church.

5
The Pious Novice

THE IRISH JESUIT NOVITIATE was a grand mansion in the little village of Emo, the very center of Ireland. It had extensive grounds, with yew trees stretching down to a lake in which novices could swim in the warm summers and skate in the cold winters. There were bees and beehives, providing a rich diet of honey for the community. The surrounding countryside was beautiful.

All this may sound luxurious, but the life of the novices was austere, insecure, and isolated. We were like Buddhist monks who leave house and home and everything to follow the way of Buddha in what is called *shutte*. Only we Christian novices had left everything to follow Jesus in obedience to the words of the Gospel that "the one who hates not father and mother, yea and his own life also, cannot be my disciple."

When I arrived in the novitiate there were between thirty and forty novices. They had been more numerous, but some had left because they were unable to endure the daily rigors. This was a life that could be sustained only by one who had an authentic vocation and a real call to prayer.

I was immediately introduced to the white-haired novice master John Neary, who was in his fifties but looked ancient. He had been a missionary in Hong Kong. Then in New York he had broken his leg in a traffic accident, so he walked with a slight limp. He was assisted by a younger Jesuit whose main job was to make life unpleasant for the novices. And this he did rather successfully.

After a short probation I was given a Jesuit gown and introduced to the community, a pleasant group of young men, some of whom would later became close friends of mine. In the novitiate, however, we were always in groups, sometimes talking in Latin, obediently speaking about the "topics about which ours may speak in time of recreation." Apart from Barney O'Neill and myself who were from Belfast, and Brendan Woods who was from Armagh, the novices were soft-spoken South of Ireland youngsters who had never crossed the border into Northern Ireland and knew nothing, and cared little, about their rugged fellow countrymen in Ulster. In some ways I was a foreigner. The novice master quickly saw this and said to me, "Don't take these South of Ireland people seriously!"

A second-year novice, Brother Dennis O'Connell, was my *angelus*—that is to say, my "angel"—who taught me the practicalities of noviceship life. I was assigned to a room with five other novices. Each of us had a table and a prie-dieu and a bed. On the table was a big Bible—the Douay version—in which was a sheet of paper with the words, "Passages of the Bible which novices are not permitted to read."

Every minute of the day was regulated. The bell wakened us at 6 AM and we rose immediately to wash and dress and to make an hour of prayer—kneeling for fifteen minutes, standing for fifteen minutes, sitting for fifteen minutes, and kneeling again for ten minutes. Then came Mass, celebrated by the novice master and followed by fifteen minutes of thanksgiving. And then came breakfast.

Let me here say that I found this hour of prayer in the morning to be of supreme importance, not only as a novice but throughout my life. Without boasting I can say that I have observed this practice all my life and it has been the greatest treasure I received in my noviceship. I learned to pray, and without this prayer I could not have persevered. In the novitiate it was supplemented by two fifteen-minute examinations of conscience and thirty minutes of prayer in the evening before the Blessed Sacrament. But let me return to the order of time.

After breakfast we went out for voice production, that is, singing, humming, breathing, and so forth. Then there were indoor works, outdoor works, reading of a big tome on spirituality by Alphonsus Rodriguez, an exhortation by the novice master, and the reading of the life of a saint. We were all given a knotted cord called a discipline with which we flagellated ourselves on certain nights, while the head novice in the room recited the *De Profundis*. We also were given a small chain that we put on our arm or on our leg as a means of mortification. In addition to this, there were small rules about not going up or down the stairs two at a time and not using our umbrellas as walking sticks. Then there were rules of modesty, which told us to observe custody of the eyes and to be careful of how we walked.

There were certain "experiments" in which we visited the sick or worked in the kitchen. But by far the most important experiment was the thirty-day retreat during which we went through the Spiritual Exercises of St. Ignatius. Let me speak briefly about the Exercises.

I confess that it is not easy for me to speak about the Exercises, since I have been fighting with them all through my Jesuit life, always searching for authentic Jesuit spirituality. The Exercises, as we got them, were a series of meditations that led to union with God. They began with "The Principle and Foundation," which told us the meaning of life. Then we were told to renounce all sin and to follow Jesus Christ in a meditation called "The Kingdom of Christ." Then came the meditation called "The Two Standards," in which we reflected on the standard of Jesus and that of Satan. There followed a meditation on Jesus utterly humiliated. Here we were invited to follow this Jesus in what is called "the third degree of humility." Then came meditations on the passion and death and resurrection of Jesus; and finally the Exercises reached a climax in an offering ourselves completely to Jesus. Here we novices sang vigorously "Take, O Lord, and receive my whole liberty, my memory, my understanding, and my whole will, whatever I have and possess." It was a total oblation made with great joy and enthusiasm.

We made these meditations with "the three powers of the soul," that is to say, with the memory, the understanding, and the will.

These Exercises, practiced once in the noviceship, were a great grace for me. The problem was that after a short time in the novitiate and a few subsequent years I felt drawn to a new and different form of prayer. I felt called, in a way I could scarcely resist, to recite an ejaculation or a mantra such as the word "Jesus" or "Sacred Heart of Jesus, in Thee I trust," and later I recited "Come, Holy Spirit." I recited my mantra again and again and again with great joy. Moreover, I was entranced by a little book on the "Jesus Prayer" written by an Eastern monk.

Saying this prayer I would sometimes feel drawn into a deep silence or emptiness without any words at all, like the prayer of St. Paul who, in the Epistle to the Romans, tells us that his prayer consists in "sighs too deep for words." Where was the Kingdom of Christ? Where were the two standards? Where was the third degree of humility?

Fortunately, there was in Emo a retired Chinese missionary whose name was Father McDonald. "Pa Mac," as we called him, taught Latin and went on walks with the novices. He was deeply contemplative and spoke constantly about the French Jesuit Jean-Pierre de Caussade who taught "the sacrament of the present moment." One should live in, and get grace from, the present moment throughout the day.

In the novitiate, moreover, there was a little library of spiritual books. This is where I found the book on the Jesus Prayer. I spent most of my free time in that library, reading books about prayer. I read everything I could get my hands on, particularly about progress in prayer. The Carmelite mystics (wisely, I believe) were not in our library. But I read Joseph de Guibert, Garrigou Lagrange, Columba Marmion, and a host of others who let me see that the affective prayer in which I repeated an ejaculation and sometimes entered into deep silence was not exceptional. It was an ordinary part of the spiritual journey.

Nevertheless, I did not speak much about my prayer to the master of novices, feeling that he would not understand. He sometimes said that Ignatius preferred ascetics to mystics, and he told us that Father General in Rome was worried by mystical tendencies within the Society. I had a feeling that my way of prayer might lead to mysticism, so I instinctively kept my mouth shut.

Yet during my noviceship I was plagued with turmoil and panic. Why?

For one thing, I was lonely without my mother and father and Jakie McMullan, who had treated me like a little king. Here in Emo I was zero. In the South of Ireland I was a foreigner. The master of novices was as cold as ice—or so he seemed to me. I just could not like him. I began to wake up at 3 AM, frightened and trembling, unable to get back to sleep. I told the novice master tearfully, "I couldn't sleep last night," and he would smile and say, "Well, sleep tonight!" Wisely he gave me no sleeping pills and little sympathy. Yet I was afraid he would throw me out of the novitiate.

One time I could not eat the food. It was heavy as lead and did not attract me, accustomed as I was to the rationing of the war-torn North. The novices complained that I was fasting without permission. The novice master roared at me. I was told that his voice echoed down to the first floor, "You must take your nourishment or home you'll have to go!"

In all this I was able to keep my balance thanks only to my prayer, which became deeper and deeper as I repeated my mantra. With Jesus at the depth of my being and present in the tabernacle, I was at peace. Some other novices just could not take it. They left the novitiate and went home. But I was convinced of my vocation and kept on.

John Neary was master of novices for twelve years, and I believe he did a good job. He was very shrewd. He never urged novices to stay and sometimes he would even say, "The door is open," inviting them to get out if that is what they wanted to do. To me he once said, "I have never regretted persuading a novice to leave, but I have frequently regretted persuading them to stay."

I think he liked me. Once when I was all forlorn about separation from my family he said, "If only you could see them now. They are probably drinking beer and laughing, while you are weeping your eyes out here!" And on another occasion he said, "It's obvious you have no sisters! If you had sisters they would have admonished you and kept you in order!" I told this to my mother who laughed and laughed. She even told her friends about this Jesuit novice who had no sisters, to the amusement of everyone.

As I LOOK BACK on my noviceship in Ireland, I see that the strong point was that first things were first. That is to say, the main thing was our Jesuit vocation and prayer. "When you go up to university in Dublin," we were told, "be sure you keep the S.J. Never mind about the B.A."

This was good advice.

6

The Jesuit Marriage

SINCE COMING TO JAPAN I have been amazed at the similarity between Christian and Buddhist monasticism. Christian monks go East and Buddhist monks go West, finding they have much in common and much to learn from one another. While it is true that the Jesuit novitiate is not a monastery, it has taken much from monasticism, particularly the notion of total renunciation for the kingdom of God. The Jesuit novice expresses his total renunciation in the three vows of poverty, chastity, and obedience. The Buddhist *unsui* (that is to say, novice) practices rigorous poverty, chastity, and obedience, and his commitment focuses on the goal: enlightenment for self and for all sentient beings. The Buddhist vows are not controlled by canon law, but one who has put his or her hand to the plough must not turn back.

This similarity between Buddhist and Christian religious life has led to a wonderful dialogue in which I have played a tiny part. I have come to agree with those who hold that in the third millennium only dialogue and cooperation between the great religions will save our world from destruction.

At the same time, it is not helpful to ignore the radical difference between Buddhism and Christianity. The great Buddhist mystics, like Dōgen and Hakuin in Japan, were rooted in a long Oriental tradition. Even when they entered into silence and emptiness without words and concepts, the sutras and the experience of their forebears were in their blood and shaped their conscious and unconscious minds. And in the same way the Christian mystics were rooted in their scriptures and their tradition. "Thou shalt love the Lord thy God with thy whole heart and soul and mind and strength and thy neighbor as thyself" was in their blood and shaped their unconscious. And the Christian mystics did not neglect the Song of Songs. The spiritual marriage was central in their lives.

BUT LET ME RETURN to our noviceship at Emo.

The novice master's exhortations were interesting and sometimes entertaining. For him the great virtue was cheerfulness. "The cheerful man is a mortified man," he kept saying. And he quoted Shakespeare, "Assume a virtue if you have it not." This is not hypocrisy, he insisted. If you keep an exterior cheerfulness, you will have interior joy. I have never forgotten this, and throughout my life I have tried to keep smiling even when things were rough. The novice master loved to quote Tennyson, and in class he would talk about Aldous Huxley, especially his recently published *Grey Eminence,* and would laugh at Huxley's incursions into mysticism. And, of course, he greatly admired C. S. Lewis. "I pray for him," he said, meaning (for those were the pre–Vatican Council days) that he prayed that Lewis would renounce his Anglican errors and become a Catholic.

However, the aim of the novitiate was to acquaint us with the Society so that we could decide whether this was our vocation and the Society could decide whether we were suitable. For this reason it was necessary to study the life of the founder, St. Ignatius, whose biography was on our table.

I cannot say I was crazy about Ignatius. He did not have the charisma of Francis of Assisi and was not ecstatically loved like the *Poverello.* Actually, I should say that I was attracted by the *young* Ignatius who went to the Holy Land and wandered around Europe, looking a bit ridiculous. But the older Ignatius, institutional and somber, turned me off. He seemed to enjoy throwing Jesuits out of the Society when they didn't go along with his ideas of obedience. I thought he would probably have gotten rid of me. And this aggravated my fear of being dismissed, one of my principal sufferings in Emo.

In his teaching about the vows, the novice master was a man of his times and culture. Poverty, it is true, was the following of the poor Jesus: "Unless you renounce everything you possess, you cannot be my disciple." And Ignatius had told his sons to love poverty as a mother. However, in the practical order, the poverty of a Jesuit consisted in getting permission from superiors. Without this permission, everything—whether it was money or a pair of socks—had to be handed in to the community. I recall the horror of my mother who went to immense trouble to knit a beautiful sweater for me and then discovered that I had handed it in.

The superior had tremendous power. There was no dialogue and no democracy. In the novitiate we could not drink water during the day without his explicit permission. The story went that to one novice who asked for permission to drink water the novice master said, "No, brother! Drink enough water with your meals." At certain times we had to ask for "the ordinary permissions," which meant permission for everything we used.

After the noviceship, the practice of poverty was hijacked by canon lawyers, who told us how much money we could keep without sin and how much would constitute a venial or a mortal sin. The important thing, then, was to stay within the limits worked out by the canonists and to avoid sin. The danger in this was that we could become like the scribes and Pharisees, concentrating on the law and forgetting the spirit.

THE SECOND VOW concerned chastity. Of this Ignatius had written: "What concerns the vow of chastity needs no mention, since it is clear how perfectly it should be observed; that is, by preserving angelic purity in mind and in body." The novice master followed Ignatius literally: I cannot remember that he spoke publicly about sexuality. It seemed to me Ignatius meant that we must be like the angels who have no sexual life whatever. Sexual thoughts (we called them "bad thoughts" or "impure thoughts") were dangerous occasions of serious sin and were to be instantly repressed with a prayer to Our Lady. No doubt this was not the mind of Ignatius, but it is what I learned.

THE THIRD VOW, the vow of obedience, was Ignatius's ideal of *kenosis* whereby one emptied oneself as Jesus did, taking the form of a servant. In *The Spiritual Exercises* Ignatius stated the principle that "What seems to me white, I will believe black if the hierarchical church so defines." Later he insisted that a Jesuit in the hands of superiors should be like a dead body or an old man's staff that can be moved anywhere at any time. Obedience of execution alone was a poor thing; one should will and even think the same as the superior. In the novitiate a notice would go up quite unexpectedly telling us who would be head novice, who would be sacristan, who would be prefect of indoor works, and so on. Needless to say, there was no consultation. The superior had all the power.

This obedience was justified by a vertical theology from above. That is to say, the pope, the Vicar of Christ, gave his authority to the superior general of the Jesuits, who gave it to provincial superiors, to rectors, and so on. This meant that the will of the superior was the will of God and was to be followed even when the superior had given no express command. The subject could, of course, ask that the command or idea be rethought, or could make a representation with a short memorandum so that the superior would not forget. But, this done, the subject was to obey in all things, sin alone excepted.

In this whole area I recall getting a wholesome shock shortly after my arrival in Japan. I explained to a Japanese student that we find God's will in our superior. The student paused for a moment and said: "Yes, that is how we regarded the emperor of Japan before and during the war." I was reduced to silence. But I did reflect that the Nazis who pleaded innocence because they were only obeying orders were not absolved. They were responsible for their actions, as we are responsible for ours.

And then there were the rules, read regularly in the refectory during meals. The novice master told us that to break a rule was not a sin. However, the distinguished Jesuit theologian Francis Suarez said that one could not break a rule without sin, since underlying the breaking of a rule was some laziness or greed or hidden vice. St. Isaac Jogues said he would be ground to powder rather than break a rule; and the young John Berchmans was canonized because he kept the rules. We were told that someone said to the pope, "But why canonize John Berchmans? He only kept the rule." To which the pope replied, "I will canonize anyone who only keeps the rule."

DURING THESE TWO YEARS we never left Emo except to visit the sick in a nearby village. Visits from parents were permitted twice each year and at specified times we could write home (with the novice master, of course, reading all letters coming in and going out). I recall the visit of my mother and Eamon. Somehow our relationship had changed.

These were the last years of the war. While we never got a newspaper, word trickled through that the British and Americans were carpet bombing German civilian cities in thousand-bomber raids. On a walk my Falls Road anger erupted and I said to Pa Mac, "But surely this is murder." And he answered, "Of course it is murder! Crying to heaven for vengeance!" Yet I never heard any British or American bishop saying that. And later I did not hear any bishop condemning the worst bombing in human history: the nuclear destruction of Hiroshima and Nagasaki. I have heard a lot about Pope Pius XII and his silence regarding the Nazis, but I have heard no bishop condemn the ruthless unconditional surrender policy of Winston Churchill.

THE TEACHING I RECEIVED in the novitiate I swallowed hook, line, and sinker. I had no alternative. I had to accept it or get out. Moreover, I did not see it as simply novitiate brainwashing. I accepted it as the static, orthodox teaching of the Catholic Church that was to guide my whole life as a Jesuit.

But what am I to think now in the third millennium?

How the world has changed! After reading Bernard Lonergan, I have come to see that everything, or almost everything, in human life is historically and culturally conditioned. Living in the twentieth century, Lonergan saw this clearly. An immense cultural revolution, caused mainly by the rise of modern science, was turning religion and theology upside down. And Lonergan's aim was to inculturate theology in the new world.

What are we to do?

We must look to the prophets, men and women mystics who see beyond cultural and historical conditioning to the core of reality that exists in all men and all women, in all times. And in my opinion the great religiously prophetic event of the twentieth century was the Second Vatican Council, supported by a galaxy of great theologians. About this I will have more to say. Here let me simply note that I have lived through part of this revolution (I say "part" because I believe it is only beginning) and that in the novitiate I lived in a culture that was quite different from that of the third millennium.

There were some ways of thinking that pertained to a medieval European culture. There was a theology of obedience that is no longer acceptable. There was an approach to chastity that modern men and women will not accept. There was an idea of poverty that no longer attracts. There was a separation from family that modern people see as inhuman. There was a separation from the suffering of the world that would horrify modern social workers.

All this may sound critical and negative; but (and this is the important point) beneath the cultural trappings was a religious intuition that is valid at all times and in all places. This is expressed in the gospel texts, "Thou shalt love the Lord thy God with thy whole mind and heart and soul and strength," and "The one who does not leave father and mother, yea and his own life also, cannot be my disciple." In the noviceship we left *everything*. The Second Vatican Council changed a culture that was out of date but it did not change the essence of Christianity, nor did it change the essence of religious life. We must now reform the cultural and historical setting while retaining the essence.

Let me speak of the essence.

Thomas Merton quipped that the Dalai Lama had asked him if the Christian vows were going anywhere or if they were just a promise to stick around for life. No doubt the holy Tibetan was thinking of the Buddhist vow that leads to enlightenment. And he asked: "Where are your vows going?"

I believe that my vows were going somewhere. They were pointing to the hymn we sang in the novitiate: "Take, O Lord, and receive my whole liberty, my mind, my memory and my whole will, whatever I have and possess," that is to say, "Take everything. All belongs to you. I give it back to you." This is the radical detachment found in the mysticism of all the religions. And Ignatius goes on apostolically, "Dispose of them in any way according to your will," which is to say, "I do not abandon my gifts; I want you to live in me and use them as you will." And he concludes with the powerful words. "Give me thy love and thy grace; for this is enough for me." The detachment is the *nada* and this is the *todo* (all). I am praying to be filled with His love.

In short, I now see that through a lot of suffering, and through a lot of cultural baggage, Our Lord brought me in Emo to the very center of my vocation. "You have given me everything; I give you everything." This I see as marriage. But the Jesuit spiritual marriage differs from that of the pure contemplative in that it has an active dimension that is expressed in the words, "Dispose of them in any way according to your will," that is to say, "Use me as you wish."

And so, in answer to Merton and the Dalai Lama, I say that as a Jesuit I was, and am, moving toward marriage with the Word of God. I came to understand this only gradually and I was greatly helped by St. John of the Cross. The works of the holy Carmelite were not available in the first years of my Jesuit life. However, while I was studying philosophy after 1948, I got direction from a saintly Jesuit, Father John Hyde, who, I was told, had learned Spanish just to read St. John of the Cross in the original. He said to me: "Holy John of the Cross is good. But for Jesuits he has to be adapted. And to adapt a principle is not to water it down." The adaptation, of course, is found in the Ignatian words, "Dispose of them [i.e., my talents] in any way according to thy will." Here we have the call to action that is inseparable from the Jesuit vocation.

I love the poetry of the Spanish mystic and I love his spiritual marriage:

> I abandoned and forgot myself,
> Laying my face on my Beloved;

All things ceased; I went out from myself,
Leaving my cares
Forgotten among the lilies.

I left Emo in September 1945. Just before my departure the novice master said to me, "You will always need good direction—if you are humble enough to take it." Then he paused and added, "And you are!"

And so I went to Dublin to study Greek and Roman classics at University College.

7
To Dublin

I MISSED THE DUBLIN TRAIN and spent the day with the parish priest in Portarlington. He was an old man who seemed to spend a good deal of his time in bed. Anyhow, I caught a later train and arrived late at night, smiling naively and little aware of the consternation I had caused. I don't suppose the superior (whom we called "Charlie") thought I had eloped with a woman, but he was puzzled and worried. What had happened to this Belfast man who didn't even phone? I think this was typical of me. I was twenty years of age.

For the next three years Rathfarnham Castle was my home. Like most religious houses, it was a beautiful mansion with a long history that is still a mystery to me. The grounds were impressive, and eventually we young people built a swimming pool that made life livable and even pleasant. We were some forty scholastics (this was the word that Jesuits used for seminarians) and sitting opposite us in the dining room was a motley group of young priests from all over the world. They were doing their "tertianship" or spiritual year prior to embarking on their life's work. Tertians and scholastics were forbidden to talk to one another except on big feast days. Why this rule was made I do not know.

Charlie, the superior, was officially Father Charles O'Conor, known as "O'Conor don" because he was the last descendant of the high kings of Ireland. His family had wanted him to get married to keep the family line going, but Charlie, a pious man if ever there was one, insisted on entering the Jesuits. In his early days, his royal lineage was a big joke and his fellow scholastics built a huge throne for him in the recreation room. Charlie, we were told, did not appreciate the joke.

The rector was Father Hugh Kelly, whom we called "Hugo." He was a kind of mystic, and every morning when we went to the chapel at 5:30 AM Hugo was kneeling in prayer at the back. In this he has been an inspiration to me for my whole life. He was also a literary man. I recall telling him that I would spend the summer vacation reading George Bernard Shaw. His response was, "Why would you read that blasphemous old dog?" On another occasion I showed him a short article I had written on Our Lord with a reference to Shakespeare's King Henry V. Hugo was scandalized. "How can you compare Our Lord to that bragging fellow?" he asked.

After a few days I went into Dublin to apply for entrance into the university. The fellow in charge looked at my documents and told me that for people born in Ireland some knowledge of the Irish language was mandatory. I explained that I had been educated in England. He again looked at my documents and said: "You have been back in Ireland for five years. That is enough time to become acquainted with the national language." I returned to Rathfarnham and told the story to Charlie who chortled and said, "By Jove! I think I know who you were talking to!" And he fixed things up, probably with a phone call. Jesuits were very powerful in those days.

So I went to the university and specialized in Latin, Greek, and ancient history. My education in Liverpool and Belfast had been pretty good and I had no difficulty with my university classes, even though I was very tired and nervous after the trauma of my noviceship. Every day we scholastics cycled into Dublin, and I can remember standing in the bike room with a splitting headache. After morning class we had lunch at the Jesuit House of Writers in Leeson Street and made our examination of conscience in the quiet little chapel.

In Emo the novice master had told us that the so-called examen need not strictly be an examination of conscience; it was enough to return to our morning meditation in the midst of a busy day. This I did. And the examen became a time of great consolation. At first I began by recalling the presence of God. After a while, however, I came to realize that God was already present within and around me. His was an abiding presence. I repeated a favorite ejaculation such as "Sacred Heart of Jesus, in Thee I trust." I think it was at this time that I entered into a deep unitive silence. That was restful.

In the university (we called it "the acad" from the Latin *academia*) there were all kinds of clubs and activities, but we Jesuits did not take part. We were in the university only with special permission from Father General in Rome, and we were not to indulge in worldly amusements. In our own house in Rathfarnham we had a debating society, a Sodality of Our Lady, a Sacred Heart club, our own magazine, and other activities.

But it was on the long Sunday walks that we really grew to be close. In Emo we had always walked in threes, but now in Rathfarnham we went out in twos to the mountains. There we gathered together around a fire in winter, swam in the lake in summer, and returned in the evening with different partners.

From childhood I have always had friends. In Liverpool, Willie Hall and Francis Cullen and I were inseparable, and now in Dublin I again made close friends. In particular when we went for holidays to Balbriggan, Bob Kelly and I became good friends. We walked along the beach and cycled in the mountains. For me this was extremely therapeutic. Coming from Emo I had been exhausted, tired, strained, and not sleeping well. Now I began to sleep. As soon as my head hit the pillow, I was out until the next morning. I have heard of homosexual relationships in monasteries, but I saw nothing of this in Rathfarnham. We did have "particular friendships," which we called "PFs." These were emotional and, in my opinion, they were good and healthy.

There were interesting people in that community. Just before I arrived the brilliant Malachi Martin had moved on to study philosophy. It was said that Malachi would learn a new language to read a footnote. Little did we know that his future would be so tragic. In wretched circumstances he left the Jesuits and wasted his immense talents writing vitriolic books about the church. Yet the Irish Jesuits forgave Malachi and celebrated a requiem Mass for him in Gardiner Street. May he rest in peace.

In the novitiate there were certain "forbidden topics" about which we had not been allowed to speak. One of these was the discipline. Now, in Dublin, the young scholastics talked about nothing else. One bright, intelligent, and good-humored scholastic said that Charlie was a saint but a bloody fool. Calling the discipline "a doings" he rhymed:

> Charlie, I've been awful lax
> I hate those folks who whack their backs
> I'll ram their doings down the jacks.
> Charlie, what have I done now?

This reminds me of a story I heard when I was a boy at St. Francis Xavier. A student asked the Jesuit retreat giver if it was a sin to say "damn." The retreat master paused for a moment and replied: "It isn't a sin; but it is so bloody vulgar." We had a good laugh at that. Some scholastics were disedified by talk about the discipline. However, the spiritual father, Father Mortimer Glynn, said, "In France, where I studied philosophy, they used to say, 'That fellow takes the discipline with a silk stocking!'" This silenced the disedified.

I myself came in for a good deal of flack. My face was very red and flushed and I had red hair. Scholastics ridiculed me for having high blood pressure. In fact, my blood pressure was normal and the red face was caused by a hormonal imbalance, but I suffered very much from the jokes about my appearance.

Though we had plenty of friends among ourselves, we had no women friends. Charlie, I think, was afraid of women and had tremendous sexual hang-ups. No records with women's voices could be played on our gramophone. At the university a young Jesuit made funny comments meant to be overheard by the women students who were sitting in the benches just in front of us. Charlie took the occasion to give us a high-powered talk on the sanctity of sexuality and the goodness of the sexual organs.

As for myself, it was only decades later that I came to appreciate the beauty and richness of celibate friendship with women. Over the course of my life, friendship with women has helped and healed me tremendously. But I did not come to experience such friendship until long after my life in Rathfarnham.

Kevin and Eamon and my mother came to visit, and those were the few times when I had a chance to see anything of Dublin. Kevin, after leaving the navy, was not happy in the civil service. He thought he was being discriminated against because he was a Belfast Catholic. So he left the civil service and, with a grant from the British government, he studied dentistry at Queen's University. On one occasion he came with his charming girlfriend Caroline, and we had coffee and meringues in Grafton Street. As a little boy, I had known Carrie at the Dominican kindergarten in the Falls Road. Now she pointed to a scar on her forehead and said: "Do you see that scar? That came when Billy Johnston pushed me against a piano." I might have been a rough kid, but I had no memory of that. Kevin and Carrie did not get married, but later she and I became good friends.

In Rathfarnham our life of prayer was carefully regulated. Charlie was like a policeman, standing outside the chapel when we filed out, making sure that everyone was present at morning oblation and litanies and Mass, giving permission to those who wanted to sleep for an extra half hour in the morning. During meditation, made in our rooms, one of the scholastics, appointed as "visitor," opened each door to make sure that the occupant was duly praying.

I recall Hugo asking me at manifestation of conscience, "Do you give the time to prayer? I'm not asking what you do. I'm simply asking if you give the time to it." I said that I did, but I told him that I didn't like the Bible very much. I preferred *The Imitation of Christ.* "Ah, that shows a certain immaturity," he said. It probably did. It was only much later that I came to read John and Paul with great joy.

SHORTLY AFTER I ARRIVED in Rathfarnham we scholastics were given a three-day retreat by the well-known Father Ernest Mackey. He was a tall man, bald, with a red face, so that one of the scholastics called him "a walking sanctuary lamp." I found him easy to talk to and I poured out my soul as never before, telling him things I could not say to the master of novices, much less to Charlie. He asked about my noviceship and the novice master. "A bit nun-ish," he commented, hinting that John Neary was like a nun. When I told him about my difficulties he said, "Your nerves are in rags!" And he recommended what he called "the vegetative life," using the Latin *vita vegetativa.* "But you have a sense of humor," he added. "Keep that!"

Naively I told the story to Charlie, who hit the roof. "I think that Father Mackey would agree that I know you better than he does," he said. And he went on: "I presume you would not have taken your vows if you were not happy." This hurt me very much, because I had no doubts about my vocation.

We agreed that Charlie would talk the matter over with Mackey. Of course he did not know me better than Mackey. He did not know me at all. Mackey spoke to me frankly about everything, including sexual matters, and let me see that I was an ordinary young man. For this I am grateful to him.

IN ADDITION TO SCHOLASTICS AND TERTIANS, there was an "upper community" of older men, some of whom were retired, and some of whom went out regularly to conduct parish missions. I have a keen memory of one white-haired old man, Father Mulhall (we called him Muller), who crouched on a seat at the back of the chapel all day long. Muller never celebrated Mass, never received Holy Communion, and never did apostolic work. He was tortured by scruples. Hugo was kind to him and at the celebration of his fifty years as a Jesuit gave a fine speech on the biblical theme "This sickness is not until death." Hugo loved the Latin *Hic mor-bus non est usque ad mortem*. Before the end, I heard, Muller received Holy Communion and died in peace.

Yet Muller was a lesson to me. I tended to be scrupulous, especially about sexuality, and here was a man whose life had been ruined by scrupulosity. Nor was he alone. I came across a number of priests who, overcome with fear, had great difficulty in uttering the sacred words of consecration during Mass. And so I made up my mind to get rid of all scruples. Basically I succeeded. But my real liberation took place only many years later, after I had gone deep into my unconscious through counseling and read the works of Carl Jung. About this I will write later.

At this time, however, I was greatly helped by writing my journal. I had always been interested in writing, something I inherited from my father and mother. Now I began to write a page every day about my morning meditation. Soon the page became two pages and then three. Needless to say, these pages were not for publication, and I tore them up regularly. Since then I have published a number of books, but what I have published is only a tiny fraction of what I have written.

What precisely I wrote in Rathfarnham I do not now remember. All I can say is that I was possessed by what Jung calls "the demon of creativity," that my writing came out of my deeper consciousness and it was extremely therapeutic. I think I can say that the three things that healed me and enabled me to remain a Jesuit were prayer, friendship, and writing.

TIME CAME FOR ME TO LEAVE Dublin and go to study philosophy in the village of Tullabeg, known to Jesuits as "the Bog." Yet I had seen little of Dublin's fair city. From childhood I had heard glowing stories of "the Rising," and the Post Office in O'Connell Street, and the Four Courts, and the Abbey Theater. But for the past three years I had been locked up in Rathfarnham with little chance to go outside the door.

These were the years 1945–1948, when the world was learning about Auschwitz and Hiroshima, when Stalin was building the wall in Berlin, when Eastern Europe was in turmoil. But about this I heard almost nothing. Even about the running of our house I cannot remember that I was consulted about anything. These were years when the scholastics, separated from the world, were to pray and to study.

I had done well in my studies, getting first class honors in Latin, Greek, and ancient history; and that was the time when special students could spend another year in Rathfarnham getting the master's degree, the M.A. Would I be chosen?

I was not. When I met the provincial, Tommy Byrne, he said pompously, "You are good, but not first-rate." This, no doubt, he had heard from Charlie; and it was true. I was too tired and nervous to be first-rate.

However, I asked the provincial about my future, what kind of work I would be doing. He paused and said, again pompously, "Colleges! That's your work." My heart sank. The thought of spending my life in Belvedere or Clongowes knocked me out. There and then I decided unconsciously that I would get out of Ireland and go somewhere else. Of course I said nothing of this to the provincial. At a previous meeting I had asked him if I could go to France for philosophy and he had answered, "Child, you are discontented. I wonder if it is a divine discontent." So I thought it was better to leave him with the impression that I was like a dead body or an old man's staff.

I said good-bye to Charlie. After a rather rough relationship we had finally become friends. I could have told him that in Emo, while the novice master roared at me, I felt that he trusted me and even liked me. But in Rathfarnham I did not feel trusted. However, I did not say this because Charlie, filled with "the dead body or old man's staff" mentality, would not have understood.

Hugo was encouraging. "Now you are going to what I can only call a mental thrill," he said.

And so I left Dublin for the Bog, to enjoy the mental thrill of metaphysics.

8

The Bog

IN 1948 WHEN I LEFT Dublin, I was twenty-three years old. I recall quoting Milton in a letter to my mother, "How soon hath Time, the subtle thief of youth, stolen on his wing my three-and-twentieth year." Now I know that my poor mother felt the passage of time even more acutely than I did. Her children were growing up and going their own ways; and I, "the baby," the Benjamin, was far off in the bog of Ireland. Many years earlier my father had warned her: "They'll all go away and you will only have me!" Prophetic words indeed.

The philosophate was typically Jesuit. It was a large isolated mansion in the middle of Ireland, with a road stretching through the brown bog to a lake in which we scholastics swam during the summer. There was also a brown river and a canal up which we rowed big boats on our vacation days. The community was cheerful and the studies were not uninteresting. We had well-trained professors who mixed freely with the students. All in all, it was restful, and I recovered the strength I had lost in Emo and Rathfarnham. Now I am glad that the provincial, Tommy Byrne, refused my request to go to France for philosophy.

Most of the students were old Irish friends from Rathfarnham days, but we also had a number of foreign Jesuits who had come to Ireland to study philosophy and English. Some were appalled at the cold wet weather and the dull skies. One young Egyptian said to me that a day without rain was as common as a meal without potatoes. He said it in French: "*Un jour sans pluie est aussi rare qu'un repas sans pommes de terre.*" Another, a Frenchman, said he could not understand how the Irish were so cheerful when they lived in such a climate. When they had emerged from Russia in those pre-historic days they should have gone south rather than north!

Another Frenchman who was to become a good friend was more insightful. He said to me, "You have your own way. Follow it. People will criticize you, but don't mind. Go your way!" This was helpful. My Liverpool days had made their mark. Deep down I had a hunch that these would be my last years in Ireland.

Hugo had spoken of the mental thrill I would have in Tullabeg. Was it really so?

It was certainly an introduction to an esoteric world of being. Following the lead of the Gregorian University in Rome, of which we were a faculty, we were staunch Thomists holding to the real distinction between essence and existence. How we proved this or even what it means I cannot now remember.

But scholasticism taught us how to think rationally and how to *prove* things with the syllogism. "All men die. John is a man. Therefore John will die." How could one dispute it? One seasoned scholastic philosopher said confidently, "We'll smash our adversaries against the rock of the syllogism."

But some philosophers did dispute it. Preeminent among these was the eighteenth-century Immanuel Kant, whose theory of knowledge upset the applecart and created the so-called critical problem: Can we have objective knowledge about anything? At first, I did not understand Kant's idealism and was satisfied with the old wisecrack that if you smash your head against a wall you will be pretty sure the wall is there. But an intelligent French scholastic spoke of the "Kantian crisis" he had experienced before coming to Ireland. And this made me think.

My respected professor John Hyde claimed that the famous Canadian Jesuit Bernard Lonergan had answered Kant in *Insight*. But since I could make neither head nor tail of *Insight*, this did not help me much. Only when I came to Asia did I begin to see an answer to Kant in the Gospel. Then I began to understand something of that saying of Jesus that the lamp of your body is your eye. If your eye is simple, your body will be full of light.

In Japan I came to see that this eye is the third eye, symbolized by the colored circle that we sometimes see on the foreheads of Indian women. This is the eye of wisdom, in comparison with which these two eyes that we all have are like foolishness.

I began to see that the third eye is very important in Zen. If my eye is simple (i.e., "one-pointed," in Japanese *seishin toitsu*) then my whole being is filled with the light that becomes enlightenment (*satori*). And so I sat on my Zen cushion with my eyes half open and my back straight. I regulated my breathing and came to one-pointedness, and then the energy rose to the surface of my consciousness with great power. I wondered if this was an awakening of the third eye, the lamp which the Gospel says fills the body with light.

But what kind of wisdom comes from the third eye? I believe it is "the coincidence of opposites," the fact that things are and are not at the same time. This is the frightful paradox at the heart of reality, and it is well understood in Zen. The Zen master Uchiyama Kosho says that life and death are one. He is right. But life and death are also two. So also morning and evening are one, but they are also two. In short, we cannot say diametrically that something is, because it is also true that it is not. And I wonder if this is the answer to Kant.

The coincidence of opposites is also found in the Western mystics, from Nicholas of Cusa to Meister Eckhart and the author of *The Cloud of Unknowing* and St. John of the Cross. And, of course, they get it from the Gospel. I ask myself if the coincidence of opposites will take the place of the principle of contradiction as the basis of Christian philosophy.

BUT LET ME RETURN to the Bog.

Even in the 1940s there were some rebels. Joe O'Meara, professor of metaphysics and the history of philosophy, spoke of Teilhard de Chardin, Henri de Lubac, Yves Congar, and others as departing from the orthodox line of scholasticism to meet the modern mind. Well do I remember the day he bustled into the classroom and told us excitedly that Pius XII had issued an encyclical, *Humani Generis*, in which deviating theologians were brought to task.

Almost twenty years later, at the Second Vatican Council, those theologians were vindicated. Indeed, they were among the architects of a council that was the first since the Middle Ages to abandon the scholastic framework in order to speak to the whole of humanity. It has been called "Newman's Council," after John Henry Cardinal Newman, a convert from Anglicanism, who knew little about scholasticism. Furthermore, from that time the Catholic Latin Church has drawn closer than ever to the Greek Orthodox Church which was untouched by scholasticism and which preserved the mysticism of the Greek fathers.

For me personally the problem with scholasticism was that it was too wordy, whereas my life of prayer was going beyond words and reasoning and thinking into silence. I got tired of affirming and denying and distinguishing; I wanted to be at the depth of my being in the presence of the Great Mystery. We now know that consciousness is multilayered and that the greatest wisdom lies at a deep layer of consciousness where one attains enlightenment. But scholasticism, as I learned it, was all at the top level. I suppose I was looking for mysticism and the syllogism was not my cup of tea.

Nor was I satisfied with the Spiritual Exercises of St. Ignatius as they were given in our yearly retreat. These also were wordy and encouraged wordy prayer wherein one thought about some topic or imagined some scene from the Gospel and then talked to Jesus or Mary who were outside. The happiest prayer for me was after receiving the Eucharist when I was silently united with Jesus within. The Exercises, as I received them at that time, were on the top level of consciousness. "Words, words, words," as Hamlet said.

I hope I will not be presumptuous if I say that my struggle with scholasticism was not unlike that of the mystic Bernard of Clairvaux and the brilliant thinker Peter Abelard in the twelfth century. Bernard claimed that Abelard was too rationalistic, that he wanted to prove everything clearly and that his thinking could not be reconciled with Paul's claim that we now see in a mirror dimly. Here I take the side of Bernard (though I abhor his ruthless treatment of Abelard) because he took the side of mystery. Scholasticism was talking too much and proving too much.

But I had to talk to someone.

In Tullabeg there was an old priest whom we called "Cap" because he always wore a skull cap. Cap would smile and talk about the moment he received infused contemplation, though I am not sure he used that terminology. "I had it; and I knew I had it!" he would squeak with glee. We scholastics laughed at Cap and many thought him a bit gaga. But I went to see him and found someone who understood me very well. He encouraged me in silent contemplation without words, but he advised me to continue to recite the rosary and to pray to Jesus. "Too far East is West," he said with a smile, "so keep the ordinary devotions."

Then I discovered St. John of the Cross. The Spanish mystic was not in the libraries of Emo or Rathfarnham but here he was in an old beat-up translation. I spoke to Father John Hyde, professor of theodicy, who read St. John of the Cross in the original Spanish, and he advised me commonsensically: "Read St. John of the Cross. If you understand him, go ahead. If you don't, then stop!" This was good advice for me.

From St. John of the Cross I learned the signs of a genuine call to contemplation. These are that one is unable to think during prayer (or, at least, has great difficulty in doing so), that one cannot fix one's imagination on a particular object, that one wants to be alone in loving awareness of God.

I also came to see that the human unconscious contains not only wisdom but also fears and anxieties and hidden trauma from childhood that can be healed in the dark nights. But it was only much later that I came to understand the "all and nothing" and the coincidence of opposites and so many points in St. John of the Cross that resemble Buddhism. And it was only much later that I faced the challenge of reconciling Jesuit and Carmelite spirituality.

THE BOG, HOWEVER, was a mental thrill not just because of the science of being but much more because of interpersonal relations and friendship. On vacation days we went on long walks through the bog, sometimes discussing profound philosophy and at other times griping about the rector and the food. We went in twos, gathered in groups of six or eight around a fire in winter, and tried to keep warm as we ate our lunch and talked and joked. In summer a number of scholastics liked to "thud"—that is to say, swim naked—in the lake or in the brown river. The "thudding" became a characteristic of Irish Jesuits. When I came to Japan I remember meeting a German Jesuit who had studied in Ireland. With great glee he told me how at the beach he saw a naked scholastic kneeling before a newly ordained priest and receiving his blessing. St. Patrick, foreigners said, had driven the snakes out of Ireland, thus eliminating temptation!

On big feasts we went to a nearby convent for dinner and to entertain the nuns. The dinner was always delicious, with rich trifle (but no wine) and ice cream. One of our scholastics, Joe Marmion, a grandnephew of the great Blessed Dom Columba, was a brilliant pianist and musician. He put to music the beautiful poem of the Irish poet, "I see his blood upon the rose and in the stars the glory of his eyes...." Barney O'Neill sang this in his beautiful tenor voice. How well I remember the climax when Barney put all his strength into the concluding words, "His cross! His cross! His cross is every tree!" Joe and Barney were both consummate artists and the audience was awed by their performance.

They also sang Gilbert and Sullivan. I recall Barney looking up and singing with tender beauty and relish about the "pair of sparkling eyes": "Take my counsel, happy man, take and keep them if you can ... happy man, happy man!" Many of the nuns became quite gooey.

I myself sang "The Protestant Boys." As a kid I had quite a beautiful voice, but here in Tullabeg I was a flop. How could I compete with two geniuses? Besides, these South of Ireland people could not understand the intricacies of the North. They were silent and mystified.

IN MY SECOND YEAR in Tullabeg I decided to write an M.A. thesis on some aspect of philosophy that I liked. The best theme seemed to be contemplation (in Greek *theoria*) in Aristotle. With the approval of John Hyde, who agreed to direct me, I applied to the Philosophy Department of University College Dublin. However, U.C.D., as we called it, answered that since my primary degree was in classics my M.A. should also be in classics. So I decided to apply to Queen's University in Belfast. The Department of Philosophy, headed at that time by the young Cahal Daly who later became the distinguished Cardinal Daly, accepted me.

What I wrote in that thesis I do not remember, but I do recall that I wrote it with great joy and enthusiasm and it was a preparation for my future interest in mysticism. Aristotle, I realized, was not just a maker of syllogisms; he was a mystic of sorts. He spoke of moments when the human person seems like God—and then returns to his ordinary self.

Cahal Daly came to Tullabeg and we welcomed him with open arms. He liked my thesis and wrote to me that "as sure as the sun rises over Japan, so surely you will get your M.A." John Hyde, of course, who was at once a scholar and a mystic, read each chapter with approval.

And then came the crash! The extern examiner, O'Doherty from Dublin, would not accept my thesis. He turned it down.

John Hyde, all forlorn, said, "I blame myself!" Cahal Daly said the thesis was a bit pious. I myself knew I would be leaving Ireland, and I was able to laugh. I saw that my writing was not thesis-like. And when I returned to Ireland for tertianship in 1958 I rewrote the whole thing in a dull, academic style. It was then accepted. The lesson I learned for myself and for my future students was: Don't write attractively if you want your thesis accepted.

When I got to Sophia University in Japan in the 1960s I discovered that an M.A. from Queen's was not enough. I needed a doctorate. So I eventually wrote a doctoral thesis on *The Cloud of Unknowing*. But my thesis on Aristotle was in the background of all my subsequent studies.

ALL GOOD THINGS come to an end. Time came to leave Tullabeg for wider pastures. Those three years in the Bog really were a mental thrill, not because of scholasticism but because of prayer, friendship, my thesis, and the direction of John Hyde, who was to me a friend, a scholar, a mystic, and a saint.

Another significant friend was the Frenchman François Besses, who had spent some years in South India and spoke Tamil fluently. Frank, as we called him, was fascinated by Indian culture and philosophy and mysticism—so much so that he criticized the church establishment bitterly and was told to leave India. It was a terrible blow for Frank to leave hot India for cold Ireland, and he suffered sadly from insomnia. But he never lost his smile or his love for India.

My long conversations with Frank turned my eyes toward Asia. Japan was in the news. The famous Jesuit Hugo Lassalle, who had suffered in the bombing of Hiroshima, visited Tullabeg with the arm of St. Francis Xavier, asking for prayers for Japan. This prompted Father Janssens, the superior general of the Jesuits, to appeal to the whole Society of Jesus for volunteers, making special mention of the Jesuits' Sophia University in Tokyo. Japan, he wrote, would be an international

The Johnston family before my departure for Japan.

mission of the Society of Jesus, and anyone who felt called to join should write directly to him.

After talking to John Hyde and Frank Besses I wrote to the provincial, Tommy Byrne, asking to go to Japan. The provincial refused. Our personnel are already stretched, he said. We had missions in Hong Kong and Zambia. How could we afford to send someone to Japan?

Again I talked to John Hyde and Frank Besses. Then I wrote to the superior general in Rome. And that was that.

Before going to the missions we were permitted to spend a couple of weeks with our families whom, it was then thought, we would never see again. So I went to Belfast to say good-bye to my parents and family. At that time the assumption was that I would never return to Ireland, or even to Europe. My commitment to Japan would be irrevocable and forever.

9
The Lure of Asia

IN 1951, AT THE AGE OF TWENTY-SIX, I left Ireland and went to Asia. This was an earth-shaking event in my life. The Jesuits in Japan had sent me a big document from SCAP—"The Supreme Command of the Allied Powers"—giving me permission to enter Japan, which was occupied at that time by U.S. forces and ruled by General Douglas McArthur, the American Caesar. This document got me into places that would not look twice at an Irish passport. It indicated that America was top dog in Asia.

And yet, to one who had eyes to see, the tide was already turning. Yes, Japan had been defeated and utterly humiliated. But Russia was hostile. The Korean War was in progress. Mao Zedong had swept through China with his Communist army. America was threatened. I did not know then what I know now: that the decline of America actually began on August 6, 1945, when the first atomic bomb fell on Hiroshima.

To me Japan was a mystery. I had picked up a few books by Lafcadio Hearn in our library, and I had read a few articles about the atomic bomb. And that was it. My missionary education came mainly from my fellow student Frank Besses who, with his deep love for the Gospel and a remarkable appreciation of Indian culture, said to me, "Don't neglect China!" And how right he was! Many years earlier, Francis Xavier had realized that to convert Japan he first had to go to China. He had died alone on an island off the coast of China, looking toward the country he would never reach. The key to Japan, I now see, is China.

ON MY LAST VISIT TO BELFAST to say good-bye to my parents and family before leaving Ireland, I found mother's house a bit rowdy. In growing older she had made more and more friends, some of them literary people like the novelist Michael McLaverty who wrote a powerful and painful book about the so-called "troubles." His *Call My Brother Back* made a deep impression on me.

A frequent visitor was the former president of St. Malachy's College, the jovial Jakie McMullan, who laughed a good deal. But even more good-humored was a Cork girl called Biddy who came with her mother and her boyfriend. She was a doctor, intelligent and uproariously funny. Her "high powered conversation," as my father called it, shook the windows. I heard afterwards that she said about me with a touch of romance, "Isn't Billy lovely! Sure you wouldn't charge him anything!" Gerry Bourke, who was going with me to Japan, also came to my mother's house. My brother Tom went to Queen's University where he eventually qualified as a doctor. My brother Kevin had been at sea in the British navy and was now studying dentistry at Queen's; Eamon was in the London police; Billy was going away never to return. This was a hard time for my mother. I think it was the beginning of her dark night.

In all the uproar my prayer was a bit different from that of the young scholastics who studied and prayed in Dublin and in the Bog. Yet those semi-monastic years had built up something in me. Now in noisy Belfast I went to St. Teresa's church for daily Mass and spent an hour in silent meditation. During the day I went upstairs to my little room, to quietly make my examination of conscience and read a spiritual book, such as that of Dom Columba Marmion. In the evening I spent fifteen minutes in prayer before going to bed.

I had learned to recall at the beginning of my prayer that God was present. Now the sense of God's all-pervasive presence had become habitual. I experienced God as present in all places and at all times. God was present in the very depth of my being and it was not necessary to make a special act, recalling that He was with me. In short, in Belfast I discovered that I was becoming contemplative in action. What a grace that was!

BACK IN DUBLIN I made final preparations for the journey. Gerry Bourke and I left Dun Laoghaire by "the mail boat" with five Irish Jesuits bound for the mission in Hong Kong. We sailed to Holyhead and got the train to London where we stayed in the Jesuit Southwell House. This was my first time in England since 1940 during the war. Now I was a foreigner. I was an Irishman in England.

After a few days in London we left by train and boat for Amsterdam where we got the plane—an old, rickety propeller plane it was—for the first leg of our air journey to Hong Kong. Ordinarily Jesuits went by

P&O liner from Southampton, but our Jesuit procurator had messed things up and we ended up going by plane. For me this was a fortunate mistake.

In Holland we stayed with the Jesuits, who gave us a great welcome. At that time Holland was a vibrantly Catholic country with lots of Jesuits. Their recreation room was filled with cigar smoke, so dense that I could scarcely breathe. Yet this was a thrilling experience, because it was my first visit to continental Europe about which I had heard so much. Some Dutch Jesuits, referring to the Korean War, said, "Courage! Courage! You have great courage!" It had never occurred to me that going to Japan was courageous.

In 1951, just before I left Ireland for Japan.

From Amsterdam we flew to Rome. This again was a thrilling experience. I remember standing in St. Peter's and looking up at the high ceiling and thinking (how naive I was!), "Now I am at the heart of Christendom!" I saw Pope Pius XII carried gloriously into the cathedral in a big chair and blessing the crowds of people who kept shouting, "*Viva il Papa! Viva il Papa!*" We visited the *Gesu* and saw the room in which St. Ignatius died. Little did I realize that this splendid medieval Roman Catholic Church was on the brink of the greatest crisis in its history, and what the future held no human person knew.

We left for Abadan and went East of Eden to Bombay.

Now I was in Asia. We stayed in St. Stanislaus College. Don Donnelly, the Irish rector, guided us through the crowded, poor, yet colorful streets of Bombay. Then we left for Calcutta and Bangkok. Finally we arrived in Hong Kong.

Flying down between those massive mountains to the airport at Kai Tak, I knew that the long journey would soon be over. After this we would travel to Tokyo. But before that we spent a pleasant week with the Irish Jesuits, traveling through the extraordinarily busy streets of Hong Kong, crossing the bay on boats of the Star Ferry (how they reminded me of my childhood trips across the Mersey!) and driving by car through the beautiful New Territories. We drove to the very border of Red China, that mysterious country, the great enigma of that time. A few naive Jesuit students had wandered across the border, only to be seized by the Red Guard. After some days (during which these three hefty men were confined to one little room with a bucket) they were released through negotiation; but this was a shock to the Jesuit community.

NOW I REALIZE THAT I was in a world that has since died. The Irish Jesuits were part of a huge Western movement that imposed its culture and even its languages on Asia. Thus the Dutch in Indonesia, the French in Vietnam, the Portuguese in Macau, the Spanish in the Philippines, the British in India, and the Americans in Japan—all so proud of their native countries that they tried to instill their cultures, their customs, and even their languages in the countries they conquered. After all, the West was superior.

And often the missionaries followed suit. Vietnamese children stood to attention to sing "God bless France!" Japan became known not as the "Far East" but as the "Far West." And the special characteristic of the Catholics in these countries was that they were also subject to Rome. Sometimes the missionaries adopted a language of "conquest." They were conquering lands for Christ.

Hong Kong was a British colony. The Irish Jesuits ran schools that were financed by the colonial government. Classes were taught in English and many of the students emigrated to the English-speaking world. Some Jesuits also taught in the university. Moreover, the Jesuits ran the seminary in which young men from all over China learned Latin and studied St. Thomas Aquinas. Some Jesuits spoke Cantonese, which they had learned in a language school in Canton prior to the arrival of Mao Zedong, but for most Jesuits, knowledge of the Cantonese language was a luxury rather than a necessity.

When I arrived in Hong Kong, however, signs of change were already evident. Asian nationalism was rising. On the eve of October 1, 1949, Mao Zedong, with a pride that sounded like arrogance to the West, declared, "The Chinese people, one quarter of humanity, have stood up. . . . No one will ever humiliate us again." Who had humiliated the Chinese? Surely it was the British, the French, the Portuguese, and the Japanese colonials; but the missionaries too had played their part, cooperating with the colonials, and frequently sharing their sense of superiority.

Now the Communist People's Liberation Army occupied Shanghai and Canton and came to the very gates of Hong Kong.

In one of the most fierce persecutions in Christian history, comparable only to the fierce persecutions in medieval Japan, foreign missionaries were imprisoned and expelled, while the Chinese priests and Catholics were executed or sent to prison camps. This persecution reached a climax with the horrendous Cultural Revolution in 1966 and lasted until the death of Mao in 1976. The heroism of the Chinese church at this time will be one of the great pages in Christian history.

Meanwhile, the Christian missionaries were beginning to realize that the only approach to Asia was that of three great Italian Jesuits: Alessandro Valignano, Matteo Ricci, and Robert de Nobili, who had put all their efforts into adapting to Asian culture. These missionaries had learned the Asian languages, studied Asian philosophy and literature, and tried to see Christianity in an Asian context.

Now in the twentieth century a Jesuit "visitor" to Hong Kong insisted that all the Irishmen learn Cantonese fluently. In the mainland all Chinese Jesuits were to stay and face martyrdom: there would be no running away. A couple of Chinese Jesuits, I have been told, were already on a ship in Shanghai preparing to leave the country when the Jesuit superior, a foreigner, got on board and ordered them back. They obeyed and joined the church controlled by the Communist government.

As I made my way to Japan it became clear to me that Christianity is deeply rooted in Asia and has a big future. In the 1980s, with a group of priests and sisters, I visited the Island of Sancion where Francis Xavier had died. When the people of the surrounding islands heard there would be a celebration of the Eucharist, they rowed into Sancion in big black boats, whole families fasting from midnight in order to receive Holy Communion. I was immediately reminded of the Nagasaki Catholics who held tenaciously to their faith for centuries without priests and without foreign help. Many, it is true, quietly stepped on the crucifix to satisfy their persecutors, but in the mid–nineteenth century, when missionaries were again allowed into Japan, they found a small band of Christians who for almost three hundred years had secretly preserved the essence of their Christian faith. And this faith was equally evident in Nagasaki in 1945 when the atomic explosion liquidated the city. Christianity will never be uprooted from China and Japan.

In 2004 I again visited China to give a "contemplative retreat" in Hong Kong. Most of the retreatants were Chinese laymen and laywomen, although there were also foreigners who had come down from mainland China to make their retreat during the Chinese new year. All were deeply contemplative. I was also invited by the local bishop to give some talks to the seminarians on prayer. These were translated from English to Chinese by a Chinese sister who was fluent in both languages.

Now it is clear that the main challenge confronting the Chinese church is reconciliation between the underground church and the so-called open church. This latter, founded in the 1950s to work with the government, was at first branded as "schismatic," but church authorities decided that this terminology was not appropriate and now assert that there is one Catholic Church in China with two "directions" or thrusts.

WHAT DOES ALL THIS say to us today?

After more than fifty years in Japan I begin to see that Asia will accept the successor of Peter not as a wielder of power but as a symbol of unity. The successor of Peter will always be in union with bishops throughout the world who acknowledge him as "the first among equals." This will surely bring great unity to Christianity and will increase Christian influence everywhere. Here is an area in which Catholics can enter into more and more friendly dialogue with Protestants in Europe and America, with Orthodox Christians in Greece and Russia, with Asians in India and China. Can we not hope that a "universal Christianity" will then enter into dialogue with Islam, Buddhism, and Judaism to work for peace in the world?

GERRY BOURKE AND I boarded the British Airways plane at Kai Tak, heading for Japan.

Mount Fuji, symbol of Japan.

10
Japan

I FIND IT DIFFICULT to write about Japan without emotion. I have lived in this country for more than five decades. When my Japanese friends threw a party and wrote a book to celebrate these wonderful years, I said that Ireland is my mother and Japan is my wife. And doesn't the Bible say that a man shall leave his father and mother and cleave to his wife and the two shall be one? They are one indeed. But even the most successful marriage can be stormy, as was that of my parents; and my marriage with Japan has had its stormy times.

It all began on the plane as we approached Tokyo's Haneda airport. A fellow nudged me and pointed out the window. And there it was: Fuji San floating majestically above the clouds! Fuji, the symbol of Japan! How many times since then have I trudged through the mountains looking at the snow-capped peak that brought me into the presence of God. One time I saw a group of children climbing out of a bus and exclaiming, "Fuji San! Fuji San!" Surely there was something religious in this.

We landed at Haneda airport and were met by two Jesuits: the Spanish Francisco Hermoso and the American Jack Slater. It had been six years since the war had ended on the Feast of the Assumption 1945. Japan was still poor, and we were jolted this way and that as we drove along the potholed road to the language school. But we finally got there—to Taura, near the big U.S. naval base of Yokosuka that I had heard about from my brother Kevin, who had been on the first British ship to enter Yokosuka after the war. His ship's previous assignment (which it never carried out) had been to mine the Yellow Sea. Then the atomic bomb exploded over Hiroshima. That awful bomb may have saved my brother's life.

We arrived at a large complex of buildings that had belonged to the Japanese navy during the war and was now a Jesuit language school and a high school. Japan was an international province of the Society of Jesus. This was the wish of the superior general Arnold Baptist Janssens, who had heard from Father Hugo Lassalle about the wonderful possibilities for conversion to Christianity in this country. And so Gerry Bourke and I found ourselves in the middle of a motley, yet cheerful, group of Germans, Spaniards, Italians, Americans, Canadians, and Belgians. The rector was from the United States, his assistant was from Spain, the prefect of studies was from Germany, and the language of the community was English.

In Ireland I had always liked "the foreigners" and I quickly made good friends here. I particularly remember the brilliant Italian Pier Paolo Del Campana who was an extraordinary linguist and became a Buddhist scholar. Pier Paolo was not unlike Matteo Ricci in his high ideals for missionary work in Japan. He completed for me the missionary education I had begun with Frank Besses in the Bog. Then there was my friend the charming Spanish Carlos Norena, whose later departure from the Jesuits made me very sad.

I was incredibly bad at the language. In fact, I learned Japanese well only much later, when I translated *Silence* by Shusaku Endo and *The Bells of Nagasaki* by Takashi Nagai. Here in Taura, divided into groups of four or five, we learned orally from Japanese professors who came to the school each day. Every week we had a written examination that I usually flunked.

I was tired and nervous. The change from Ireland to Japan was almost more than I could take. The climate was warm and muggy and made me perspire. Millions of mosquitoes, or so it seemed to me, surrounded my net at night. Gerry, with whom I shared a room, seemed to snore and I could not sleep. I told this to the rector and he immediately switched me to a single room and gave me a sleeping pill. This was very decent, but he put a Mexican Jesuit into the room with Gerry and the relationship was not good. Poor Gerry protested that he didn't snore and that I had been imagining the whole thing!

Each week we had a free day on which we were given money to go out and see Japan. This was great. The scenery around Yokosuka is magnificent, particularly in October and November, and we went in twos to the island of Enoshima or to Hayama from which we could look across the clear blue sea at snow-covered Fuji San rising up into the cloudless sky. We used our stumbling Japanese to talk to people and found them uniformly cheerful and kind.

I recall once visiting a school with Pier Paolo. The headmaster kindly invited us into his room and offered us green tea. He had been some kind of commander in the Japanese army. "But it's different now!" he said with a smile. As we left I thanked him for the green tea. "Not at all!" he said in impeccable English. "We call it 'the cat's urine.'" Pier Paolo and I really laughed at that.

I THINK THE POLITE and repressed Japanese genuinely liked the back-slapping Americans. Douglas MacArthur was a hero until he said at a dinner in the United States that the mentality of the Japanese was like that of thirteen-year-old adolescents. He lost clout on that. But his treatment of the emperor of Japan won him popularity. Then there was the Yasukuni shrine, the central symbol of Japanese nationalism and the burial site of many of Japan's greatest soldiers. MacArthur, the rumor has it, was going to raze this shrine to the ground and was stopped by a German Jesuit, Bruno Bitter, whom he consulted about many of his decisions. This also won McArthur popularity and after the Occupation the grateful Yasukuni shrine gave Father Bitter a prize.

I never heard bitter criticism of the annihilation of Hiroshima and Nagasaki. I heard no criticism of the brutal bombing of Tokyo, when one hundred thousand civilians died in a single night. Wounded and broken ex-soldiers sometimes boarded the trains and cried out, begging for money. Disheveled, dressed in old uniforms, carrying crutches, these poor fellows represented millions of Japanese soldiers who were ridiculed, beaten, tortured, and killed throughout Asia. They got little sympathy from the world. From their own people I heard only the cry for peace. The Japanese said: "We have suffered from the atomic bomb. We know what it is. Our vocation is to ensure that Nagasaki will be the last atomic bomb."

THE LANGUAGE SCHOOL was a typical, pre–Vatican II Jesuit house. The rector, John S. Forster, was a tall, middle-aged, smiling American who had come to Japan immediately after the war. He had made desperate efforts to learn the language, and even wanted to teach it. But anyone who tries to learn Japanese after the age of six will have problems. Much more will one who comes in middle age.

Forster, who was greatly loved and respected by Arnold Janssens, ran a tight ship, much to the chagrin of Pier Paolo, who was his head novice. Forster read carefully the letters of the community, both coming in and going out, sometimes asking questions about the content. Every six months he had us do a manifestation of conscience. We were told to write an inventory of all our possessions and show it to him. He looked at it and graciously gave permission. This was holy poverty. It gave some people great satisfaction, he said, to know that they had permission for everything they had. And, of course, the bells rang for prayers and litanies and everything that happened in daily life. A "visitor" was appointed to look into our rooms at time of prayer, as was the custom in the Society at that time.

We took it for granted that the American victors were right: "the cruel Japanese" were justly punished by the International Military Tribunal of the Far East. Douglas MacArthur exercised the strictest censorship. Takashi Nagai's book on the Nagasaki bomb was published only on condition that it contain an epilogue about Japanese atrocities in the Philippines. I heard no mention of the morality of the bomb. I confess with shame that I, like most of the Jesuits, jumped on the American bandwagon and even envied those who had American citizenship.

Across the road from the language school was the high school run by four German Jesuits collaborating with excellent Japanese teachers. Some of the Germans had come to Japan as novices, and they spoke Japanese fluently. They had endured the horrors of the war, and they knew Japanese life and culture. Led by the energetic Gustav Voss, who had studied in America, they wanted to build a first-class school that would get students into the prestigious Tokyo University, previously known as the Imperial University, which educated the leaders of Japan. To call it a mission school would not help, so they were content to call it "Eiko High School."

The Germans were embarrassed and irritated by Spaniards in long black cassocks walking in the campus, reciting the rosary. It was not that the Germans were against religion. In fact they gave extensive religious instruction, baptized students, and celebrated Mass. But they did not want the school to be known as a religious institution. That was their missiology. But it did cause misunderstanding and tension. In the refectory we read Charles Boxer's classic book *The Christian Century in Japan*, which describes two approaches to mission: one, that of the Spanish Franciscans, who preached the Gospel openly and baptized; the other, that of the Portuguese Jesuits, who took a more subdued approach. These two visions of missiology have remained in Japan until this very day.

LANGUAGE STUDY CAME to an end. Two hard years! "If we had put this amount of time and energy into German or Spanish," quipped Pier Paolo Del Campana, "we would be university professors by now! And look at us!"

Leaving the language school was like escaping from prison. Only my prayer helped me to survive. Not that my prayer was very special. But I could enter into a deeper level of consciousness where I experienced rest and peace in the presence of God. In addition to this I had friends, and the spiritual father, an old German with a long beard (we called him *O-Hige Sama* which means "The honorable bearded one") could listen to me with understanding. He was radically conservative, but that did not worry me.

The problem was, What next? Where would I go?

Eiko wanted an English-speaking teacher, but not me. The Germans were looking for an energetic Japanese-speaking young Jesuit who would teach hours and hours of English, march around the grounds with the students, and go to the mountains and the sea. I was a nervous wreck. So they chose Gerry Bourke, and I went to Sophia University. To teach in Sophia had been my dream. This was what I had always wanted and I was happy indeed, especially as Pier Paolo Del Campana and Carlos Norena were going with me. And when I arrived, I found myself in an exhilarating community with Frank Mathy and Tom Johnson and all kinds of students.

Sophia University (known in Japanese as Jochi Daigaku) had been founded at the beginning of the twentieth century with the blessing of Pope Pius X and entrusted to the German Jesuits. It was to be a beacon of Christian light and wisdom for Asia, but when I arrived in 1953 it was still a small school, Catholic and friendly. We Jesuits wore black suits and Roman collars, and the priests were called "Father," even by students speaking Japanese. All the students and teachers were male. When I walked through the campus each student would greet me with a slight bow and a smile, "Good morning, *sensei*!" (The Japanese word *sensei* means teacher or master.)

My job was to teach English and to be sub-prefect of the student dormitory, which consisted of a group of Quonset huts in which the students froze in the winter and perspired in the summer. My boss in the dormitory was Franz Bosch, a vigorous, rotund German Jesuit who spoke brilliant Japanese and whom the students called "Oyaji," which is the Japanese for "Daddy." He gave religious instruction, baptized a lot of students, and lectured to enormous numbers on the ethics of sex. He was a wonderful man, and his statue can be seen on the campus today. But I could not like him and felt uncomfortable when he was around. No doubt this was my fault, not his. Later a counselor quietly observed that

I was never comfortable with anyone who had authority over me. Was that why I had been uncomfortable with my master of novices?

Several years later, Franz came to Yokohama to see me off when I left by boat for tertianship. Little did I realize that I would never see him again. He died suddenly at the age of forty-eight while I was in Ireland.

AT THE FOOT OF MOUNT FUJI our Jesuit community had a small house to which we went to rest and relax. We would play cards and go for long walks. One time I was there with Tom Johnson and Carlos Norena and a number of the brethren. In the morning I walked outside to make my meditation, but since the sun was hot I returned and continued my prayer in a small room at the front of the house. And then it happened. There was a deafening crash like awful thunder. In fact, it was a landslide in the very place to which I had been walking. The brethren rushed out of the house. Where was Johnston? They came back, and I walked serenely out of the front room. What a relief!

For me this was an experience. Yes, God had preserved my life, and for this I was grateful. But what shocked me was the equanimity with which the brethren had accepted my apparent death. "Well, there's nothing we can do about it," said one of my friends, as he raised his camera to take a picture of the place where I seemed to lie buried.

My stay at Sophia University was brief but eventful. The provincial procurator Bruno Bitter got into trouble with the authorities about money and even spent a week in jail. This was too much for the provincial, Paul Pfister, who had a great love for the Society, the church, and Japan. His health broke down and he was seen wandering around the campus late at night.

A change had to come. The obvious man to be provincial was the saintly mystic Pedro Arrupe, who was master of novices and had vigorously trained the young Japanese Jesuits in prayer and in the spirit of St. Ignatius. A Spaniard who had studied theology in Germany, Arrupe was loved and respected by almost everyone. Well do I recall the day he walked into our refectory and took the provincial's seat, to the joy of the Spaniards and the chagrin of some Germans. He often spoke to the young Jesuits and he had vivid and humorous stories about the war, during which he had been imprisoned. After the war he met an ex-soldier who, having treated him harshly, was ashamed to meet him. "Not at all!" said Arrupe. "Thank you! It was for this that I came to Japan!" The ex-soldier's eyes filled with tears.

I was in Sophia for only a few months when Arrrupe sent for me. "There is a place in the theologate," he said. "Would you like to go?" I had reckoned on another year at the university but I said, "It's okay with me. One way or the other." The next day I got a letter telling me to go to the new Japanese theologate in Shakujii. Pier Paolo was going also. I recall how we went for a walk and he said enthusiastically: "Bill, in three years we will be priests!"

We were priests in three years. But Tom Johnson left the Society and got married. Carlos Norena left the Society and got married. Pier Paolo, after a long stay in Japan, got Alzheimer's and returned to Italy. What will happen to me I do not know.

But my short time at Sophia University went well. I recovered the energy I had lost in Taura. I began to speak Japanese. I met interesting students and professors. I got a glimpse of Japan.

"In three years we will be priests" was good news indeed.

11

The Shack

AT SHAKUJII a new era in my life opened up. How different I would be if, like Gerry Bourke, I had returned to Milltown Park in Dublin for those four years of theology. Instead, I went to the new theologate at Shakujii (I had studied philosophy in "the Bog" and would be studying theology in "the Shack") where the infant Jesuit province was planning to train hundreds of students, secular and religious, who would gloriously convert Japan to the Gospel. Thousands of German marks and American dollars had been poured into splendid buildings. But God had different plans. It was the Filipino nannies who would teach the Japanese children to make the sign of the cross, while our plush unused buildings would crumble to the ground.

We were the same motley crew as in the language school, except that we now had Japanese Jesuits studying with us. The head scholastic, Hayashi Shogo, had been an orderly in the Japanese army. Baptized and trained by Pedro Arrupe, he entered the Society and eventually became a provincial superior. Then there was Kono Yoshinari who had been a mechanic in a Japanese submarine, Oki Akijiro who was preparing to be *kamikaze* pilot when the war ended, and Tsuchida Masao who had been in the Japanese navy. These were excellent men, formed in the Japanese army to lay down their lives for their country and their emperor. An Irish Jesuit in Hong Kong told me that when the Japanese army occupied their school, a soldier quite unexpectedly asked him in Latin: "*Tu es sacerdos?*" ("Are you a priest?"). And, calling him into a small room, the soldier laid aside his rifle, knelt down, and asked for absolution. That soldier was a seminarian.

In our theologate there was a lot of talk about inculturation, but Rome kept tight control of what was taught. Our courses in dogma, moral theology, canon law, sacred scripture, spirituality, and the rest were little different from the courses taught in New York or Dublin or anywhere else in the universal Catholic Church.

For higher studies, promising young Japanese were sent to Rome or to Germany; only a few of the theology students were interested in Buddhism and the Asian tradition. After all, there was an index of forbidden books, and we were not allowed to read anything that might endanger our faith. To read a Buddhist book one needed permission from the bishop. We were right and they (even the Protestants) were wrong. We must have no truck with them. And nothing must change! What a shock to the church and to the world was the Second Vatican Council's appeal for dialogue.

Within the framework of that time, our professors were reasonably well qualified. For them, the important thing was to teach accurately the truth of the Catholic Church outlined in Heinrich Denzinger's book, which set out clearly the definitive church teaching that everyone had to believe. If anyone questioned an article of faith, God help him. The fate of George Tyrrell, the Irish modernist who was excommunicated and died outside the church, was hanging over our heads like the sword of Damocles. Someone might write to Rome! I was told that Pope Pius XI, asked to dispense a priest from his vow of celibacy because the priest would marry anyhow, said: "*Pereat!*" ("Let him perish!"). Such was the climate of fear that enveloped theological study at that time.

However, a young professor who had studied in Rome brought some changes. He began his lectures not with Denzinger but with sacred scripture. This caused alarm and consternation. Then one day he asked the question (only asked!) if, since bread and wine were the foreigners' food in Asia, could the church give permission to celebrate the Eucharist with rice cake and rice wine? This was in the 1950s, and the question was not well received. One elderly professor said to me, "He should shut up!" No doubt the young professor was thinking of the Eucharist as a meal in which Christ is truly present. Perhaps he was thinking of that time at the Sea of Tiberius when the Risen Jesus said to the disciples, "Come and have breakfast." And he took the bread and the fish and gave it to them. And they knew it was the Lord.

COMMUNITY LIFE IN SHAKUJII was pleasant. Heinrich Jokiel, who had fought with the German army in Russia, and Kono Yoshinari, who had been a submariner, and I, who had been born to the sound of guns in Belfast—together would walk on the roof at night and talk and laugh. We seldom spoke about war. Sharing my room was Pier Paolo, who had been a soldier in the Italian army. I studied theology with Luciano Bertagnolio and we discussed the theses we would be called on to defend. In the summer we went to Mount Fuji and the Spanish brethren sang their beautiful native songs while we rowed boats on the lake. The melodious rhythms of those Spanish songs still haunt me today.

Yet I was getting depressed and sad. Why? What was wrong?

I must speak about my prayer. I was praying in silence, sometimes reciting a mantra, such as the word "Jesus," which filled me with the sense of God's presence. But now that sense of presence was becoming bitter and dry. And beneath all this my repressed unconscious was causing trouble. My subliminal fears, anxieties, anger, violence, and sexual drive were affecting me in an obscure way. Indeed, I was projecting my anger and fears and anxieties onto the people around me. This made them say that I was very emotional.

But why was my unconscious no longer totally repressed? It was because my contemplative prayer was sweeping away the reasoning and thinking of the upper level of consciousness, leaving it silent and empty and thus enabling the lower level to arise. This lower level contained great wisdom, but it also had its dark side. Every day I wrote in my journal, but now I have no remembrance of what I wrote.

The Spanish rector was the obvious person to talk to. He was young (he became rector at the age of forty) and he had studied mystical theology at Woodstock in the United States and written his doctoral thesis on St. Teresa of Avila. He loved America and was familiar with Garrigou Lagrange, Joseph de Guibert, Juan Arintero, and all the current mystical theologians. He was, moreover, an amateur psychologist.

But the rector had his own problems, one of which was an insatiable desire to know the inner lives and the emotional thrusts of his subjects. He loved to listen to our manifestation of conscience. This irritated me no end.

When I told him about my prayer, he was a little surprised at my "infused contemplation" and very curious. As we talked, his own fears and anxieties and repressed sexuality were unconsciously influencing him; and this led to a clash of emotions. For me it was not unlike the clash I had had with my novice master many years before. During the rector's class (for he taught theology), I felt uncomfortable and ill-at-ease and he noticed this. He also was ill-at-ease. I began to feel intense anger against him and fear. What was this all about?

Only a few years later, when I met a great spiritual director in Rome, the Belgian Jesuit Michel Ledrus—only then did I begin to understand what I was experiencing. "You are in the night of the senses," said Ledrus, "and you will go into the night of the soul." Ledrus, spiritual father to the Jesuit seminarians, lectured on St. John of the Cross at the Gregorian University.

Now I see the night as a process of purification found in all authentic mysticism and having much in common with psychoanalysis and deep counseling. Indeed, to go through this night (and I don't think I will ever be completely through it) I needed the help of mystics like St. John of the Cross, the author of *The Cloud of Unknowing*, Theophane the Recluse, and a counselor familiar with modern psychology.

I have written about this in my little book *Letters to Friends*, particularly in my letter to Thomas. In Shakujii I thought I was angry with the rector—and I was—but I was also living out childhood anger at someone else. "Did he remind you of someone?" Ledrus kept asking. It was this childhood dimension that made the anger excessive and called for healing.

However, the dark night is more than a healing of childhood traumas. It brings us into a deeper dimension of reality where we become aware of the good and evil spiritual forces of which Paul speaks, telling us that our struggle is not against enemies of blood and flesh, but against the rulers, against the authorities, against the cosmic powers of this present darkness, against the spiritual forces of evil in the heavenly places. Paul, using the terminology of his day, speaks of a very real psychic world of good and evil spirits. The Bible speaks constantly of this world, as do the scriptures of all the religions. Spiritual writers like Ignatius of Loyola and John of the Cross, too, are aware both of the deceits and machinations of the evil spirit, the enemy of our soul, and the loving guidance of the good spirit who inspires peace and unction and love of God.

For many years I asked myself if this psychic world really existed. I wondered if Ignatius's talk about good and evil spirits was a poetic way of talking about the good and evil quirks of human nature. When I heard Malcolm Muggeridge, the great English convert, saying that he had seen the devil, I was inclined to pooh-pooh the whole thing.

But now I believe in the reality of good and evil spirits. I believe in the reality of what the Second Vatican Council calls "personified Evil." Without in any way denying the great insights of psychology, I am conscious that a spirit of evil has at times influenced my life and actions and I have been deceived. ("He has studied you well," said my master of novices). Nor am I alone. I see the action of the evil spirit in Afghanistan and Iraq, in America and in Britain. The evil spirit works not only in evil people but also in good people, deceiving them, causing division, and robbing them of peace. I see this happening in church leaders throughout history and also today. The evil spirit, says Ignatius of Loyola, knows our psychological weak points and attacks us there.

When I read Bede Griffiths and Fritjof Capra, when I came in touch with Buddhism and Hinduism, when I read something about modern science and philosophy and the New Age, I began to see that Europe, since the Renaissance, has lost its sense of the psychic world and become hopelessly materialistic, atheistic, and mechanistic. It is preoccupied with the material world and no longer sees the psychic and the spiritual. I do not say this of everyone nor of really great scientists like Newton and Einstein; I simply say that materialism is part of the general scene in the West.

And now, at the period of history in which I write, I see more and more people going beyond the material to the psychic and spiritual worlds. In my room or even in the chapel, as I call on the Holy Spirit who, I believe, is really present within me, I see (or I imagine I see) this crude little fellow, half human and half beast, growling and cackling and trying to cause disturbance in my human relationships. Yet I am not afraid. Once I recognize him I know that he is a chained dog and cannot injure me. I remember how Ignatius drove him away with his staff. The problem is only when I do not see him and think that only the material world exists.

I know that this little fellow (for me he is masculine) is one of a horde of demons who are acting on the human unconscious in Ireland, Iraq, North Korea, Sri Lanka, Britain, America, India, China, Japan, and everywhere else.

The forces of evil can work on the collective unconscious. They can bring about an eruption of the collective unconscious that no human being can control. If a catastrophe like nuclear war is coming, it will come not because any human being wants this appalling suffering but because no one can stop it—we will have lost control of our unconscious, which will then be governed by forces of evil.

Please do not think that I am being pessimistic. As always, I am simply following the Second Vatican Council which, already in the 1960s, spoke of the magnified power of humanity which threatens to destroy the human race. It further spoke of a monumental struggle against the powers of darkness that pervades the whole history of humankind. And, referring to the parables of the Gospel, the council insists that this struggle will continue until the end of time.

Nor does this obviate the scriptural words, "Greater is the one who is in you than the one who is in the world," or the saying of Julian of Norwich that "all shall be well." Even if there is a great storm, good will triumph. On our part, we must cooperate by being open to the wisdom that enables us to see and to discern between good and evil psychic forces. We must learn the basic wisdom that lies at the root of all religions. As Alcoholics Anonymous teaches it, that wisdom means we need to recognize our own weakness and call on "a higher power." We must have our ear to the ground to listen to the prophets of our time: Mahatma Gandhi, Mother Teresa of Calcutta, and the Dalai Lama.

Above all, we must learn to go—or, more correctly, we must let ourselves be carried—beyond the material world, beyond the psychic world, to the world of spirit. This is the world beyond reasoning and thinking and imagining, the world to which all religions finally point. It is the world of mysticism. False or half-baked mysticism stops at the psychic world and for that reason is very dangerous. In the popular meditation movement that is spreading through the world we stand in need of skilled teachers who will lead meditators beyond the psychic to the spiritual dimension of reality.

BEFORE ORDINATION TO THE PRIESTHOOD in Tokyo we had our eight-day retreat given by a prophetic Jesuit, Hugo Enomiya Lassalle (Enomiya being the name he had taken on becoming a Japanese citizen). Already known for

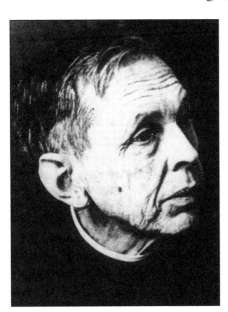

German Jesuit Hugo M. Enomiya Lassalle, S.J., founder of the Christian Zen movement.

his practice of Zen, he had the appearance of a mystic, lean and tall and charismatic. When the atom bomb was dropped on Hiroshima, he had been critically wounded, and the story goes that as he lay exhausted on the road he had gasped: "Give me a cigarette!"

In our ordination retreat Lassalle said nothing about Zen but followed the Spiritual Exercises of St. Ignatius quite literally with little reference even to sacred scripture. Getting a chance to speak to him personally, I told him about my silent prayer. "Perhaps you don't need Zen," he said.

Lassalle was a practical man. He saw Zen as a good thing that led to a deep religious experience;

and so he practiced. He even boasted that he had not taken a single course in Buddhism at any university. All his knowledge came from experience and the guidance of Zen masters. Someone said to him, "But what about theology? Where does Christian theology fit in Zen?" and he answered, "I don't care about theology."

"You don't care," said his questioner, "but other people do," hinting that Lassalle might get into trouble. And he did get into trouble. Letters went to Rome, and he said sadly, "I can't write for the people. I have to write for the censors!" Yet he was shrewd; he was never condemned.

I once said to him, "Where is Christ in Zen?" and he answered almost sternly, "Father, practice Zen and you will find Christ!" And he did find Christ. Wherever he went to practice Zen, whether in a Buddhist temple or a private house, he brought the bread and the wine and celebrated Mass with great devotion.

I see Lassalle as a prophet of the twentieth century, ranking beside Thomas Merton and Daisetsu Suzuki. It was not that he had very profound enlightenment—some people question the depth of his Zen experience—but he opened a new path in the dialogue between religions. In the 1950s when theologians were arguing about "the salvation of the infidel" and "*communicatio in sacris*" he was meditating with Buddhists. He could do this because he had found something that Christians and Buddhists have, or can have, in common. This is *satori*, or enlightenment.

Lassalle had read widely in the Christian mystics. He knew Eckhart and *The Cloud of Unknowing*. He spoke about Nicholas of Cusa. He visited Mount Athos to meet the Orthodox mystics. And he practiced Zen.

All kinds of problems, theological and Christological, remain. We did not face them in Shakujii, but mystical theologians of the future, East and West, will be challenged by Lassalle.

12

More Theology

IN THE TOKYO THEOLOGATE of the 1950s we were living in the old Society of Jesus, the old Catholic Church, and the old world. Our study was based on the European scholasticism of the thirteenth century. The giant, of course, was Thomas Aquinas. Sacred scripture was good and wholesome, but we were warned to beware of Protestant critical scholarship that might deflect us from the infallible and unchanging teaching of the Holy Roman Church. More important than scripture was the manual of Heinrich Denzinger. Thomas Aquinas himself was a mystic, but his followers were not. Consequently, our teaching, dualistic and anti-mystical, was conducted at what I call "the top level of consciousness."

Times have changed. We have had a Second Vatican Council; we have come in contact with the mystical religions of Asia; we have discovered relativity and quantum theory; we have begun to study Freud and Jung. We have entered into a new culture, in which an increasing number of people meditate and are aware of the mind-boggling mystery of the universe. Is it possible that many of our problems can be solved only by mysticism, by a mystical intuition of the unity of being and the coincidence of opposites? Will the movement started by Hugo Enomiya Lassalle be central to the theology of the future?

EXAMINATIONS WERE IMPORTANT for us, examinations in which we were confronted by four grim, bespectacled professors. On these examinations depended not only our ordination to the priesthood but also our position in the future Society of Jesus. Following the customs of his culture, St. Ignatius had divided his society into grades or classes. First were the professed who took, in addition to the vows of poverty, chastity, and obedience, a fourth vow of special obedience to the pope. These were the core of the Society and they alone took part in the central meetings of Jesuits; they alone could occupy certain positions such as rector of a major house. Assisting them were "spiritual coadjutors" who would say Mass and hear confessions. Then there were lay brothers who did not study but had to be content with the role of Martha.

At the end of theology there was a big exam called "Ad Gradum" which determined whether one would be a professed father or a spiritual coadjutor. I passed that exam by the skin of my teeth (the results were secret, but the provincial's secretary told me I had gotten two sixes, a seven, and an eight) and I know that I would have been bitterly hurt and disappointed if I had flunked. Other Jesuits were more reasonable. They saw it didn't really matter if one flunked: they would be content to live (as they jokingly called it) on the periphery of the Society.

Let me here skip a few decades to say how the Society of Jesus changed.

IN 1965 OUR JAPANESE PROVINCIAL, Pedro Arrupe, was elected superior general of the Society. He was a Basque mystic, enormously charitable and prayerful. So charismatic was Arrupe that we called him Don Quixote because he was always chasing windmills. When the election for superior general was to take place, his time as provincial was coming to an end and we were asking: "What will we do with Arrupe?" It was said in Japan that Gustav Voss and Emmanuel Gonzales were sent to Rome as Japanese representatives to ensure that Arrupe would not be elected general. They failed in their task.

In Rome, after the Second Vatican Council, Arrupe called a general Congregation and in answer to many requests—we called them *postulata*—he led the Society (or was led by the Society) to modify in some way the Jesuit vow of special obedience to the pope. Many Jesuits felt that in our democratic society it was not good to have grades and divisions so that the professed were "up" and the spiritual coadjutors were "down." Could we not follow the example of orders of women who had done away with the distinction between mothers and sisters? And it was suggested that not just a few but everyone in the Society of Jesus should take the vow of special obedience to the pope.

Pope Paul VI , scrutinizing the Congregation documents with the utmost care, refused permission to make this change. And when the fathers made a representation, he again refused quite angrily.

How did this affect me?

I myself took my vow of special obedience to the pope in Tokyo in 1961. I took it hush-hush in a secret little chapel surrounded by a few friends after pronouncing my ordinary vows in public. I don't remember what was in the vow and I am not sure that I knew then. I had my personal vocation. I wanted to follow our constitutions by devoting myself to my own perfection and the perfection of my neighbor by praying, by teaching others to pray, and by writing. My ideal Jesuit was Pierre Teilhard de Chardin.

Then came the fuss in Rome about the fourth vow: the anger of Paul VI, the hurt of Arrupe, the confusion of the Jesuits, and all the hubbub. It didn't affect me at all. It seemed so unimportant. What would this fourth vow mean to the people around me? What would it mean to the Japanese? I recall going for a walk in busy Tokyo with Pier Paolo. We stopped for a few moments of silence and watched the traffic whirling around—the cars, the huge trucks, the motor bikes, the hooting police cars, and the ambulances with their screeching sirens. After a few moments of silence, Pier Paolo turned to me and said: "And the pope is worried about our fourth vow!"

I laughed. It was so good and so typical of Pier Paolo.

We were both Jesuits, committed Jesuits. And all this talk in Rome seemed to me (and still seems) utterly irrelevant. Besides, no one had asked my opinion. I had learned in the novitiate that we should accept the superior's decision as coming from the hand of God, without asking any questions. Pope Paul was all for this.

A similar situation arose when Arrupe got sick in 1985 and John Paul II personally appointed Paolo Dezza and Joseph Pittau to lead the Jesuits. Most Jesuits did not bat an eyelid. We had our personal vocation in accordance with the end of the Society to sanctify our own souls and that of our neighbor. Why worry about the fuss in Rome?

BUT LET ME ADDRESS a new topic that affected my ordination.

One thing I cannot understand is the frequency with which I have fainted. As a small boy in St. Francis Xavier's I fainted a few times during examinations. I think it happened when I was taking examinations that I could not face or that I was going to fail. Yet the same thing occurred in Dublin University during an English exam in which I was doing pretty well. At another time I was praying silently at the back of the chapel and intolerable darkness rose from the depth of my being; I got up and went out, only to fall into a faint on the ground. I have also fainted in the morning before breakfast when I was trying to fast.

I still had this tendency in Shakujii when, during an oral exam in moral theology, one of the professors attacked me and I almost fainted and had to stop. Later I repeated the examination and was warmly received by my former opponent.

Time came for my ordination to the priesthood by the Japanese Cardinal Doi at the church of St. Ignatius in Tokyo. I was nervous and scrupulous. I felt I had to have the right intention, because otherwise the sacrament would not be valid. During the ceremony I began to fear that I would faint. Pier Paolo was standing just behind me and I heard him whisper, "He's going to faint!" He kindly took my arm and brought me to a seat at the side of the altar and said, "You are united with them," as if to say, you will be ordained with them.

But the damage was done. I went up for imposition of the bishop's hands, fearing that my ordination was doubtful. Perhaps I had withdrawn my intention. My old scrupulosity had caught up with me.

Immediately after the ceremony I met the provincial, Father Arrupe, who was bubbling with energy and all smiles. "I want to talk to you sometime," I said. "Now!" he responded characteristically. So we went into a small room and I explained my problem. Again he smiled and said, "Father Johnston, don't worry. You were there like everyone else." And I felt relieved.

I was grateful to Arrupe for this, and I still am grateful. My novice master many years before had said, "You will always need good direction— if you are humble enough to take it...and you are!" And he was right. I took Arrupe's advice. For cases like mine the old scholastic theology also had a good phrase, "*Supplet ecclesia*," meaning the church will supply what is necessary. I like this.

And so I was ordained a priest. None of my family from Ireland came for the ceremony. At that time it was unthinkable. A nun from a nearby convent told me afterwards that she took the place of my mother. The next day, the feast of the Annunciation, I celebrated my first Mass, assisted by Father Joe O'Brien, who was one of the founders of the Columban mission to Japan.

WHILE I WAS IN THEOLOGY one of the big events was the departure from the priesthood and the Society of Peter Herzog, the German rector of Sophia. Herzog married his secretary. This was in the 1950s, a time when priests did not leave. I had, of course, heard of the Irish Jesuit Boyd Barrett who had left and subsequently returned, dying peacefully in the Jesuit infirmary of Santa Clara in California. But now Peter Herzog. Why?

Precisely why Herzog left I do not know. I heard plenty of rumors. But rumors are rumors and I prefer to leave them that way. To me his departure was a big shock because I knew him as a priest who prayed for a few moments in the chapel before going to his classes and for another few moments after they were over. Now, I was told, he had given up all religion. How could he do it? I did not understand.

One of his supporters was the Catholic novelist Shusaku Endo who was baptized as a young man by Herzog and whose mother was an ardent admirer of the holy Jesuit. She had already died when Herzog left the priesthood and Endo had to work out his problems alone. He said to me many years later with conviction, "Father Herzog did not lose his faith!"

In a short story in which he does not use Herzog's name, Endo tells the story as he saw it. Herzog's illicit love was at first an awful shock to Endo; but eventually he came to see its beauty. By chance he saw Herzog in a restaurant, no longer the handsome, well-dressed cleric but a slightly disheveled old man who, at the end of his meal, blessed himself. Was he not much better, much more humble than the proud prelate of the past?

Deeply impressed, Endo tells us that he made Herzog the hero of some of his novels. In the novel *Silence*, the noble misfit tramples on the image of the Christ whom he loves—not to save his life but to save the lives of his Christians. The hero does not lose his faith. He steps on the cross for love. This is Endo's Herzog.

Likewise, in his last novel, *Deep River*, Endo writes of the Japanese priest misfit who is constantly at odds with his colleagues but heroically carries dead bodies to the Ganges. This time Endo shows a wonderful appreciation of the celibate love between this priest and the woman who breaks down in torrents of tears when he dies. Their love is celibate and powerful.

Many Jesuits in Herzog's community, however, cannot agree with Endo's "apostasy for love" theory. Herzog, they say, should never have been rector of Sophia. And there were bitter problems in the community that drove him to leave and get married. God alone will judge us all.

Peter Herzog lived to be very old. Decades after he left, with my Jesuit friend Dan McCoy I visited him and his family several times. Dan was a red-hot pentecostal and after a chat about all kinds of things he suggested that we pray. Rather sheepishly Herzog agreed, and Dan poured forth his soul, praying that Herzog and his family would be happy and filled with peace.

Then Herzog got sick and, as he lay unconscious, a German Jesuit friend gave him absolution for all his sins and administered the last rites with the cooperation of his wife and children. Herzog was buried in the Jesuit church and his ashes lie with those of his Jesuit brethren.

EVENTUALLY THE TIME CAME to leave the theologate and move on. Plans were made for young Jesuit priests to get high-powered degrees in literature or religion or economics in Germany or America. Arrupe did not quite know what to do with me. "You have many qualities," he said. "But it is difficult to know how to use them." I think of the Irish provincial Tommy Byrne telling me I was good but not first-rate.

Arrupe, forever chasing windmills, distinguished between the big-time scholars and the people who would work with students. I belonged to this latter class. I think the theology professors looked on me as a pretty good journalist but not a big scholar.

Then the Irish provincial Luigi O'Grady visited Tokyo on his way to Hong Kong. Luigi was a prince, and he made a big impression on the Jesuit community. He and I got on well, traveling through Tokyo and postwar Japan. One day he said to me: "The young Irish Jesuits in Hong Kong come back to Ireland for theology, and I have not met one who regrets it. Why don't you come back for tertianship?" He said he would pay the expenses so it would be no financial burden on the Japanese province.

I liked this idea. The Japanese province was struggling to establish its own tertianship, but I was tired and depressed and I liked the idea of getting out of Japan for a year. I spoke to Arrupe, and that was that. My colleague Tsuchida Masao, later to become president of Sophia University, would go with me to have a chance to see Europe.

Before leaving for Ireland, however, I had a few free months and these I spent in Fukuyama in southern Japan. The parish, run by an old-time Dutch missionary, Hubert Peeters, was small but bustling with activity. It was my first time working as a priest, and I was happy saying Mass, teaching scripture, hearing confessions, and meeting the people. French sisters—with a few Japanese—had a big school near the church. There was a secular high school to which my old colleague Franz Bosch came down from Tokyo to give an inspiring lecture in his brilliant Japanese about the new Europe.

Peeters and I went to see *The Bridge on the River Kwai*, starring Alec Guinness and Setsue Hayakawa. That was an experience: Alec Guinness as the brilliant British officer and Hayakawa, an American Japanese, weeping gently and fondling his dagger as if preparing for suicide. It was a war movie—or perhaps I should say a peace movie, for it was a tragic plea for peace—and I was surrounded by an audience of Japanese who watched intently. At one point a young Japanese soldier fell dead and from his pocket there slipped a small photo of his beautiful child. This was in 1958. The memory of the war was still alive. What, I asked myself, are the Japanese thinking?

Reviews said that the Japanese liked the movie and found it fair. I believe the Japanese love their country very deeply, but I cannot figure out their attitude toward the Americans after the war. I only know that if the Brits had dropped that atomic bomb on Dublin, Irish bards and poets would have been composing songs and sagas for centuries, whereas most of the Japanese have already forgotten the bomb. The rest of the world composes the tragic stories while the Japanese get on with their business. But this is a subject to which I shall return.

As I LOOK BACK on those happy days in Fukuyama, I see that Vatican II still needs implementation in Asia. The little flock was happy in its own way, but it was living in a foreign country. The people learned about three persons in one nature; they studied a lot of Tridentine theology that was very foreign to their Asian archetypes and religious sensibility. What large crowds flocked to watch Alec Guinness in *The Bridge on the River Kwai*, leaving our catechism classes to a few stalwart souls!

Forty years later we are still asking if Japan and China can find their own theology based on the Gospel and the Christian tradition, a theology that will not separate them from their own people, their own religions, and their own saints.

There is hope. We have at the Tokyo cathedral a Japanese international Mass with Filipino dancing, Spanish singing, and the Japanese drum. People from all countries in the world pray and sing and dance together. Will the time come when we welcome people of other religions to pray for peace as happened at Assisi in 1986? This surely is the ideal toward which we must strive.

TIME PASSED QUICKLY and soon I was at Yokohama, boarding the boat for Marseilles.

13
Enlightenment in Rome

THE FRENCH LINER steamed out of Yokohama and we said good-bye to Japan. I had arrived in 1951 and now it was 1958. Those seven years had changed me completely, but my short stay in Rome would change me even more. It was nothing short of a revolution in my life. I was thirty-two years of age.

On the ship were all kinds of people, and during the five weeks of our voyage we formed a sort of community. There were several missionaries returning to their native soil in Europe. I recall an elderly Capuchin, dressed in brown robes, playing table tennis on the scorching deck with a little girl. Then there were we three Jesuits, the Hungarian Viola, the Japanese Masao Tsuchida, and myself. There were a couple of young Frenchmen and two Japanese girls going to Europe for study. We all had a good time together, the Frenchmen telling me I was lucky to speak Japanese. In fact one of the Japanese girls was quietly beautiful and as we walked on the deck I fell in love with her. Not that we touched one another. I don't think we even shook hands. But the encounter was important for me, as I shall explain anon.

We stopped at Hong Kong and Saigon (now Ho Chi Minh City), where we were welcomed by energetic Jesuits who had little idea of the earthshaking events that were on the horizon. Then on to Columbo. As we came into the Mediterranean the air was fresh and cool. Finally we arrived in Marseilles, where we said good-bye. I went alone by train to Rome.

On the ship my incorrigible addiction to writing came to the fore. I wrote a little book about my experience in Japan. I think it was beautifully written—in my heart I secretly compared it to James Joyce's *Portrait of an*

Artist—but I was young and it was naive and the Roman censors turned it down. What happened to that manuscript I do not now remember.

My reason for going to Rome was to study Aristotle and to rewrite the thesis that had been rejected seven or eight years earlier in Ireland. I stayed in the Bellarmine College with students from all over the world who were studying at the Gregorian University. It was a new experience for me. I had not known that Jesuits in Italy drank so much wine. And I had a chance to meet Bernard Lonergan, who quoted Aristotle in the original Greek with great vigor. I cannot say I learned a lot from the great Lonergan at that time. In fact I could not understand what he was talking about.

More important for me than Lonergan was the spiritual father Michel Ledrus, whom I mentioned earlier. His room was close to mine. Shortly after my arrival I called to see him and to make my confession, and after receiving absolution I sat down and we began to talk. I told him about my difficulties in Japan and about Peter Herzog's departure and my fear that I might do the same thing. Why was Japan so difficult? People said that by going to China one could become a saint, but with Japan one had to be a saint before going. Then there were difficulties with the language and with the people. I told him about the Japanese girl I had fallen in love with on the ship.

After a while, Ledrus took out a notebook and began to write. "I have so many people coming to see me," he explained, "that I have to check on who said what. But what you say is absolutely confidential."

In hindsight I now see that in our talks my repressed unconscious was coming to the surface. This had started when I was a theology student in Shakujii. And now I had a real guru who could listen and understand and help. Ledrus was a rather small Belgian Jesuit in his early sixties. He taught spirituality and lectured on St. John of the Cross.

I have heard of a Jesuit psychiatrist who said, "In my therapy I am an atheist," meaning that psychology is psychology and he would not mix it with spirituality. Ledrus was not like that. He knew psychology well (and this was before the Second Vatican Council, at a time when Freud and the rest were "forbidden books") but he was also interested in my prayer and my relationship with God. His approach was holistic.

And so we talked and talked. My stay in Rome was short—only six weeks—but we met every day and I bared the depths of my soul. He simply listened and said occasionally in French, "*Bon!*" Many of the Jesuits in Japan had studied in Rome and Ledrus knew them well. He knew my friend Pier Paolo and was familiar with his big plans for inculturation.

But it soon became evident that my problems went much deeper than Japan.

We spoke about sex and sexuality. Here Ledrus was a rock of common sense. As an adolescent I had been tortured by scruples and had gone to confession again and again, until I read a little book telling me that unless I was absolutely certain that I had committed a sin I could assume that I hadn't. This had helped, but some anxiety had remained and I had never talked frankly about sex to anyone. I recall my novice master looking into space and saying, "But of course you have discussed all this with a priest." And I had to answer, "Yes." He made no offer to discuss it.

I recited three Hail Marys morning and evening for "the virtue of holy purity" and I avoided all "dangerous occasions of sin." I once looked at the picture of a nude woman and I called this my "big sin." When I told Ledrus this, he simply said, "A sin of curiosity!" I had loved women, but never in a sexual way, and my love quickly became guilt-ridden. "Why are you scrupulous about sex and not about anything else?" asked Ledrus. "In an otherwise balanced character you have this unbalanced anxiety." He told me that I had been spared the coarser temptations of the flesh and the energy had flowed into my emotions. This was a valuable insight.

We talked about my dreams and about my childhood and my father and mother. I was afraid to look at the nude statues in Rome and even to look at my own body. Ledrus told me to go to the museums and to contemplate the statues. "There is nothing pornographic in Rome," he said. I came back and we discussed my experience.

And then in a dream it all became clear. I had a mother fixation. I was bogged down in the Oedipus conflict. I had heard something about the road to Thebes and how Oedipus loved his mother and murdered his father. This seemed to me to be esoteric and absurd. But now I realized that Freud was a genius and that Sophocles also was a genius, seeing in the outer world a drama that is enacted in the unconscious of millions.

My growth, particularly my sexual growth, had been arrested at an early age. And now it had begun to develop. Over a few days I got a whole new vision of my past life. I saw how I had climbed into my mother's bed where she had told me stories about George Bernard Shaw and William Butler Yeats. I saw Liverpool and St. Francis Xavier's College and the Mersey Tunnel. I saw my novice master with whom I had had so many problems. "Your father without your mother!" said Ledrus. And so the story unrolled. I saw my whole unconscious that had been crushed. I realized I was more Clearkin (my mother's maiden name) than Johnston. "One woman" said Ledrus, meaning that my mother was the only woman in my life.

"The change in your face!" said Ledrus, smiling with glee when I saw the light. He understood that my experience was not just a psychological insight; it was more like an Asian enlightenment. It was a Zen *satori* or a Christian conversion of heart. It was possible only because I was praying constantly before the Blessed Sacrament in the chapel.

In fact it was an experience of healing and of growth. It was the beginning of a road on which, liberated from childish clinging to my parents, I could start to move toward authentic love for them and for others. From then I began to understand how so many people come to love and appreciate their parents only later in life when their parents are already old or dead. Earlier in life most people are not capable of authentic love.

Was it also the beginning of an authentic, celibate love for the opposite sex? Ledrus said nothing about this. Only ten or twelve years later, when I met another great Jesuit, Yves Raguin, did I come to realize that authentic celibate love is not just a concession to human weakness that needs the companionship of the opposite sex, but can be a truly mystical way to God.

I have found it helpful to make a distinction between what I call horizontal prayer and vertical prayer. The Spiritual Exercises of St. Ignatius, as I had learned them in my noviceship, had taught me horizontal prayer. That is to say, they had drawn me through a series of meditations at the top level of consciousness, encouraging me to reflect on the call of the Divine King, the standard of Christ and the standard of Satan, and the three classes of men—all leading me to make a choice about my future life. Vertical prayer, on the other hand, draws one down into the deeper, unconscious levels of the personality. It leads one into the cloud of unknowing where one is frequently silent, in love with God.

I was already practicing this vertical, contemplative prayer when I went to Rome, and my experience under the direction of Ledrus led me to break through to a new and deeper level of consciousness. I began to read more of St. John of the Cross and found that I was distancing myself from standard Jesuit spirituality, following Ledrus who insisted that St. Ignatius wanted his sons to be mystics. Ignatius was himself a mystic. He did not spend his life going through the Spiritual Exercises.

Ledrus, I have said, told me I was in the night of the senses and would go into the night of the soul. This still puzzles me.

The night of the senses deals with the personal unconscious—with the fears and anxieties of childhood, with childhood relationships with father and mother and family, with any traumas that may have happened during life. All these come to the surface of a consciousness that is being emptied with great pain but at the same time is being greatly healed. St. John of the Cross writes that there are plenty of books about this first night and he will not waste much time writing about it.

The second night concerns the purification of the collective unconscious of the whole world. It is the purification of Jesus when he took on himself the sin of the world in Gethsemane. Perhaps the mystics of today are called to atone for the Middle East and Europe and America and all the sin we now face. For St. John of the Cross, this night is the rising of God who is night to the soul. Not that God is night in himself (God is transcendent light), but God is darkness to us because we are blinded by this light. We cannot endure the vision of God, and even in the next life we will need a special grace from God to enjoy the beatific vision.

To describe this night, St. John of the Cross speaks of "nothing"—*nada, nada, nada*—and of emptiness. His *todo y nada* (all and nothing) is so similar to the *mu* (nothing) and *ku* (emptiness) of Asia that he has been called a Buddhist in Christian disguise. To this I would say, however, that the Buddhist *mu* and *ku* may well be an experience of the same unknowability of God. Perhaps mystics of all religions are called to unite in atoning for the ugliness of the world and facing the unknowable mystery that cannot be put into words.

Still, an even more important point needs to be made. One who reads the poetry of St. John of the Cross can only marvel at the influence of the Song of Songs. The poetry is filled with the ecstatic joy of the lover who goes forth to meet the beloved. "Upon my flowering breast which I kept wholly for him alone, there he lay sleeping . . . ." I like to express the theology of St. John of the Cross in Lonergan's terms—my being becomes "being-in-love." Here there is no subject-object distinction but a true coincidence of opposites.

WHEN THE TIME CAME to leave Rome, I said good-bye to Ledrus with gratitude but without sadness, for I knew we would soon meet again. Brimming over with newly acquired energy I went by train to London, where I stayed with my brother Eamon who was in the London police. Then north to stay in Newcastle-on-Tyne, where Tom was living with his wife Anne and his little boy Eamon and working as a doctor. Then on to

Belfast where Mum and Dad were showing signs of age, and Kevin, working as a dentist, was proud of his growing family. After my long absence, it was a great reunion.

In Dublin it was good to see the old familiar faces. We tertians were living in Rathfarnham Castle where I had stayed while studying classics at University College. Hugh Kelly, my rector in 1945, was now in 1958 my tertian instructor. He was older and more mature, and he was just the superior I needed. The tertianship, he told us, had not changed for three centuries. It was a time when young Jesuits, just ready for activity, were told to spend a year in prayer. We would have plenty of time for prayer.

Hugo gave a conference each morning on Jesuit spirituality, and he invited other competent Jesuits to do likewise. He directed the thirty-day retreat during which he himself got up with us to make the midnight hour of prayer. But he offered no counseling nor did he interfere in our lives to make us obey the rules. "I am not a policeman," he said.

For me this was ideal. I thought I had had enough counseling from Ledrus to last me for the rest of my life. I say "I thought" because the reality turned out to be different. My subsequent life was in fact filled with storms, one after another, and each book I wrote was the outcome of some crisis. I needed, and got, counseling after tertianship. But at this period of my life I was glad to be left alone to get myself sorted out.

Living in the same house were twenty or thirty young scholastics studying at the university. One of them remarked to me that tertianship is a good time for making up for lost sleep. Such was the reputation of the tertianship.

And the tertians were the same old gang with whom I had suffered in Emo and Rathfarnham and the Bog. We were the same and different. Now we had new stories. Joe Conway and Bob Kelly talked about Zambia. Jack Brennan and Joe Marmion had stories about Germany. Johnny Russel and Arnie Hogan had had adventures in Hong Kong. Paul Jenkins had been in Malaysia. I could talk about Japan. Then we had a Spanish artist and a Portuguese mystic. And so we hiked through the Dublin mountains and had a hilarious time. I am still grateful to the Irish provincial Luigi O'Grady for having invited me to Ireland for tertianship.

But my deep unconscious, awakened in Rome, kept coming to the surface and I was overwhelmed with sexual energy. This happened not only when I was in bed at night but even during my prayer. I wrote to Ledrus and he answered immediately that this "should have been foreseen," adding that "everyone has his problems, so don't worry: this will pass away." It did pass away, but only after many years. Meanwhile, it left me with the conviction that while celibacy is my calling it is not the calling of all priests. Optional celibacy would be good.

Before returning to Japan I wanted to do some study. My rewritten thesis was accepted by Queen's University in Belfast and I asked Arrupe if I could study for six months at the newly established catechetical institute Lumen Vitae. Arrupe agreed and I left Ireland for Brussels.

14
The Search in Brussels

I WAS GLAD TO BE ABLE TO STUDY in Belgium for seven months from September 1959 until April 1960, exciting months leading up to the Second Vatican Council. The professors at Lumen Vitae were mildly and cautiously progressive, though what they said would be old hat today. I was an Irishman and I soon saw that Irishmen, particularly Irish bishops, were laughed at as bulwarks of the old traditional church that was bursting at the seams. This was a time when liturgy was changing so that priests could offer Mass facing the people. And the big joke was that Irish priests said the rosary facing the people. Ha! Ha!

I knew, however, that not all Irish men and women were submissive servants of Rome. This became even clearer to me a few years later when I taught English literature in Tokyo. While my English colleague Peter Milward read with his students the work of devout and committed English Christians like John Henry Newman, Gerard Manley Hopkins, and T. S. Eliot, all the time insisting that Shakespeare was a Roman Catholic, I had only George Bernard Shaw, whom my rector Hugh Kelly had called "a blasphemous old dog," and James Joyce, whose *Ulysses*, proclaimed the novel of the century by people who had not read it, was to me a gigantic leg-pull. And then the Irish tradition was carried into the twentieth century with Frank McCourt's *Angela's Ashes*. Enough said.

The fact is that the time had come for me to get out of the narrow nationalism in which I had been raised and to find my true self. I see now that my meeting with Ledrus, while a tremendous breakthrough, was only the first step in what was to be a long journey. It was a death— or should I say a resurrection? A whole area of my consciousness that had been repressed was now opening up. All my childhood memories, my relationships with my father and mother, my sexuality, my love for women, my confrontations with death—a whole world had to be sorted out.

The seemingly progressive professors of theology did nothing for me. I cannot now remember anything they said. Indeed I was little interested in the theology I learned in Brussels or in Tokyo. It was almost all at the top level of consciousness, with little place for mysticism. Besides, I think that we Irish, like the Japanese, are literary rather than philosophical. "You are a literary man," said my friend Heinrich Dumoulin. And perhaps he was right.

Let me say again that I make a distinction between horizontal thinking and vertical thinking or, more correctly, between horizontal prayer and vertical prayer. Horizontal prayer is at the top level of consciousness whereas vertical prayer descends to deeper levels of the psyche. It is contemplative and even mystical. This vertical prayer I found in the Christian tradition (even though our Jesuit tradition was rather reticent about it) and in Pierre Teilhard de Chardin and Bede Griffiths. It was the basis of my theology.

In Brussels I spent a good deal of time in prayer in the big church close to our school. My prayer was contemplative, at a deep level of consciousness where I found God dwelling within—within me and within the universe. At a more superficial level the sexual turmoil continued, but it did not worry me unduly. My guru, Michel Ledrus, came from Rome to visit his native Belgium and we had a good and cheerful chat. I learned that sexual thoughts or thoughts of hatred and anxiety and the rest could go their way at one level of consciousness while at a deeper level I was united with God. Ledrus was down-to-earth. "If you commit a sexual sin, confess it and go ahead," he said.

Then I discovered Carl Jung, who gave me a modern framework in which I could understand my own experience and even perhaps elaborate a new theology of mysticism. I loved Jung. I read him again and again, and many years later when I went to Australia and found myself stranded in Canberra with nothing to do, I reread him. Here I found the mysterious world of dreams.

I was fascinated by that dream where Jung found himself in the top story of a house and went down to the lower stories, one by one, until he came to the ancient cave-like basement where he discovered two skulls.

Freud did not understand Jung's dream. He wanted to interpret the skulls as a death wish. But Jung, rejecting the interpretation of his master, saw the dream as an image of his psyche; he came to realize that he contained in himself the history of humanity. Was this his collective unconscious? For me, Jung's interpretation of his dream was a marvelous insight, and I began to see that the whole history of humanity, the whole universe, and God Himself—all this I could find within me. Could this be true?

Now I ask myself if Jung anticipated the Second Vatican Council which, in *Gaudium et Spes*, says that the human being is not just a speck of nature. By reason of his interiority he outstrips the whole sum of things. When he enters into his own heart God awaits him and he discerns his proper destiny through the eyes of God. "Man judges rightly that by his intellect he surpasses the material universe, for he shares in the light of the divine mind." The same document says that anyone who searches for the truth with a humble mind is, even unknown to himself, guided by the Spirit of God. Was Jung such a person?

I have on my table an article by Aniela Jaffe entitled, "Was C. G. Jung a Mystic?" Aniela Jaffe worked with Jung on his autobiography. She really knew him. And she hints that he was in fact a mystic.

I also loved the archetypes, particularly the *anima* or feminine dimension in man. It was clear to me that Jung had a strong sense of his own *anima*, though he was less at home with the *animus* in woman. Then there was the "shadow," which taught me something about the dark night of the soul and what we call original sin.

Here let me say, however, that while I have read Jung with great interest and great joy, I do not consider myself a Jungian scholar nor have I received Jungian analysis. I have understood Jung in my own way. And thanks to him—and thanks to my own experience—I know that the mind is multilayered. Beneath the top layer that preoccupied the old scientists, scholastics, and spiritual writers are many layers that contain both positive and negative material. The positive material is wisdom that culminates in enlightenment; the negative material consists of the fears and anxieties, the hatred and violence that are repressed in the personal and collective unconscious. I believe I have encountered both the darkness and the light. I am still being healed from the tormenting darkness. Thanks to Jung, I have interpreted dreams in a way that has changed the course of my life.

AT THIS TIME some development took place in my prayer. As a novice I was introduced to the Spiritual Exercises as a process of meditations. I was encouraged to reflect on sin and the following of Christ, then I would pray to the Father or to Jesus or Mary and make resolutions for my future life.

This, I was told, was the basic spirituality of the Society of Jesus. Every year we had to go through this process, sometimes listening to three or four lectures each day. To follow the teaching of the Exercises was part of the rigorous obedience demanded by the Society.

From my early days in the Society, however, I felt called to abandon this process so as to enter into a deeper level of awareness where I found true wisdom and enjoyed the sense of presence. I simply repeated an ejaculation like "Jesus" and, when called to silence, I accepted the call. I loved this kind of prayer; but I did not have the courage to speak at length about it to retreat directors. I could not admit that discursive prayer and "the process" no longer interested me.

At about this time I began to read about mantra meditation that was coming into Europe and America from the East. Particularly important was Transcendental Meditation taught by the Maharishi Mahesh Yogi from India. This was not religious, we were told; it was a psychological practice wherein one received a mantra or sound that one was to repeat again and again and again. Piercing to the deeper, unconscious levels of the psyche, this meditation liberated people from addictions to drugs or alcohol or tobacco or whatever. Needless to say, many devout Christians were up in arms, claiming that the Maharishi was trying to convert Christians to Hinduism.

I met the Maharishi (I cannot remember where or when) and I was impressed by him as a sincere and good man. I never opposed his movement. "TM," as it came to be called, was made famous when the Beatles went to India to study under the Maharishi, but serious scholars at Harvard and other universities were converted and claimed, with interesting research, that this meditation really did help people.

Now, as I look back, I see Transcendental Meditation as one of the first steps in a movement to separate spirituality from religion. Many people were turned off by religion—by its encouragement of wars and its extremely ethical thrust. Its emphasis on law reminded people of the teaching of the scribes and Pharisees. These people wanted spirituality. And they found it in the East.

And so there arose a number of meditation movements within Christianity inspired by TM, Asian methods of prayer, the teaching of the ancient desert fathers, and the mystical Christian tradition of the Byzantine and Orthodox worlds. Think of Thomas Merton, John Main, Abhishiktananda, Bede Griffiths, Tony de Mello, and a host of others influenced by the mysticism of Asia. These taught a way of prayer that was acceptable to modern searchers.

But what about the Spiritual Exercises of Ignatius?

As I have already indicated, I was tired of going through discursive meditation on the doctrine of hell, the call of the temporal king, the two standards, the three classes of men, the third degree of humility, and all the rest. This had been great in my noviceship but now I wanted something deeper. Back in Japan I had spoken to the provincial, Pedro Arrupe, saying that I preferred St. John of the Cross to St. Ignatius. Arrupe, who was an extrovert mystic, smiled and said, "I don't think John of the Cross will satisfy you." It was a good answer, and now I see that he was right.

I read Joseph de Guibert on the spiritual teaching of the Jesuits. Himself a mystic and a mystical theologian, de Guibert points out that the early Jesuits were mystics. Our problem had begun with John Roothaan, a Dutchman who became superior general after the restoration of the Society in 1829. Something of a dull dog, Roothaan put all his chips on a literal interpretation of *The Spiritual Exercises*, which quickly became "the way" of Jesuits. I recall telling an instructor of tertians that I did not intend to follow the Exercises in my annual retreat and he answered, "Well, well . . . ."

St. Ignatius outlines his interior life in his autobiography, but what interests me is his diary. This was written while he was composing the constitutions of the Society, and in it we find a peculiarly Ignatian mysticism. Whereas the mysticism of St. John of the Cross concentrates on emptiness and nothingness, revolving around the famous *todo y nada*, the mysticism of Ignatius has content.

There are two levels of experience. At the deep level God is vividly present as Ignatius celebrates the Eucharist. At another level the content of the constitutions is present. Ignatius is constantly discerning, asking what is the best way to practice poverty, searching for the right path in which to guide his Society. In fact, the constitutions come out of Ignatius's mystical experience.

Now, while I have had immense help and inspiration from St. John of the Cross, I am finally drawn to Ignatian mysticism. My writing and my work have frequently been the overflow of my prayer, and sometimes I have composed the chapter of a book or an article for a magazine while sitting before the Eucharist and practicing contemplative prayer. I justify this by thinking of Ignatius composing the constitutions as he celebrated Mass. Only my discernment has not always been good. Not infrequently I have written things that I later regretted. Discernment is the key to Ignatian spirituality and mysticism.

And what about the world in which we find ourselves today?

We are living in a new age both in the world and in religion. We are living in a new age of Christian spirituality. It is an age when searching people see that most of the discursive work can be done by computers. Human beings want mysticism. Unless we Jesuits refine and develop our mysticism we will not survive. Already it is clear that searchers of the new age are not interested in us. Vocations to the Jesuits are at an all time low. If people are looking for mysticism, how can we ask them to work with the three powers of the soul (memory, understanding, and will) and to reflect on the three classes of men?

THROUGH JUNGIAN AND ASIAN THOUGHT and through what Bernard Lonergan calls "the shift to interiority" I have found a new approach to the Bible. Take that passage where Jesus tells us to go into our room and shut the door and pray to our Father in secret. I understand this as the inner room that the Hindus call "the cave of the heart." It is here that we will secretly meet our Father.

Or again, Jesus tells us that the kingdom of God is within. This surely applies to the inner cave of the heart.

Or again, think of that striking passage in John's Gospel where Jesus tells us that if we believe, rivers of water will flow from within. The original Greek does not say "from within" but "from the belly." I like the literal translation of the King James edition, which runs: "He that believeth in me, as the Scripture hath said, out of his belly shall flow rivers of living water." I imagine a stout Japanese bodhisattva sitting gloriously in the lotus posture while rivers of *ki* (energy) flow from his *hara* or *tanden* (belly) to the entire universe.

Again, this process of going down, going down to my true self has taught me a new approach to morality. I see that the truest morality is not fidelity to a set of rules and regulations that I learned from the catechism, but fidelity to my true self. This has liberated me to some extent from the old scrupulosity.

But how, you may ask, am I to find my true self? And how am I to know that this inner voice is indeed the true self and not my vicious superego?

Aye, there's the rub! I will have more to say about this later. Here let me simply note that we must give more time to silent prayer and meditation and discernment. Let us remember that it has been only a hundred years since the West discovered the unconscious. Before that, it is true, we knew of this inner world through the mystics, but dull theologians surrounded the mystical world with an aura of mystery that made it forbidden territory for the ordinary person. Now we are in a new era of history when the ordinary Joe Blow and Mary Anne are aware of their unconscious. They will no longer be kept at the top level of consciousness. We must give them mysticism or perish. This is an important message for us Jesuits.

MY TIME AT LUMEN VITAE came to an end. I got a big certificate marked "Satisfactory." No doubt this was the first stage above failure. But I was happy with it.

I said good-bye to my many friends and took the ship across the rough Atlantic to New York. On the way, we stopped at Cobh in the south of Ireland. This was 1960 and, as the poor Irish clambered on board, I saw that the old tradition of tearful emigration was still alive. These people were going across the sea to a distant land from which they would not return, though they might sigh, "I'll take you home again, Kathleen!" On board we had Irish dancing and ceilidh music. It was fun! Hilarious!

I was introduced to the captain and, when he heard that I was Irish, he said with a smile or a smirk, "These Micks are everywhere." It was the first time I had heard myself called a Mick.

We landed in New York. The famous United States of America! Since everyone spoke a sort of English I felt more at home there than in Belgium. After a night with the Jesuits at Fordham University I went to Philadelphia to meet the Clearkins, my mother's relatives from Ballybay in County Monaghan. They seemed awfully numerous. Kids were climbing all over the place. The Clearkins were builders—they had constructed big buildings all over Philadelphia—and they seemed to have done well in America. They gave their Irish cousin a wonderful welcome.

I worked in a New York parish for a couple of weeks. Then I gave a retreat. What that retreat was like I just don't remember. I don't think I said too much about mysticism. But when it was over, I took the plane to California and back home to Japan.

15

The Search in Asia

THE SOPHIA UNIVERSITY to which I returned in 1960 was very "Catholic." The Jesuits, faithful to the wishes of the founders, wanted it to be a beacon of Catholic light throughout Asia.

So, with red hair (and later a red beard) and wearing a black suit and a Roman collar I strode forth confidently from our beautiful residence, home to almost one hundred Jesuits, ready to confront Japan with the unshakable truth of the Christian tradition. We Western missionaries would liberate Japan from paganism, making it the great Christian nation of Asia.

Alas and alack, the world changed. The Catholic Church changed. The Jesuits changed. I changed. The Second Vatican Council (1962–1965) told us that all authentic religions issue from the same primitive perception and from people asking the same questions: What is a human being? What is the meaning and purpose of life? What happens after death? Where are we going? Religions bound up with cultural advancement have struggled to answer these deeply human questions in refined concepts and in highly developed language. But in the very search for answers there arises a profound religious sense (and I myself call it a mystical sense).

The council then urged us to be faithful to the teaching of Jesus, who is the way and the truth and the light, while accepting and promoting the good qualities found in all religions. This opened our minds and hearts to the beauty of Buddhism, and we began to see with the old missionaries that Japan is not a country for mass conversions. Might it not be better to engage in "pre-evangelization"? That is to say, could we not teach the basic truths of the Gospel, allowing people to remain Buddhist as long as they wish?

The mills of God grind slowly. More than twenty years later, in 1986, leaders of the world religions gathered at Assisi to pray for peace. Does their meeting say that prayer transcends the religions? Is it prayer for peace that will bring us together? The big distinction now, remarked Heinrich Dumoulin, is between those who believe in something and those who believe in nothing.

And all the time the church was changing its old practices. I recall the sniggers of the students when first I appeared in a white shirt and black trousers. Then I wore a tie. And finally I appeared in the classroom dressed in a suit like any other human being. Time was moving on.

IN THE UNIVERSITY I was kept busy. I lived in the student dormitory, where my job was to keep discipline, seeing that the students got up in the morning, came home at night, and generally behaved themselves. I also taught religion (at that time it was a compulsory subject) to a large class. I remember telling the students about the glories of matrimony as described in the book of Genesis and the Christian tradition, and one student, to the delight of the class, asked, "Then why don't you get married?"

Then I was in charge of the Catholic Students' Club, which had sister clubs in all the Japanese universities, and this turned out to be my most challenging work. In addition to this I taught English to students in various parts of the university, and I got a job teaching English conversation to the students of the prestigious Tokyo University. These students, the future politicians and ambassadors of Japan, were very intelligent. Talking to them was fun.

At this time I also began to give religious instruction with a great German Jesuit. Helmut Erlinghagen was tall, strikingly handsome, blond, and proud of his doctorate in ethics from Fordham University. Highly admired by the young people, whom he got to distribute handbills all over Tokyo, he put together a team of Jesuits to teach Christianity under his leadership. And he helped me a lot. "Johnston," he said, "don't teach anything you don't believe yourself! We all have lacunae in our faith. So if there is something you don't believe, leave it to someone else."

Big crowds came to our lectures. On the first night I spoke about Graham Greene and referred to his belief in hell. "My God, Johnston," said Erlinghagen. "You spoke about hell on the first night! Don't you realize that no one outside the Catholic Church and very few inside it believe in hell?" I had a good laugh at that.

Erlinghagen, however, knew that my lectures were pretty good and we became friends. I also made other friends among the Japanese students, both men and women, and they remain close to me today. I baptized the future archbishop of Tokyo and his two sisters. All in all, Erlinghagen's project was great.

At the height of his fame, Erlinghagen was sent back to Germany. Many years later I met him again. He was waiting for me at the station in Germany when I arrived from Holland. We had a glass of good German beer and a long chat. Then we said good-bye. I never saw him again after that. When he died suddenly, his friends and disciples celebrated a big Mass for him at the cathedral in Tokyo. May he rest in peace.

SHORTLY AFTER MY ARRIVAL at Sophia University I found myself in the middle of an awful student riot about the Security Treaty with the United States. It was basically anti-American, though the whole country boiled up in anger against Prime Minister Kishi. There were snake dances through the streets, with people chanting the slogan "*Ampo Hantai, Ampo Hantai, Ampo Hantai...*" *Ampo* meant the Security Treaty and *Hantai* meant "No!" So the message was: "No Security Treaty!"

It was a peaceful demonstration, though one young girl, Kamba Michiko, was trampled to death in a stampede and became something of a martyr. But I walked outside and watched the crowds chanting *Ampo Hantai* and no one molested me or even threatened me. Some even smiled at me. The students at that time were basically nonviolent. But I feel now that the anti-American feeling crushed by MacArthur in 1945 was beginning to emerge.

I knew almost nothing about politics. This was a time when Jesuits were little interested in social problems. I had learned a lot about Alessandro Valignano and the early Japanese martyrs, but not much about the society in which I lived. We Jesuits knew very little about the Security Treaty and assumed that the demonstration was a Communist plot. We paid little attention to the Japanese diocesan priests, some of whom sympathized with the demonstrators. Alas, we Jesuits, anxious to preserve our university, didn't think much about justice. Only much later did "justice and peace" come into our vocabulary.

In the dormitory where I was working I put up a notice inviting students to a discussion about the current unrest. Not one student turned up. This was a lesson for me, telling me that I was a foreigner and should keep my mouth shut about the internal problems of Japan. "*Sensei*, this is a Japanese problem," said one friendly student. And I decided to keep my Irish passport.

Let me say here that a number of my colleagues have taken Japanese citizenship. I decided, however, to remain "a yellow-haired foreigner" (in Japanese *komojin*) and to stay with Ireland. A Belgian missionary has written a book entitled *I Would Like to Be a Japanese* (in Japanese *Nihonjin ni Naritai*) and he reaches the conclusion that he cannot become a Japanese. It would be quite impossible. Now I find that to remain an Irishman who loves Japan, admires the culture, and speaks the language is greatly appreciated by the Japanese. Besides, I find that the Japanese expect a foreigner to bring something from his or her own country, even from a country like Ireland.

After a while, however, I became dissatisfied. With so much activity I was not able to settle down and pray. At times of prayer I would find myself restless and preoccupied with other things.

But my dissatisfaction was not only about prayer. The provincial, Father Arrupe, had divided the young Jesuits into two groups. There were those who would study at prestigious universities and impress the intelligentsia of Japan; and there were those who would slog around with students. I belonged to this second group. Arrupe assured me that he himself had no big degree and made an impression only by the force of his personality. No doubt he did.

But Pier Paolo was studying Buddhism in Chicago. Peter Milward was studying English literature in Oxford. Others were studying in Berkeley and in Germany and getting doctorates in Rome, while I was digging students out of bed in the morning. What would my mother think? I was still my mother's spoiled child. I wanted more.

So I asked to join the Department of English Literature. And I kicked up such a shindy that my request was granted. With the students I enjoyed reading *The Waste Land* and T. S. Eliot's plays, particularly *The Cocktail Party*. I also wrote two little religious books in Japanese and several articles for Japanese magazines. I had always wanted to be a writer, and here was my chance.

And then it happened.

One day, while browsing in the local bookshop, I found the Penguin edition of *The Cloud of Unknowing*. I began to read and I could not stop. This was it! This was the Christian mystical tradition, written two centuries before St. John of the Cross and in a delightful style. I decided then and there that I would write my doctoral thesis on *The Cloud* for our theologate in Shakujii. I would ask my old friend Tony Evangelista to direct me. And that was that.

Evangelista wanted me to study St. Ignatius, but I insisted on *The Cloud*. I loved *The Cloud*, and I felt that the anonymous English author was my friend. His sentences outlined my own contemplative experience. I could harmonize with every word. Here was a fourteenth-century mystic saying the things that I had read about in the libraries of Emo and Dublin, that I had learned from the holy John Hyde in Tullabeg, and that I was trying to experience in my everyday life.

And so I set to work. I wrote to Oxford University Press for the original fourteenth-century text of *The Cloud,* got some advice from James Walsh in England, and visited Evangelista every week in the theologate. Soon I was writing my thesis. I continued to teach at the university, but—horror of horrors—I forgot to tell the rector about my darling project. Klaus Luhmer caused no problems. He was a bit cynical—the kind of rector I liked.

Besides writing the thesis I had to take a few courses. One with Heinrich Dumoulin meant reading Daisetsu Suzuki on Zen. Together, Dumoulin and I went to one of the old man's last lectures on Pure Land Buddhism. Suzuki was more than ninety years of age. Coming back, Dumoulin asked me what I thought, and I said, "It was a lecture on the Sacred Heart." I meant it. It really was a beautiful lecture on what Christians might call the love of God.

I defended my thesis during the council years, and the professors were happy with it.

Next came the problem of publication. From the very beginning I was determined to have my thesis published as a book. But how was that to be done? God provided a way.

I was invited to give a course at a university in New York and while I was there I wandered into various publishing offices, carrying my big thesis under my arm. Everywhere I met with polite rejection until I found the French publisher Desclée, where the editor was looking for an English book. I offered him my thesis, *The Mysticism of "The Cloud of Unknowing."* And that was that. In the course of our discussion the editor insisted that we get a preface from a famous author, and I suggested Thomas Merton.

I was interested in Merton. In the 1940s we read *The Seven Storey Mountain* in the Jesuit refectory in Dublin. An elderly father there remarked that he was wary of "this young man." But Merton kept searching and growing until he turned to Asian religion. His dialogue with Daisetsu Suzuki, published as *Zen and the Birds of Appetite,* shows real insight.

Trappist monk, Thomas Merton.
(JOHN LYONS)

Dumoulin was writing about Zen, and Merton wrote a sharp and critical review of one of his writings. Dumoulin, always sensitive to criticism, wrote a letter of protest, and Merton answered humbly that he was not an expert and had no intention of crossing swords with a great writer like Dumoulin. Mollified by this humility, Dumoulin wrote again, inviting Merton to Japan. He, Dumoulin, had spoken with the Trappists in Hokkaido and they would love to receive Merton. Besides, if he did not come to Japan, Merton's writings on Zen would lose credibility.

Merton answered immediately that he would love to come to Japan. But what was normal for a Jesuit would be very extraordinary for a Trappist. Would Dumoulin write to the Trappist superior in Rome and ask for permission?

Dumoulin promptly wrote to Rome. There was no response. Finally, after a long, long delay, the Trappist superior answered in French: *Non!* The exigencies of Trappist silence did not permit such a thing. Instead of Merton, could the Jesuits invite Dom Aelred Graham?

Dumoulin, wise old politician, laughed. He knew immediately what had happened. Now he understood the delay. The Trappist superior had written to Merton's monastery in Gethsemani and gotten the answer, "No!" And he had passed it on. It was another instance of the old conflict between Thomas Merton and his superior, Abbot James Fox. I traveled to Gethsemani, and Merton was glad to see me because I came from Japan and knew something about Zen. He agreed to write a preface for my book but shrewdly observed, "Tell the publisher to send me the proofs." Obviously he did not want to write a preface for a book that would not be published.

At this time Merton was in crisis about his deep love for a nurse he had met in the hospital, but of course I did not know this, and our meeting in the monastery garden centered on Buddhism and Christianity.

Merton was obviously a searcher. He was searching, searching, searching, and saw that Asia had a lot to offer.

Was Merton a mystic?

I see two kinds of mysticism. One is like that of Padre Pio in Europe or Ramakrishna in India. Marked by the extraordinary, this type of mysticism baffles the psychologists. Merton does not belong here. The second kind of mysticism is like that of Dōgen in Japan or Meister Eckhart in the West. Merton, as I see him, is more at home here. About these two types I will speak later when I come to "the uncreated energies" and *kundalini* or "the serpent power."

But let me add a few more words about Merton.

Under the next abbot, Flavion Burns, Merton got permission to visit Asia in 1968. While on that trip he was electrocuted by an electric fan in Bangkok, just after having completed a lecture with words of dramatic irony, "So I will disappear."

I recall going into our Jesuit recreation room after breakfast and there it was. In the *Japan Times* a short article announced the death of Merton in Bangkok. Both Dumoulin and I were shocked. We had known about the meeting in Thailand. Our colleagues Hugo Enomiya Lassalle and Shigeto Oshida were there, and we were preparing to welcome Merton to Japan at last.

We always kept our interest in Merton. He is surely one of the leaders of today's meditation movement and its dialogue with Asia. When his biography by Michael Mott appeared, Dumoulin was at first shocked by Merton's apparent love affair. But after reading the biography carefully he remarked, "To condemn Merton would not be fair either to Merton himself or to Mott. For a long time Merton had been reflecting on his relationship with women."

Perhaps in this too Merton was prophetic.

MY BOOK, *The Mysticism of "The Cloud of Unknowing,"* appeared with Thomas Merton's preface. It was well received and got a rave review from the great Benedictine historian David Knowles. After forty years, it is still in print with Fordham University Press and some people have told me it is my best book. I don't agree. But that's what they say.

16

The Mystery of Endo

A SHORT TIME AFTER MY RETURN to Japan I grew depressed. I felt I just did not fit in. The German who was head of the English Literature department did not like me, and I did not like him. Peter Milward, a graduate of Oxford, was the expert on Shakespeare, and Frank Mathy had a doctorate in comparative literature from the University of Michigan. There were big-time Germans who ran the university and there were little people like me who were hangers-on. I became prematurely old. Perhaps I was a misfit in the Society of Jesus as it existed at that time. Or perhaps I was, as Michel Ledrus in Rome had suggested, in the night of the senses.

I was not helped by the development of student problems in Japan. As 1970—the year for the renewal of the Security Treaty—drew near, the student world became violent. Influenced by the so-called prophet Marcuse, Japanese students united with student movements throughout the world. They created the famous, or infamous, Zengakuren. Rebellious students took over the universities and smashed school property. I recall seeing a tall student, wearing a steel helmet and carrying a long pole, threatening a teacher who cowered before him. We Jesuits were shocked and afraid. What was happening? A Jesuit brother architect who had designed our buildings died of a heart attack. Another got sick and returned to Germany.

After the 1960 riots, which had almost caused a revolution, the Japanese government had carefully created an efficient riot police unit. But the law did not permit these men to enter a campus unless invited by the university authorities. And all the universities wavered.

Then Sophia took the lead. Our president, a Japanese layman (influenced no doubt by the foreign Jesuits), called in the police. Armed with helmets and shields and big truncheons, the riot police entered the campus slowly and methodically, catching dissident students and throwing them into vans, while other student groups gathered around shouting, "Riot police, go home!"

Was it a good idea to treat the students this way? The foreign Jesuits were all for it, but some of our Japanese Jesuits did not like it. Certainly the relationship between students and the establishment changed overnight. No more "Good morning, sir." No more greetings. Only stony silence. The university was locked up for the vacation. We became a business and have remained so until this day.

Small wonder I was depressed.

During this time I often spent weekends at the small vacation house we Jesuits had in Hakone at the foot of Mount Fuji. I would walk alone through the mountains and around the lake and in the evenings I would listen to Beethoven and Schubert and Chopin. Those long walks with the vision of snow-white Fuji rising majestically to heaven were a time of contemplative prayer for me. I had a strong sense of God's presence there.

A nun who knew me well, seeing my gloom, said I was depressed because of my creativity. "Creative people, like artists and writers, are always misfits," she said.

Be that as it may, I was coming to realize that my immensely valuable talks with Michel Ledrus had truly been only the start of a long journey. I had broken my childhood addiction, it is true; I had been liberated to some extent from fears and anxieties and scruples. But I was still faced with a struggle that would last a lifetime. Would creativity be the answer?

WRITING MY THESIS on *The Cloud* had been a creative experience and it had eased my depression. The next step was to be my translation of the controversial novel *Chinmoku* (its English title would be *Silence*) by Shusaku Endo. I did not consider myself a professional translator; I simply wanted to study more Japanese. After almost twenty years in Japan I was always trotting out the same words, more or less understanding and more or less understood. So now I was searching for a good Christian book to translate while at the same time spreading the Gospel. An eminent Catholic, I was told, had written a book about the Japanese martyrs of the seventeenth century. This was my chance.

I had read about the Japanese martyrs in Charles Boxer's book about the Christian century in Japan. In 1597 twenty-six Christians were crucified in Nagasaki, and in the subsequent century four thousand Christians were put to death. Since the ordinary death penalties won only admiration for the martyrs, the persecutors concentrated on making apostates. Among the cruel tortures that they devised was "the pit." Here the victim's body and arms and legs were tightly bound with rope and he was suspended upside down in a pit filled with refuse and garbage. A hole was drilled in his temple to permit the blood to fall drop by drop and thus prevent a rapid death. Sometimes this torture lasted for an entire week before death took place.

Christianity was apparently stamped out, but on March 17, 1865, the French missionary Père Petitjean discovered in Kyushu a small community of "hidden Christians" (*kakure kiristan*) who for generations had secretly practiced and handed down their faith.

Endo was familiar with all this. He loved Nagasaki, where today a monument to him has been erected. Besides, he had accurate information from Jesuit historians, even though he distorted some of the historical facts to suit his thesis.

I first met Endo at a showing of *Ogon mo Kuni (The Golden Country)*, his little play about the martyrs, translated into English by my friend Frank Mathy. Here Endo tells the story of Christopher Ferreira, the Portuguese Jesuit provincial, who, after five hours hanging in the pit apostatized by putting his foot on the *fumie* (a copper tablet with a likeness of Jesus on which suspected Christians were ordered to step). The Christians were shocked. Particularly dramatic is the play's conclusion, where the persecutor Hirata rushes excitedly onstage with the news that a rider has just come from Fukuoka with a message: "Four Christian priests have just landed.... They came over in a small boat rowed by Chinese and managed to land under cover of night."

So faith goes on. I liked this conclusion. I took it as a sign of resurrection.

At this time I had not read *Chinmoku*, but its theme, I had heard, was more or less the same as that of *The Golden Country*. I asked Endo if he would be interested in having it translated and he said he was looking for a good translator.

In fact, I soon discovered that *Chinmoku* does not have the triumphant resurrection of *The Golden Country*. It begins and ends in sadness. It tells the story of the Portuguese priest Rodriguez who, having courageously come to Japan to atone for the sin of Ferreira, is overcome by the awful suffering of the Christians and the silence of God. All through the novel the excruciatingly psychological suffering of Rodriguez is so vividly described that the reader shivers. There is no letup. "My God, my God, why hast thou forsaken me?" And the climax comes when he places his foot on the picture of Jesus whom he loves. But why does he do this?

He does it in answer to the cry of Jesus, "You may trample! You may trample! For this I came into the world!" And so he steps on the picture of Jesus, not because he is tortured in the pit but to save the Christians who, the persecutors have told him, will be saved if only he gives this sign of apostasy.

The novel was much loved and appreciated in Japan, but many Christians were upset, thinking that Endo was glorifying apos-

Novelist Shusaku Endo gazing at the fumie, *or picture of Christ, on which Christians were obliged to trample.*
(COURTESY OF JUNKO ENDO)

tasy. In the first printing Endo had added a postscript, saying that his ideas might be more Protestant than Catholic. But many Protestants were so angry at this that he omitted the postscript in subsequent editions.

Some Catholics complained to my provincial that a Jesuit should not translate such a book. I explained to Father Provincial Martini that I had promised the author to translate the book. Besides, I had asked for and received permission. Martini smiled and said, "Well, it's your responsibility, not mine."

Later I got good news. A Carmelite sister in the United States who read my translation wrote, "This is a book about prayer." She went on to quote the Gospel, saying that Peter and Paul, Mary Magdalene and Thomas—all had denied Jesus and then came round to accept him. Rodriquez, she said, was the same. He did not lose his faith. *Chinmoku* was his dark night of the soul. I told this to Endo and he was delighted. "Father, give me a copy of that letter!" he said.

I began to see her point. *Chinmoku* ends with the emptiness or *kenosis* of Jesus who cries out that he came into the world to be trampled on. It ends with the *kenosis* of the priest who, out of compassion and love, empties himself completely. And now I believe that *Chinmoku* is a story of the *kenosis* of Endo himself.

In short, I see in Endo the *kenosis* of the Epistle to the Philippians, where Jesus empties himself, taking the form of a slave, becoming obedient unto death, even death on the cross. I see in Endo the *todo y nada* of St. John of the Cross, the "all and nothing" of *The Cloud of Unknowing*. I now realize that most of Endo's works center on the weak Jesus who emptied himself, and Endo, always conscious of his own sinfulness and admitting that he would have stepped on the *fumie*, looks on himself as the weak follower of Jesus. The glorification of weakness is at the very center of his work.

But Endo was a complicated person (in this he was very Japanese) and *Chinmoku* is a complex novel. And Endo did have his personal problems.

As I have previously recounted, Endo's first problem was that Father Peter Herzog, the good and pious rector of Sophia who had baptized Endo, had left the priesthood and married his secretary. This was in the 1950s, and to Endo it was a terrible shock. He could not fathom it. Yet, over time, he came to believe that Herzog still had faith. According to Endo, the proud, almost arrogant, priest who had baptized him had undergone *kenosis* and was now a better, humbler man.

Is *Chinmoku* a defense of Herzog? Is Herzog the man who abandons everything for love?

A second problem for Endo was that Christianity, apart from the tiny group of Christians in Nagasaki, had been totally banished from Japan. Why?

Over the years many historians have tackled this problem. Some say that the leaders of Japan, afraid of Portuguese and Spanish influence, wanted to get rid of Christianity and create what was later called "a closed country"—in Japanese, *sakoku*.

Endo, however, has his own answer, drawn from his own personal struggle. Japan is a swamp (in Japanese *doronuma*) which cannot accept a foreign religion without changing it. This comes out in the important dialogues between Rodriguez and his persecutors, in which Endo is in fact talking about himself. He was baptized as a child into this foreign religion.

He tried to reject it but could not. So he wants to exchange his Western dress for a Japanese kimono. He wants a Japanese Christianity.

Endo's writings revolve around the struggle between his Japanese self and his Christian self or, as he himself puts it, between "the white man and the yellow man." This struggle, his dark night of the soul, may have begun in France where he studied as a young man after the war and was not greatly appreciated. Yet it made him greatly loved by the Japanese people. His first novel, *The White Man* (*Shiroi Hito*), won him the much coveted Akutagawa literary prize.

For Endo there was no question of rejecting Christianity. He says that *he could not* reject Christianity. His eyes were always fixed on Christ, whom he loved and for whom he was always searching. The Christ whom he found and with whom he identified was the humiliated Christ who was a misfit, the Christ who emptied himself, taking the form of a servant. What Endo rejected was the dualistic Western framework that put God "up there" and constantly made separations and divisions. I myself think he was looking for the God of the mystics in whom we live and move and have our being.

However, let me be honest.

As I was translating *Chinmmoku* what irritated me most was that Endo seemed to be saying, "You foreign idiot! You came to Japan to convert the Japanese and you failed utterly. Ha! Ha!" I am not saying that Endo said this or even intended it. I simply say that this is how he came across to me as I sweated over the work of translation. And, worst of all, I felt it was true!

Yet we became friends. He invited me into his little literary circle of intellectuals who called him "the godfather." He was charming and full of fun. On one occasion I joined him at a Chinese restaurant for an interview with an English journalist. After asking many innocuous questions, the journalist suddenly asked, "Mr. Endo, you are an admirer of Graham Greene?" Endo nodded in agreement. "But Greene," said the journalist, "had many problems with the Catholic Church. What about you, Mr. Endo?"

Endo answered with a smile, "I have had problems. They appear in my books. But my mother died a Catholic. My brother died a Catholic. And I would like to die a Catholic too."

Of course, he did admire Graham Greene and was influenced by *The Power and the Glory*. Once when Endo was in London he ran into Graham Greene by accident in a hotel and this was one of the big days in his life. Yet there were differences, pointed out to me by a bishop in Finland who was a fan of Endo. The bishop said that Greene was a novelist who happened to be a Catholic, while Endo was a Catholic who happened to be a novelist. This may be true. Still, both of these authors worked out their religious problems in powerful novels and will go hand in hand through the centuries as honest but committed Catholics.

While in Australia I was asked by the university in Sydney to give a talk on Endo. I refused, saying that he was a prolific writer and I had only read a fraction of his books. However, when they insisted, I agreed to speak about two books: *Silence* and *Deep River.*

I said that in *Silence* Endo was searching for a Japanese Christianity, but by his last novel, *Deep River,* which takes place around the Ganges, Endo has grown. Now he was looking not just for a Japanese but for an Asian Christianity. As a traditional Catholic, he had started his search in Israel, but what he really wanted he found in India with the sisters of Mother Teresa of Calcutta and the young Japanese priest who (once more Endo's favorite theme!) is a misfit in the universal church.

"I would like to die a Catholic too . . ."

I last met Endo in 1996 when he was in the hospital dying, with his faithful wife Junko sitting beside his bed. I asked if he wanted to receive the sacraments and he said, "Yes, Father! Please! Please!" So I administered the sacrament of the sick and gave both of them absolution. Then I brought the Eucharist.

We had a beautiful memorial Mass for Endo in St. Ignatius Church. The actress who had played the heroine in the movie of *Deep River* wept. The cardinal was also present, saying he had come not because Endo was a great novelist but because he was a friend.

I asked Junko if she was very lonely. "No," she said, "he is always with me." And then she added that in his last hours her husband had shared in the passion of Christ.

ENDO WAS ONE OF JAPAN'S top writers. His thesis that Japan is a swamp that cannot absorb Western Christianity made a deep impression not only in Japan but on readers throughout the world. A Japanese professor told me that an Englishman had asked him, "Can you Japanese really believe in the Christian God?"

After many years in this country I believe that the Japanese can accept the God of the Christian contemplatives and mystics. This is the God who is present at the depths of the universe, giving existence to all things. This is the God we meet in the silence of contemplative prayer. I am grateful to Shusaku Endo for stressing this aspect of God.

As I write at the beginning of the third millennium, however, another insight comes to me. I see that the Japan of Endo's day is fast disappearing. Born in 1923, Endo was raised in a Japan that was still something of a *sakoku,* or closed country. This was a Japan in which foreigners were rare birds (when I came to Japan we were still called "funny foreigners"—*hen na gaijin*) because we stood out in an extremely well organized society. Western Christianity also stood out as a funny religion, run by funny foreigners.

Now Japan has changed. With the fall in population, Japan, like the Western nations, needs foreign labor for economic survival. We see a huge influx of workers from the Philippines, Brazil, Peru, Vietnam, and a host of small countries. The migrants bring their own language, their own culture, their own religion. Some get married to Japanese and have their children baptized. Now in the Japanese Catholic Church we have more foreigners than Japanese.

I have had the privilege of celebrating the Eucharist for large congregations of Filipinos. How I enjoy their beautiful singing, their uninhibited devotion, and their charismatic joy! As in Italy, Britain, Germany, Spain, and France, this migration brings enormous problems that I cannot speak about here. Only let me say that the Japan of Endo's days is rapidly giving way to a new Japan.

TO RETURN TO TOKYO of the 1960s. With the student turmoil, a few of us younger Jesuits felt that our big residence was not a good place to live. We were about one hundred Jesuits, almost all foreigners, living in something like a castle. Could we really understand Japan? Could we really come in contact with the Japanese world?

We proposed to the provincial that we move to a small house in Hongo near the prestigious Tokyo University. The older Jesuits thought we were rebels. They called us "the young Turks."

Anyhow, the provincial agreed and we moved to Hongo.

17
Dialogue with Zen

MOVING FROM THE BIG JESUIT RESIDENCE to the little house near Tokyo University was a wonderful experience. Since entering the novitiate in 1943, I had lived in religious institutions where the rector was the big boss and I got my money from the minister. Toothpaste and soap and the like were available in a common room. Newspapers and magazines were in the recreation room. If I wanted to travel outside Japan I submitted an application that the rector discussed with the house consultors and sent on to the provincial. If there was discernment, I was not part of it.

Now in our little house in Hongo I was liberated. Here I lived in an ordinary Japanese house as an ordinary human being with a few Jesuit friends. We were subject, it is true, to the rector in the big residence, but this was Father Giuseppe Pittau who was reasonable and far away. Instead of asking for money, we had a "green box" in the kitchen from which each of us took what he needed and into which we put the money we did not need. I began to understand the spirit of poverty as opposed to its legal ramifications.

Every day we went to the Sophia University to teach our classes. Sometimes we went by train, but more often I cycled through Tokyo. We had lunch with the Jesuit community—some said we were getting the best of both worlds—and in the evening we came home for dinner. This was cooked by an elderly lady who also cleaned the house. Sometimes I stopped off to eat rice and tofu and vegetables at a Chinese restaurant.

In the 1960s this way of life was a bit revolutionary, but now in the third millennium it seems to be the way in which religious life will go in the future, if religious life has a future.

Most of our rooms had straw matting (*tatami*) and we slept on the floor. We also had a chapel where we could sit on the floor on Zen cushions. I liked Hongo from the very beginning. It was great to live without a rector breathing down my neck. We did our own shopping and had some contact with our neighbors. On the main road were the two main gates of Tokyo University. All in all, I felt that for the first time I was living in Japan!

I DID A LOT OF WRITING in that house, sitting on the floor in front of my typewriter. Here I wrote *Christian Zen*, which I dedicated to my community: "For George, Isidore, John, Rich, and even for Pier Paolo."

Yes, Pier Paolo, my lifelong Italian friend, was a community member. A fine Buddhist scholar, he read my book and remarked with a smile, "There's not much Zen in that book! But people will read it and it will do them good!" In fact, my intention was not to write a book about Zen; it was to write about Christian meditation in dialogue with Zen. I wanted this to be a practical book from which Christians would humbly learn from Zen and the East while being totally committed to the Gospel. I still think that *Christian Zen* is such a book.

In Hongo we tried to have "an open community" to which people could come at any time, walking freely into the kitchen to talk.

I STARTED A PRAYER GROUP with some friends whom I had baptized. We sat on the floor for an hour in Zen style before the Blessed Sacrament, ringing the little bell at the beginning, middle, and end. Then we had Mass and finally we drank green tea and engaged in conversation.

The leaders of our group were Christians, but anyone was welcome. The only qualification was the willingness to "sit"—either in the lotus or the half-lotus or back on the heels or on a pile of cushions. We asked aspiring meditators no questions about their belief in God. We made no enquiries about their morality. We did not ask if they were divorced. "Just come and sit with us, and believe what you want."

I began to see (and now I realize it more and more) that the Asian tradition of meditation is practical. It teaches people how to sit with the back straight, how to breathe, how to relax, and how to enter into a deep level of awareness. The Japanese who came to our prayer group could do this almost automatically. Perhaps the "ways" that are deep in their culture— the way of tea, of the flower, of the bow, of Zen, and the rest—teach them. The foreigners, on the other hand, remained at the top level of consciousness until they were taught to enter more deeply into the inner world.

Sitting in the lotus position around the Eucharist.

I began to see also that my vocation in Japan was not to teach English or even to give religious instruction. It seemed that I was being called to pray or meditate and to teach prayer and meditation. For me personally this meant prayer before the Blessed Sacrament, rooted in the Bible; but I did not expect this of every one. People could believe what they wanted and we could all meditate together.

Here let me say that when I pray before the Blessed Sacrament, Jesus, the Bread of Life, is not "out there" separated from me. We—the body of Christ and I—are at the same time two and one. This is the coincidence of opposites that in the Jewish and Christian tradition is centered on love. This is how I understand Genesis, that a man shall leave his father and mother and cleave to his wife and the two shall become one. They are no longer two but one because they love one another—and yet they are two. I myself, though not married, experience this non-dualism with friends who are far away. What a joy it is to receive a letter and to know that we are not two but one, even while remaining two!

WHILE IN HONGO I made contact with the Zen-Christian dialogue that was getting under way. The pioneer in this was the Jesuit Hugo Enomiya Lassalle who had practiced Zen long before the Vatican Council in an effort to understand Japanese culture. Now, convinced of Zen's religious

The Catholic Zen center, Shinmeikutsu, or "The Cave of Divine Darkness."

value, he set up a Christian Zen temple outside Tokyo called Shin-meikutsu, translated into English as the "Cave of Divine Darkness."

With my friend and colleague Heinrich Dumoulin I went to the in-auguration. The Catholic archbishop was present, and several Buddhist monks sat motionless in the lotus posture. The Jesuit provincial, attempt-ing unsuccessfully to squat, cut a pitiful figure.

We celebrated the Eucharist in the impressive meditation hall, using a massive rock as an altar. Lassalle, as the principal celebrant, said in his homily that his crazy dream had at last come true. The monks sat beauti-fully and unemotionally in their robes through it all.

It was truly a breakthrough in dialogue.

I SOMETIMES VISITED Shigeto Oshida, a Dominican priest who had a little ashram at Takamori in the mountains of Nagano. Oshida was very differ-ent from Lassalle. A bit of a misfit among the Dominican friars and in poor health, he went to live in the mountains where the air was pure and the water clear. Oshida was a convert to Christianity; his family back-ground was Zen Buddhist. He was a graduate of Tokyo University, and all alone he began to "sit."

Gradually men and women admirers surrounded him, and with them he sat and sat. Unlike Lassalle, who had collected millions of yen in Germany to build a beautiful and traditional Zen monastery, Oshida lived in dire poverty. He worked in the fields and he welcomed visitors, Japanese or foreigners, asking for no remuneration but only that they work in the fields to support themselves. And soon he was revered as a Zen master.

However, Oshida took direction from no Zen master. He made no claim to have reached *satori*, but he was steeped in the Christian scriptures and celebrated the Eucharist with great devotion. He also had a sense of humor. On one occasion when I was with him at a Zen-Christian dialogue in the United States, participants were asked to write down their name and profession. Oshida wrote that he was "a farmer."

Oshida had a profound knowledge of Chinese and Japanese philosophy. He had, moreover, a close relationship with Zen monks and spoke their language. At a dialogue I heard him say, "The first thing is honesty. My Zen is in the words of Jesus, 'My God, my God, why hast thou forsaken me?'" The Zen participants appreciated that a lot. Oshida loved the Gospel of John. He wrote out the whole Gospel in beautiful Japanese characters, the fruit of his devotion to Christianity and Japanese culture.

Dominican Oshida Shigeto (right), revered as a Zen master.

I myself made no claims to practice Zen as the Buddhists practice it. But many years later, when Lassalle was practicing under the great Yamada Koun, I asked Oshida for advice: "Should I join this group? Should I do Zen under this great master?" Oshida smiled: "*Ma!*" he said. "Go if you want. But I think you will find that their faith is different from yours." This was wise advice. Oshida saw that the essence of Zen is faith in the Buddha and the patriarchs, and the essence of Christianity is faith in Jesus and the Christian tradition.

I think that this question of faith was the reason why Lassalle, while he will remain in history as the great pioneer, was never highly esteemed by the Buddhists. I ask myself if he was inwardly split, trying to be faithful to both the Christian tradition and the Buddhist tradition.

Since Lassalle's time, there has been much talk of "double belonging," with people asking if they can belong simultaneously to Christianity and to Buddhism. I have always said that for me this is impossible. Much as I love the Buddha and the patriarchs, I cannot make to them the total commitment I make to Jesus. And I cannot help asking myself if Lassalle also, perhaps unconsciously, was trying to reconcile his commitment to Jesus and to the Buddha—and if perhaps for him too it was impossible.

In a letter written to me in 1967 Thomas Merton makes some very insightful comments about our practice of Zen. He says that sitting in the lotus posture is not important, and he speaks of the apophatic approach to God, citing Eckhart's comment that one can be so poor that one does not even have a God. Most important is his subtle attack on Lassalle for aiming at *satori*. Such an aim, he points out, could make *satori* impossible. In the third edition of *Christian Zen* I include a quote from Thomas Merton's letter in which he says that it is probably best to take what Zen can offer in the way of inner purification "and not to worry too much about where we get." I believe Merton here voices the authentic tradition of both Christian and Buddhist mysticism.

Then there was the great Quaker Douglas Steere who came to Japan to take part in a Christian-Zen dialogue. We all sat on the floor in Zen—or perhaps I should call it meditation. Then the Protestants had a Bible ceremony, and finally we Catholics celebrated the Eucharist for the whole group. Important in our meeting was the brilliant Carmelite Ichiro Okumura, a graduate of Tokyo University, who was steeped in St. John of the Cross and had a profound grasp of the Buddhist sutras. We also had several fine Zen practitioners. And, of course, Lassalle, Dumoulin, and I were present. Only later did we have the Jesuit Kakichi Kadowaki who, after his practice of Zen,

Japanese Jesuit Kakichi Kadowaki has practiced Zen intensively.

wrote a pamphlet on "Zen and the Spiritual Exercises of St. Ignatius." This pamphlet (which I translated into English) describes his efforts to synthesize Zen and the Exercises.

THE CHRISTIAN-ZEN DIALOGUE was very successful. I attended its follow-up in the United States to which Douglas Steere invited eminent Buddhist practitioners.

Yet Zen has not made much progress within Christianity in Japan. I now see little "pure Zen." I do not see any Japanese priest or pastor or sister claiming to be a roshi (Zen master). What has happened?

I always come back to Oshida's "I think you will find their faith is different from yours."

The core of religious meditation is faith. There is a long tradition of Buddhist faith in the Buddha, the dharma, and the sangha. Often when they break through to enlightenment, Buddhists will cry out, "The patriarchs have not deceived me!" And often the Christian coming to conversion will cry out, "Jesus is Lord!" In both Buddhism and Christianity there is a long tradition and a long series of transmissions. Now these two traditions have met and are learning from one another.

The Jewish scholar Zvi Werbalowsky, who often had lunch with us in Hongo and was deeply committed to dialogue, used to say, "I take Buddhist metaphysics seriously." He did not mean metaphysics like that of Aristotle. He simply meant the sutras, particularly the *Heart Sutra* and the *Lotus Sutra*. In other words, Zen is more than *satori*, just as Christianity is more than conversion of heart.

Japanese Christians, then, have not given up the dialogue. Throughout Japan one can find Christians sitting before a crucifix or before the tabernacle. They are learning many things from Zen and are coming to experience the coincidence of opposites; but that is different from practicing Zen. Like Shusaku Endo, they are coming to a Japanese Christianity.

And what about myself?

Before coming to Japan I had been familiar with the apophatic tradition in Christianity. I loved St. John of the Cross. Then in Japan I discovered *The Cloud of Unknowing*. I have read Jung's magnificent articles on yoga and Zen. Like Jung, I see much in common between East and West, and I love the dialogue. It will certainly continue, to the mutual enrichment of both Buddhists and Christians.

AFTER A SHORT TIME in Hongo I felt the urge to go to the United States. For me at that time America was the center of the world. It was at the forefront of evolution in both science and religion. There was interest in meditation, particularly in Zen—a fad, no doubt, but a fad that interested me. Also, since the war America had exerted enormous influence in Japan. Even our university was modeled on American universities. For all these reasons I felt that I wanted to go to the United States.

My brethren in the Jesuit community, however, had their own interpretation. This restless Irishman, they thought, cannot sit still. He cannot stay in one place. He wants to travel around the world.

I could not deny this. I was a restless Irishman. My forebears—at least the Clearkins on my mother's side—had gone from Ballybay to Philadelphia and even to California. Perhaps travel was in my genes. Yet I do not see this at odds with my Jesuit vocation. St. Ignatius wrote in the constitutions that it is according to our vocation to travel to any part of the world—"Any part of the world," said my Irish provincial, and he quoted it in Latin—"*Quavis mundi plaga*"—adding, "and there are some men you cannot get to cross a corridor!"

Anyhow, I heard that there was an excellent program at the Jesuit summer school of the University of San Francisco, run by Father Al Zaballa (his mother's name was O'Connor), and I asked a Californian Jesuit colleague to write to him for me. Bob Arrowsmith kindly did so, mentioning my doctorate from Sophia in mystical theology. I had just written a book entitled *The Still Point: Reflections on Zen and Christian Mysticism*, and this sounded pretty good. Al Zaballa invited me to give a course on Mysticism East and West.

So I got permission from the Japanese provincial and set out for California.

18
California, Here I Come!

OUR PLANE PUT DOWN in Honolulu. This was 1970, when a glorious air of freedom permeated the United States. And the Catholic Church, like the rest of the country, was full of self-confidence and joy. The priest, like Bing Crosby in *Going My Way*, was a jovial fellow who could do nothing wrong.

The official, looking at my Irish passport and my address at the University of San Francisco, asked, "Will you be teaching there?" I said yes. "Father, you can't teach with this visa," he said. Then he stamped my passport and ushered me through.

Hawaiian music floated through the air with the romantic voice of Andy Williams softly singing about love. I was licking an ice-cream cone—something I would not have done in Japan—when I met a student from Sophia. He, too, was going to the mainland and we greeted one another with a good laugh as we moved toward the plane. There was almost no security as we boarded. Well-wishers came right up to the entrance.

In San Francisco I was welcomed to the big Jesuit residence, which was little different from our residence in Tokyo, and after meeting the Jesuit brethren I began to look through my notes for my classes.

I had thirty or forty students, many of them priests and sisters, and what I taught them I do not now remember. Probably I followed my book *The Still Point*, which takes up the main points of dialogue between Buddhism and Christianity in a rather reasonable way. I think I still hold to what I say there. Anyhow, we had a cheerful time with plenty of laughter and fun.

In the evenings I gathered students together for meditation, which we did by sitting on the floor on Zen cushions. This was not just for my students but for anyone who wanted to come, and quite a large number turned up. Some people called it "Zen" and this earned the criticism of some conservative Jesuits. "They are doing Zen Buddhism in the chapel," exploded one elderly father. But in fact we were not doing Zen but contemplation, with some Christians repeating a mantra like the word "Jesus." Al Zaballa said nothing. I think he was glad to have some controversy around the summer school.

I know I have been criticized from the other side for not practicing "pure Zen" like Hugo Enomiya Lassalle. But I have already explained that this is not my line. I am happy with St. John of the Cross and *The Cloud of Unknowing* in *dialogue* with Zen. I have always made it clear that I speak from the standpoint of Christian contemplation, as a person who wants to learn what he can from Zen, and I have never found this an obstacle to authentic dialogue. In fact, a Buddhist monk once said to me laughing, "I have practiced for years and never got anywhere, and here come foreigners claiming *satori* after six months!"

I visited the Zen Center in San Francisco and found it very serious. Americans recited sutras in Japanese using Roman script. The inspiration came principally from the Zen monk Shunryu Suzuki whose book *Zen Mind, Beginner's Mind* is a sort of classic. Apparently Suzuki was not greatly appreciated in Japan and became well known only after he went to the United States. When I visited the Zen Center he was already dying of cancer and I had no opportunity to speak with him.

I GOT A GREAT WELCOME from my American cousin Brian who was living outside San Francisco. With his wife Carol he came frequently to the university on weekends and brought me down to his home where we talked about Ireland and about cabbages and kings. Both Brian and Carol, born in America, were very Irish and very Catholic.

When he heard that I was interested in Zen, Brian offered to drive me to a Buddhist center where there were hot springs. I liked the idea. Since Carol was pregnant at that time, she could not come, but we were joined by a middle-aged man, an old friend of Brian. And after a rough drive along a road that was full of potholes, we reached our destination.

There was an information center and a small hall where people were invited to spend some time in meditation. I think there was some kind of religious ceremony in the evening.

What shocked me was that the river and the pools outside were filled with naked men and women—stark naked—enjoying the hot water and lying in the sun. Also there were baths divided into two sections, one for men and the other for women, but people could move easily from one section to the other. Brian and his friend did not bat an eyelid and we got into the bath.

I think I was unduly upset. I had thought my problems had been solved by my talks with Ledrus years earlier, but now I realized that psychological problems are not so easily put to rest.

Back at the university I naively told some students that I had been to this Buddhist center and the whole thing went round the campus as a standard joke. This Irish Jesuit who had spent twenty years in Japan had gone to the hot springs! Ha! Ha! I felt really humiliated.

But it was a good experience and it made me think. Pedro Arrupe, when he was provincial in Japan, loved to tell stories and anecdotes. I heard him tell a story concerning his experience during the war. When he was a prisoner in Yamaguchi, a soldier called out, "*Sensei*, would you like to go to the *ofuro* (i.e., the bath)?" And Arrupe, thinking he was referring to the soldiers' bath, answered yes. But to his surprise, several soldiers with rifles marched him through the streets to the public bath. Arrupe, I have been told, related this story several times, always laughing, and I wonder if he was letting the seminarians see that the public bath was quite innocent.

FOR THE NEXT FOUR YEARS I kept going to the United States to teach in the summer school of the University of San Francisco and to give retreats and talks. So often did I go that the English Literature Department of Sophia got irritated and started looking for a way to drop me from the department. However, my good and intelligent rector Joseph Pittau quickly grasped the situation and transferred me to another section of the university from which I could travel more freely. I was happy about this.

In the United States I made many new friends. Chief among these were the Carmelite sisters in Reno, Nevada. They had enthusiastically read my book *The Mysticism of "The Cloud of Unknowing"* and, hearing that I was teaching in San Francisco, invited me to give some talks. I went by bus and was met by a couple of sisters in brown habits. From that time, Reno became my second home.

On their free day the community would drive up the mountain to the magnificent Lake Tahoe and I enjoyed that scenery more than I can say. At other times we went to the dead and motionless Pyramid Lake. Most interesting of all were our discussions about contemplation, Carmelite spirituality, and the Christian mystical tradition.

I quickly saw that the youngest nun, Sister Laureen, was very intelligent. She was well versed not only in the Carmelite mystics, John of the

Cross, and Teresa of Avila, but also in Teilhard de Chardin and the best contemporary writers. Together we walked along the mountain paths, talking about mysticism and agreeing that the mystics are in the forefront of evolution.

Laureen was open to new movements in psychology and science and their influence on meditation. This was the time when Transcendental Meditation was popular in the United States. Then there was the ongoing dialogue with Zen, which had begun in Japan. Laureen was interested in science and mysticism and the study I had done in Japan with Dr. Tomio Hirai of Tokyo University, who was interested in meditation and brain waves.

Around this time I went to the Menninger Foundation at Topeka in Kansas and had fascinating talks with Dr. Elmer Green who, like Dr. Hirai, was interested in the relationship between meditation and alpha and theta waves on the electroencephalogram. He spoke a lot about energy, particularly about "passive energy" which comes into the psyche when one is able to "let go" of all attachments and allow the energy to flow. He had meditators "wired up" in the laboratory so that he could test their brain waves in time of meditation.

All this was initiating a new dialogue between science and mysticism. I saw that professional people with little interest in religion were fascinated by meditation. Was this the beginning of a clearer distinction between spirituality and religion? And was meditation beginning to appeal to the irreligious masses?

This went into my book *Silent Music*, published by Harper in New York and Collins in London. Clayton Carlson, then a young executive at Harper, told me I was "a whale of a writer." And Lady Collins, the charming dowager, distinguishing between "best sellers" and "long sellers," told me that my book would be around for a long time. This elated me. I recall walking down Fifth Avenue in New York and saying to myself with élan, "I'm an author! I'm an author!" I knew my mother in Ireland was proud of me.

The actual writing of *Silent Music* I did in Japan. I remember how, on the long train journey between Tokyo and my new destination in Hatano, I read Laureen's long letters, containing comments on the pages I had sent to her and suggestions for fresh approaches.

The Reno Carmelites had introduced me to the Association for Contemplatives based in the Redwoods Monastery in Northern California and I gave a workshop there. I also spoke to the Trappists in Vina and gave retreats and talks to other religious communities. I was especially welcomed by the Carmelites of Indianapolis. Always I spoke about St. John of the Cross and *The Cloud of Unknowing* with references to the experiments of Dr. Elmer Green.

SINCE MY TALKS were mainly on contemplation, people began to ask, "Are you not a Jesuit? What about Ignatius of Loyola? What do you think of the Spiritual Exercises? Why do you not give talks to the Jesuits?"

For me this was indeed a problem.

As a novice I had gone through the Spiritual Exercises systematically, rigidly, and methodologically. In the thirty-day retreat the master of novices had made us think about the meaning of life and the ugliness of sin, leading to a general confession of the sins of our whole life. We had then considered the call of a temporal king and the call of the divine king, a meditation that led to a total commitment to Christ poor and humiliated. We then made, or renewed, our vocation to the religious life, meditating on the passion and death of Jesus and his resurrection. Finally we made the great "contemplation for obtaining divine love," handing over everything and asking Our Lord to use it as he wishes. "Take, O Lord, and receive . . . ."

This final meditation is, in my opinion, the Ignatian introduction to contemplative prayer. As I noted in the chapter on my novitiate experience, it resembles the *todo y nada* of St. John of the Cross, except that—in asking God to *use our gifts*, to "dispose of them in any way" according to his will—it is the prayer not of one who is purely contemplative but of one who is a contemplative in action. *And I believe that the aim of the Spiritual Exercises is to lead to contemplation in action.*

After completing the Exercises, I read many books on prayer, especially books written at the beginning of the twentieth century. These books distinguished between "ordinary prayer" that came from human effort assisted by ordinary grace and "extraordinary prayer" that was a privileged gift of God. Ordinary prayer I had practiced in the Spiritual Exercises. I saw how it reaches a climax with "acquired contemplation," which I now see is very common in Japan in the "ways" I mentioned earlier—that is, the way of tea, the way of Zen, and so on. These so-called ways (in Japanese *do* and in Chinese *tao*) are among the richest flowers of Sino-Japanese culture.

However, while still in Ireland, I had read that there comes a time when human effort becomes less and less necessary because of the action of God, and then there comes "infused contemplation," which is pure gift.

The chief characteristic of infused contemplation is the sense of presence. One is enveloped by an indefinable sense of presence, either within or around or both together, with the conviction, "I did not cause this. I could not cause this." When this infused contemplation is given, the director must never urge the praying person to think, since thinking might interfere with the gift of God, who is doing great and mysterious work at a deeper level. Rather than thinking, one must "do nothing." One must simply allow God to act, allow the process to take place.

Here there were certain theological disputes. Most Dominican theologians spoke of "the universal vocation to contemplation," saying that every baptized person is eventually called to contemplation, or what some theologians called "mysticism."

Most Jesuits were more cautious. Influenced, no doubt, by a fear of quietism, or "doing nothing" in the wrong sense, they held that infused contemplation is indeed a gift, but (and this was important) some people are called to spend their lives with the so-called ordinary prayer and should not be forced into silent contemplation. One Jesuit superior general, Claudio Aquaviva, in the seventeenth century had written a letter telling Jesuits that they might direct people who are called to infused contemplation but they were not to teach it.

Fear of contemplation or mysticism, however, remained with a large number of Jesuits. I recall my novice master with great glee quoting the novel *Grey Eminence* where Aldous Huxley lampoons the Jesuits for destroying "the blind stirring of love" with their emphasis on thinking and reasoning about this and that and the other. Huxley was no fool when he spoke about mysticism.

Yet Joseph de Guibert, in his masterly work on the spirituality of the Society of Jesus, claims that a great number of Jesuits have always been called to infused contemplation.

WHETHER OR NOT there is a universal vocation to mysticism, I was becoming more and more convinced that my call was leading me in that direction. I always liked the French Jesuits, such as Jean-Pierre de Caussade and Louis Lallement, and I viewed Teilhard de Chardin as a mystic. I also liked Joseph de Guibert and I saw plenty of mysticism in Ignatius of Loyola.

And so I had no scruple about teaching simple prayer, such as the repetition of the word "Jesus," or "Come, Holy Spirit," or some phrase from scripture. I encouraged praying people to enter into silent contemplation when called to do so. After this, those called to the dark night could read *The Cloud of Unknowing* and St. John of the Cross.

AND YET, AS I NOW WRITE from the cool heights of seventy-nine years of age, I see that in my late forties I was in turmoil and in crisis. When I arrived in relaxed Honolulu, an innocent lamb licking my ice-cream cone and listening to romantic Hawaiian music, little did I realize that I was coming to a Catholic Church that was reeling from the crash of the Second Vatican Council. The most fundamental doctrines of the church were being questioned. Priests and sisters were leaving their orders to get married. Religious orders were collapsing. Already the sexual problems that were to shake the whole church were simmering beneath the surface.

Was I questioning my vocation as a Jesuit?

Deep down I did not like the Spiritual Exercises and was not very attracted by Ignatius. I was repulsed by "obedience of the intellect" and I wondered if I should follow the least sign of the superior's will even when he gave no express command. I was not in close contact with Jesuits, either in America or even in Japan. My relationship with Sophia University had become very flimsy. Joseph Pittau, it is true, had given me permission to travel abroad, but he had told me with a smile that he had had to fight for me. Other Jesuits had gone abroad and had never returned.

Then there was my sexuality. The nudity I had seen at the Buddhist center attracted me and made me think. I had a deep attraction—almost an addiction—for some sisters. So what about celibacy?

About poverty, I don't remember how I acted. I think I led a pretty poor life but I did not bother to get permission for the money I used or the places to which I traveled.

The experiments of Dr. Hirai in Tokyo and of Dr. Green in Kansas had made me ask about the validity of our traditional spirituality. Their emphasis on levels of consciousness, their talk of passive energy, their discovery of alpha and theta brain waves in meditators—all these things made me ask about "acquired and infused contemplation."

Then there was Oriental spirituality. Coming to the fore were big names like the Dalai Lama, Hugo Enomiya Lassalle, John Main, Raimon Pannikkar, Mother Teresa. Anyone interested in spirituality was looking to Asia. Should I do Zen? What about my efforts to stay with traditional Christian teaching?

How did I survive?

I believe I survived because of my fidelity to prayer before the Blessed Sacrament. The Reno sisters made me a red *zafu*, or Zen cushion (in Japan the *zafus* are black) and I sat on this at the back of the chapel. Wherever I was, I would do this every day for an hour, and in deep contemplative prayer my problems were relativized.

What was really unique about the Society of Jesus was the name. We were the *Society of Jesus*—not the "Society of Ignatius" or "Iñiguists" or anything else—and this was a point on which Ignatius was adamant. For me this was, and is, the essence.

In light of the experience of contemplation, the experiments of Hirai and Green were not important.

As for sexuality and friendship, I survived because of common-sense friendships with the sisters in Reno and even more because of the good advice of the French Jesuit Yves Raguin, about whom I will speak in the next chapter. Celibate friendship with women and men became increasingly important to me.

I have often looked back to my meetings with my old friend Michel Ledrus in Rome in 1958. Here was a great Jesuit who was a mystic and believed in mysticism. "Your vocation is pretty deep," he had said to me. And he could criticize! Much later, after Janssens had died and Pedro Arrupe had become superior general, Ledrus said to me, "Janssens had principles. Mistaken principles, but principles. This man [and here he meant Arrupe] has no principles!" Knowing Arrupe as I did, this made me laugh. But it also let me see that one could criticize and be a good Jesuit.

I STILL HAD PROBLEMS to be worked out in practice, and I will speak about them as my book progresses. My prayer life grew, as did my friendships. I also came to realize that I could be a good Jesuit on my own terms.

19
Zen and Mysticism

AFTER I GOT BACK TO JAPAN, Pier Paolo and I were invited to Manila for a Jesuit conference on interreligious dialogue. Pier Paolo was now a recognized Buddhist scholar. He had studied Pure Land Buddhism in Chicago under Mircea Eliade and Joseph Kitagawa, but, while he loved Buddhism intensely, he had little time for the Western cultivation of Zen. "We need a moratorium on Zen," he used to say. And when Hugo Enomiya Lassalle traveled to Europe to give his Zen *sesshin* (Zen-style retreat), Pier Paolo remarked with characteristic dry humor, "There he goes to create more confusion!" I enjoyed Pier Paolo's company very much; and I think he enjoyed mine.

At our conference we heard a lecture on Zen from a distinguished Jesuit. Yves Raguin was an aristocratic French Jesuit (he reminded me of Teilhard de Chardin) who had been a superior in Vietnam and then moved to Taiwan. He never practiced Zen officially and he never sat in the lotus posture. But he had practiced his own Zen—"Zen without Zazen" he called it—and he claimed that his experience had been recognized by Yamada Koun Roshi in Japan. Raguin's talk was very fine and very Christian. He had entered into the void, and there he had experienced Christ at the very depth of his being.

I applauded this talk with enthusiasm. I understood from my own experience what he was talking about. My only objection was, "Why call this Zen?" Surely his was an experience of the Christian apophatic tradition *in dialogue with Zen,* greatly influenced by Raguin's profound reflection on Taoism. Was it not an experience of the *todo y nada* of St. John of the Cross? Was it not the experience of Eckhart and the author of *The Cloud of Unknowing,* now in dialogue with Asia?

I was confirmed in my view by the comments of my Jesuit friend Ka-kichi Kadowaki, who upset the applecart by saying that Westerners could not authentically practice Zen in which millennia of Chinese philosophy lay buried. And Carl Jung (whom I quote extensively in my book, *The Mirror Mind*) said something similar, maintaining that Christianity would have its own yoga based on the Christian message. This is the Christian contemplation that I am searching for, constantly learning from the Buddhist tradition.

HOWEVER, THE MOST EXCITING PART of this conference was my evening walks with Yves Raguin. He had just written a little book entitled *Celibacy for Our Times* in which he spoke enthusiastically about the intense love that can exist between celibate people whether of the opposite sex or of the same sex. I had been educated to believe that I must be very careful about human relations, particularly with women. Some Jesuits, it is true, had efficient secretaries with whom they worked well and sometimes drank tea. Yves, however, believed not just in cooperation and collaboration but also in *communion*. He believed that friends could love one another very deeply and lead one another to God.

About chastity Yves was adamant. While for married people sexual activity was part of the journey, any sexual compromise would make intimacy very difficult for celibate people. Expressions of affection were valuable if they were expressions of an intimacy already acquired, but if they were a search for erotic pleasure they could destroy the relationship.

We talked about this as we walked in the evening air of Manila. Yves, speaking English with his French accent, was full of enthusiasm, speaking of "the joy, the intense joy" that comes from chaste love. Celibate friendship, he held, promotes equality between man and woman. It could provide an answer to the issues regarding women's inequality that were being raised at that time. His message was important for me.

French Jesuit Yves Raguin.

IN TOKYO I HAD A CHINESE FRIEND who often came to see me in Hongo. Born in Indonesia of a Chinese father and a Japanese mother, Amy Lim had been brought up in Hong Kong. During the war, when the Japanese invaded China, she and her four sisters were saved by their diplomatic mother who spoke beautiful Japanese. Later Amy joined the Sacred Heart sisters in Japan. I first met her in Oxford where her community had sent her to study. She spoke English with an impeccable Oxford accent that she never lost.

Now in Tokyo we met often. Sometimes we went out to a Japanese tea shop where we talked for hours. What we talked about I do not now remember. I remember only that a profound love arose between us. After drinking tea or coffee, we frequently walked through the big Yasukuni shrine, sometimes engaged in conversation and sometimes in deep silence. On free days we went to Seibu Yuenchi, a big park outside Tokyo with a glorious lake and beautiful woods. It was full of children playing and laughing. We found a quiet place where we celebrated Mass together, sitting on the ground. Even now, when I see Seibu Yuenchi, I feel a pang of sorrow, thinking of the days that are no more.

Amy had an Indonesian friend, Elvira, who was married to a Japanese man. We often visited their house and together we went to the hospital to take care of an African lady who was poor and sick and lonely. I baptized Elvira's two grandchildren and her husband shortly before he died. I recall how Amy met me at the station. "I'm going to Elvira's. Her husband has just died." We went to the house, and later he was buried in St. Ignatius Church. May he rest in peace.

Now I began to read the documents of the Second Vatican Council with new eyes. One decree speaks of friendship between man and woman as "the primary form of interpersonal communion." My edition has a footnote, attributing this primary form of interpersonal communion to marriage. But the council does not speak only of marriage. Interpersonal communion is what people are looking for today. I also like the phrase in Genesis which says that "it is not good for man to be alone" and that other passage in John's Gospel (again quoted by the council) where Jesus prays to the Father that his disciples may become one "as we are one." Here Jesus compares interpersonal love to the love of the Trinity.

MANY YEARS LATER, I attended a talk on interpersonal relations in the Jesuit theologate in Dublin. The lecturer, a well-known psychiatrist, spoke mainly about the man-woman relationship, but he made an almost casual remark about homosexuality. "Is it not better for a person to have one stable relationship than to sleep around promiscuously?"

After the lecture a small group of professors came together for an informal chat. I asked the psychiatrist, "Do you not think that a person with a homosexual inclination may be called to celibate intimacy—not in the institutional sense of entering a religious congregation but in ordinary life?" The doctor seemed reluctant to answer. Then he grunted and said, "Yes, yes! If they can make it . . . !"

If they can make it! I took him to mean that usually they cannot make it. Yet I believe that thousands do make it, and that they find peace in God.

I LOOK ON YVES RAGUIN as a prophetic figure who spoke to a world searching for depth in human relations and to a Catholic Church in which many priests—I think of Thomas Merton, Pierre Teilhard de Chardin, Karl Rahner—were reconciling commitment to celibacy with intense love for the opposite sex. This was a source of anxiety and suffering for many good men and women, but it brought much more joy than suffering. It made men and women truly human.

Yves was a mystic who broke out of a narrow Jansenism and based his actions and his teaching on the Gospel. "The Lord loved women," he sometimes said with a smile. And Jesus said to his disciples, "I call you friends." He had a special love for Peter, James, and John, whom he took up the mountain to pray; and his loving affection for Mary Magdalene and the other women is very clear. Even if there was "a disciple whom Jesus loved," Jesus had many friends. And Yves Raguin stressed this point.

Following Yves's advice I have found friendship very healing. Indeed, I was in great need of healing, particularly in my relationship with my mother, and I discovered that love is the great healer. Furthermore, I found in love between the sexes, union between the yin and the yang, something I did not find in love with the same sex. I experienced, like Teilhard, that love for the opposite sex arouses a new and unique creativity and that it is a way to chastity in celibate life.

With Amy Lim at a Japanese lunch in Tokyo.

As I enter the last years of my life, I look back on my talks with Yves Raguin and my friendship with Amy as among the greatest graces I have received. And I know that Amy feels the same. I believe that if there were more understanding of this deep celibate love in the Catholic priesthood there would be much less pedophilia and fewer sexual scandals.

LATER, I SPOKE ABOUT THESE IDEAS to Al Zaballa, who quickly invited Raguin to give a lecture at the University of San Francisco. Raguin accepted the invitation and was greatly appreciated by his audience. However, in some quarters he caused something of a hubbub. I recall one nun protesting vigorously, "What right has a man to withdraw a sister from intimacy with her own community?"

I forget how Raguin answered that question.

AFTER THE MANILA CONFERENCE Pier Paolo and I returned to Tokyo. Within the Catholic Church at that time there was great interest in Zen, centered on the group known as the Sambokyodan, which flourished in Kamakura under the powerful leadership of Yamada Koun Roshi. I had written about Yamada's extraordinary *satori* in my book *The Still Point,* quoting his description of how he awoke at night laughing and laughing and laughing. And a friend of mine, a graduate of Sophia, had shown Yamada this passage in my book. So he knew something about me.

Hugo Enomiya Lassalle, after practicing under several roshi in Hiroshima, ended with Yamada. I have already mentioned that Lassalle was little appreciated in Japan, but let me add a few words about it here.

The Jesuits who lived with Lassalle and loved him agree that he was a man of great holiness. He was a pioneer or, if you will, a prophet. His greatness, it seems to me, was in introducing into Christian prayer and meditation an unconscious dimension that had been overlooked. Lassalle came to see that the unconscious contains a wisdom that the conscious mind does not have. While in the West until very recently the unconscious was known only by mystics who considered it "extraordinary," Lassalle, through his contact with Zen, saw that in Asia the unconscious has been an ordinary part of religious life for millennia. And he taught many people to get in touch with their unconscious through meditation. This was a great achievement.

Lassalle was known for his practice of Zen—in Germany he was considered a "Zen hero"—yet Yamada himself was very reluctant to recognize Lassalle's enlightenment. This may have had to do with the "double belonging" I discussed earlier. Yamada may have sensed in Lassalle an internal division that prevented him from going deeply into the inner world.

ANOTHER JESUIT WHO PRACTICED under Yamada was my close friend Tom Hand. A Californian who had taught English for many years at a Jesuit high school in Hiroshima, Tom felt drawn to more spiritual things and became spiritual director of the Jesuit students. From the language school he went faithfully to the Sambokyodan every Sunday and took direction from Yamada. Tom was interested not just in Zen but in everything Japanese. From him I learned a lot about Japan and Japanese culture. He loved Philip Kapleau's *The Three Pillars of Zen* and I recall him saying to me one day, "Bill, what we must ask ourselves is this, 'Do we see what we are told to see, or do we see what is there?'" This jolted me and made me ask myself about my faith.

Though our ideas were quite different, Tom and I became close friends. As I learned a lot about Buddhism from him, he learned a lot about St. John of the Cross and *The Cloud of Unknowing* from me. I had to show him the best, for he was inclined to pooh-pooh the Christian mystical tradition. I recall how he sniffed when I showed him a book by Garrigou Lagrange.

Tom made many Zen *sesshin*, but he never claimed to have reached *satori*. And when he went to California years later he taught not Zen but Christian meditation, always in dialogue with Buddhism. I found, moreover, that he had remarkable insight, and later when I was in crisis he showed great understanding for my psychological and spiritual suffering.

SO MUCH DID I HEAR about Yamada and the Sambokyodan that I began to think about joining it. It could do no harm to sit and breathe and recite "*mu.*" I have already told of how, when I asked the Dominican Father Oshida for advice on this, he had said that I should go if that was what I wanted to do, but that I would probably find their faith different from mine.

Now I see that my interest was not really in Zen as such but in deepening my own life of prayer. Nevertheless, I went to the temple and introduced myself to Yamada Koun Roshi and the meditators. The temple was neat and clean, well-organized, and beautifully decorated with Buddhist art. After a few sessions I accepted Yamada as my teacher.

I sat in the lotus posture facing the wall and recited the Jesus Prayer: "Lord, Jesus, Son of the living God, have mercy on me a sinner!" Sometimes I would enter into silence in God's presence, and when I got all distracted I would return to my ejaculation, "Lord Jesus...!" We all walked slowly around the room, practicing what is called "walking Zen" *(kinhin)* and I continued with my prayer, "Lord, Jesus...."

I went to Yamada for the regular interview *(dokusan)* and when he heard what I was doing he was not too happy. I saw him a second time and now he became a bit angry and scolded me. "You must do what I tell you," he said. "Then later you can turn to Jesus!" I think he wanted me to recite "*mu*" with the breathing so as to become completely empty. In this he was probably true to the Zen tradition, but I felt he was authoritarian.

I began to see that I was on a different path from the one along which he wanted to lead me. It is true that St. John of the Cross speaks of the *nada* which is the Spanish for *mu*; but he also speaks of "the living flame of love" and I believe that this had begun to arise in my heart.

> O living flame of love
> That tenderly wounds my soul
> In its deepest center...

I say it had "begun to arise," because it was still a tiny flame and had not reached the intensity that St. John of the Cross speaks of, an intensity that came later to me. Nevertheless it was very real and I did not want to (perhaps I could not) crush it.

I saw that *The Dark Night of the Soul* culminates in this love:

> Upon my flowering breast,
> Which I kept wholly for him alone,
> there he lay sleeping, and I caressing him
> there in a breeze from the fanning cedars.

Since this poem is classical and beautiful, allow me to quote the original Spanish:

> *En mi pecho florido*
> *que entero para él solo se guardaba*
> *allí quedó dormido*
> *y yo le regalaba*
> *y el ventalle de cedros aire daba*

And I saw how Christian mysticism arises when one is purified and comes to grasp the great Johannine saying that "God is love." Then one is possessed by the greatest commandment, "Thou shalt love the Lord, thy God, with thy whole soul and mind and heart and strength . . . ." This explains the mystics' use of *The Song of Songs*, the stigmata of Francis of Assisi, and the "my being becomes being-in-love" of Bernard Lonergan.

Is this what Oshida meant by faith? Was he saying that the center of the Gospel is love and the Christian mystic is possessed by this love?

I explained to Yamada that I wanted to walk the Christian path, at the same time continuing with dialogue. I think he understood very well. And we parted company.

MY BREAK WITH YAMADA ROSHI was significant. It made clear to me what I really wanted, namely, to follow St. John of the Cross and *The Cloud of Unknowing*, rooted in the Gospel. This I had wanted for decades and now my path became clear. Moreover, I saw that there is much to learn from Buddhism, particularly in the area of purification. I have much to learn about breathing, and posture, about entering the deeper areas of the mind, and about the sutras, particularly the *Heart Sutra*.

But the break with Yamada was also painful. In Japan one who enters any of "the ways" must not give up. And I appeared to have given up. Hugo Enomiya Lassalle was disappointed. Our friendship was weakened.

I moved on, yet love for St. John of the Cross and *The Cloud of Unknowing* was to cause me problems in another way, in relation to the Exercises of St. Ignatius. About this I will speak in the next chapter.

20

Knocked into Conversion

PEOPLE SOMETIMES ASK, "Has Japan changed the way you pray?" Or "Had you had not gone to Japan, would your prayer be the same?"

This question is not easy to answer.

When I came to Japan in 1951 I had no idea that Asia would teach me how to pray. I came as a Christian missionary to expel the evil spirit and bring the good news of the Gospel. I had *The Spiritual Exercises* of St. Ignatius and St. John of the Cross. I had read all the current Western literature on prayer. Hugo Enomiya Lassalle, it is true, was already practicing Zen and he fascinated me a lot. But he was highly suspect. Angry Christians were sending letter after letter to Rome in protest.

Then came the Second Vatican Council. Lassalle was vindicated. Christians were told to appreciate other religions, seeing how all come from the same good God. In 1964 Pope Paul VI established a secretariat to establish a good relationship between the various religions, and this secretariat was headed by Cardinal Marella, who was friendly with Japan, especially with Heinrich Dumoulin. The secretariat had a committee of bishops and laypeople from all parts of the world whose explicit aim was to dissipate prejudice and ignorance and create harmony.

This was an earthquake in my life. Yet I changed slowly. One critic of my book *Christian Zen* shrewdly remarked that I was on the defensive and had a love-hate relationship with Buddhism. This may have been true.

In Japan, as I have earlier said, we started a "school of dialogue." The founders were Hugo Enomiya Lassalle and Heinrich Dumoulin and soon we were joined by a number of Japanese Christians, notably, the Dominican Shigeto Oshida, the Carmelite Ichiro Okumura, and the Jesuit Kakichi Kadowaki. I, too, was privileged to belong to this group. We also had occasional visitors from abroad, including the great Quaker Douglas Steere and Raimon Pannikkar. Thomas Merton was to visit us, but he died before he could get to Japan. This was in fact the tiny beginning of a dialogue that was to spread like fire to the whole world.

We met with Buddhist masters and scholars. Together we sat in silent meditation. Then Protestant members read the Bible and we Catholics celebrated the Eucharist. We were deeply united.

I quickly saw that Buddhist contemplatives easily transcend the ego, or small self (in Japanese *shoga*), to be in contact with the big self (in Japanese *taiga*). Are they, I asked myself, entering into what we have called "infused contemplation"? The attention they attached to the body, the breathing and the unconscious—all this was teaching me something new.

And now I see that contemplation pervades this country and has got into me by a sort of osmosis. Sitting on the train that runs through Tokyo and watching the faces of the people, I cannot escape the feeling that they are in touch with their unconscious; they are living at a deeper level of reality than most Westerners. Likewise, when people clap their hands, bow their heads, and enter into a momentary silence before a shrine, they are surely in touch with their true self. Again, at any time of the day one can see a sprinkling of people sitting quietly before the Blessed Sacrament in St. Ignatius Church. The Japanese do not care about religion but they do have spirituality.

AND SO IN JAPAN I have given "contemplative retreats," encouraging my listeners to repeat the mantra of their choice and to enter into contemplative silence. I have done this also in the United States and find that many Americans, influenced by John Main or the movement of centering prayer or whatever, are searching not only for meditation but for mysticism. In my retreats I follow the four weeks of the Spiritual Exercises—healing, the life of Jesus, the passion of Jesus, and the resurrection—but I always suggest that people pray in a contemplative way, repeating their mantra or becoming aware of their breathing or entering into silence, and I do not talk about the so-called "exercises" which can sometimes sound like mental gymnastics.

Nevertheless, when I was in the United States to give retreats and lectures, I decided that I myself might benefit from a thirty-day retreat. I had heard that Vince O'Flaherty, a former instructor of tertians, was an excellent director. So I phoned St. Louis where Vince was living and he kindly agreed to take me on.

Vince met me at the airport. He had arranged for me to stay at a big Benedictine women's monastery and to drive each day into the city to meet him. This sounded good. It was my first time in St. Louis.

At our first meeting I expected him to ask me about my prayer as a sort of starting point. But he did not. I myself then said that I would like to sit in the lotus—or in the half-lotus—posture at the back of the chapel in the presence of the Blessed Sacrament and to leave things to the Holy Spirit. "Oh," he said, "if a person feels called to make the Spiritual Exercises, this is quite different from adoration of the Blessed Sacrament." So I said nothing.

Later I told him I was reciting the Jesus Prayer and I asked him what he thought. "I think it is very subjective," he said. "There is a lot of subjectivism around these days."

So we followed the book and Vince explained the Ignatian points. As we got into the first week, I said, "Please don't give me the meditation on hell."

"I could omit that meditation," he said firmly, "but I might be depriving you of some of the greatest graces of your life." And for that meditation he kept repeating, "Isolation! Isolation! Absolute isolation!"

I was unmoved.

We went through the various contemplations on the call of the temporal king and the call of the eternal king and on the standard of the evil spirit and the standard of Jesus. Then we came to the central point which was the choice of a state in life: the election. I kept asking myself what choice I should make. What would be a good outcome of this retreat? Should I ask myself about Japan? Or what?

Then quite suddenly, out of the blue—or so it seemed to me—Vince confronted me forcefully: "Your basic question is, 'Is there, or is there not, a place for me in the Society of Jesus?'"

I was shocked. He was questioning my vocation. Was he trying to throw me out of the Society?

He began to enumerate my difficulties. He spoke of my problems with obedience. He saw me as wandering around the United States and he wondered if I had permission. "Unless you had explicit permission from your provincial . . . ." This, it should be remembered, was the 1970s, just when large numbers of priests and sisters were beginning to leave.

I drove back to the convent and went to see the abbess. She was a young woman with straight white hair brushed to a knot at the back of her head. Later, after spending some time in India, she became an ardent admirer of Bede Griffiths. I had spoken to her a few times and now she was practically my director. After listening to my story she said firmly, "Sleep on it! The answer will come from your unconscious!" But I was frustrated. "I can't sleep," I said.

Yet her advice was sound. I did sleep. And I had a dream. The details of the dream I do not now remember, but it had something to do with my being in a room in a big house, feeling very happy and comfortable. I woke up in peace, convinced that this room was the Society of Jesus and I was in the right place. I had no doubts about my vocation. I was where I should be. The answer, as the abbess had predicted, came from my unconscious.

I went to Vince for my daily visit, and I said clearly, "St. Ignatius distinguishes between a mutable and an immutable decision. I know that some people do not agree with him. But I agree. I believe that my vocation to the Society is immutable." Then I paused and said forcefully, "And I want this respected!"

It was his turn to be shocked. "Of course!" he said. "Final vows in the Society are immutable. But sometimes married people make an election. It is not that they are considering divorce. It is simply that they want to re-think their relationship." This was very reasonable. But I know he was shaken. He said to me at a later date, "Some Jesuits think romantically about directing retreats. But it isn't easy!"

We went on with the retreat, praying for tears with Christ suffering and ending with the great prayer of total self-offering: "Take, O Lord, and receive . . . ."

At the end Vince congratulated me. "You're as good a Jesuit as I have ever known!" he said.

"Now he says it," laughed the abbess.

Vince and I shook hands. We never met again.

I WENT TO RENO and told the sisters about my retreat; and we all laughed. "He zoomed in on me when all my defenses were down," I said. And I added, "I wouldn't recommend that thirty-day retreat to my worst enemy." So deeply was I shaken that after a couple of months I became sick and had to go to the hospital. Whether that sickness came from the retreat or from overwork I do not know.

Yet now, at the age of almost eighty, looking back at the whole scene again I can see that earth-shaking retreat as one of the blessings of my life. Truly it was a great blessing. In zooming in on me and breaking down all my defenses, Vince was the Zen master leading me to enlightenment. He was like Jesus who said to Peter, "Get behind me, Satan." And Peter's eyes were opened.

And yet Vince's assault would have done nothing had not the abbess, a woman, told me that the answer would come from the unconscious and urged me to sleep on it. Only then did I acquire a confidence in my vocation that I had not had before. It was not that I saw many reasons why I should be a Jesuit. On the contrary, I saw many reasons why I should not. But I was knocked into the unconscious realization that my vocation, my basic choice in life, was not a rational choice. It was somehow mystical, something like an awakening. I still think that an authentic vocation is not rational—even though a rational check is very valuable—but a choice made at the depths of one's being. "You have not chosen me; but I have chosen you."

And how does all this relate to the Spiritual Exercises?

I am still wary of directing everyone at the top level of consciousness, that is to say, at the level of discursive prayer. I believe that today we are seeing a step forward in evolution. People everywhere are looking for vertical meditation whereby they can experience the deeper levels of awareness and look into their unconscious. That is why so many look to the East—toward Hinduism and Buddhism—where they can be drawn from the head to the belly (in Japanese *hara*). Vince, it is true, knocked me down to that area, but this was not because of the Exercises but because of a woman who pointed to my unconscious. Now as the masses look toward John Main's meditation,

Sitting in the lotus position.

and the Dalai Lama, and centering prayer, and Zen and yoga, it is necessary for us to adapt the Exercises to their needs.

Let me say a word about my own experience.

I have spoken of my love for St. John of the Cross and *The Cloud of Unknowing*. I have already mentioned how my director in Ireland, Father John Hyde, had said in his slow drawl, "Holy John of the Cross is very good, but for Jesuits he has to be adapted." And how, much later in Japan, when I told our provincial Pedro Arrupe that I liked St. John of the Cross, he had smiled and said, "I don't think St. John of the Cross will satisfy you."

I began to see in St. Ignatius a mysticism that was the same as that of John of the Cross and also different. Whereas John of the Cross loved the silence of the desert, Ignatius loved the mighty cities. Both John of the Cross and Ignatius of Loyola entered into mystical prayer, one to be united with God in silence, the other to work for the salvation of the world.

It is at this mystical level that Ignatius will dialogue with the East and get new insights. The Exercises may have some value for beginners, but eventually one must move beyond them into contemplation.

TIME CAME TO LEAVE the United States. Thanks to my books, my name was now becoming known, and the Australian provincial invited me to Melbourne to give a seminar to the Jesuit scholastics on the Spiritual Exercises. I would have preferred to have spoken about Ignatian mysticism, since I believed (and still believe) that the survival of the Society of Jesus depends on our capacity to refine and develop our mystical tradition. But the provincial wanted the Exercises and I agreed to his request.

When I arrived in Australia I found that there had been some confusion about dates, and I was stranded in Canberra for a month with nothing to do. But it was a great month. I spent the time with the small Jesuit community, reading Jung who fascinated me more and more.

Jung saw (and here is his great significance for Asia) the importance of the unconscious and the meaning of dreams. I began to pay more and more attention to my dreams and to write them down. This was the voice of my unconscious through which the Holy Spirit often speaks. But to discern this inner voice takes time and prayer.

Jung gave me a new approach to ethics based on the inner archetypes. What matters, I saw again, is not fidelity to rules (like the fidelity of the scribes and Pharisees) but fidelity to the true self and to the *animus* and *anima* that are longing for unity.

Jung's individuation seemed like the Zen *satori*. I began to ask myself if Jung had discovered an archetypal experience that could bring the religions together and lead to the universal wisdom that Bede Griffiths loved so much.

THE MONTH IN CANBERRA passed quickly and I journeyed to Melbourne to talk about the Exercises. It was a complete flop. The Australian scholastics were more interested in riding their bikes to the sea so they could swim than in listening to me. And I just did not get across to them. Besides, there was an older father there who did not approve of my approach to the Exercises.

And so I returned gladly to Tokyo.

Now I was assigned to teach in the Department of Comparative Culture where my friend Pier Paolo had become dean. He welcomed me with open arms.

This was the only part of the university where all the teaching was done in English, and at that time it had many Americans and Europeans as well as Japanese who had studied abroad and spoke fluent English. I was asked to teach Comparative Religion, which fortunately had become "Religious Studies." I told the students that I was interested not in comparing religions but in working for dialogue between religions. I think the students liked that.

And so I began to read the classics again. Jung, of course, was a great favorite, as were Teilhard de Chardin, Bernard Lonergan, and Bede Griffiths and, on the Oriental side, the *Heart Sutra, Gopi Krishna*, and *The Awakening of Faith*. Most important of all, I gave an elective course on meditation to which anyone, whatever their faith or lack of it, might come. All this gave me new life.

This was April of 1975 and I was approaching the ripe old age of fifty. Time was moving on.

21

Greene and Lonergan

THIS WAS MY FIRST EXPERIENCE of teaching religion to a group of Buddhists, Jews, Muslims, Catholics, Protestants, and agnostics. Obviously I could not give them the old doctrine on "the salvation of the infidel." After all, the Second Vatican Council had taken place. Besides, some students were suspicious, afraid that this Catholic priest would try to indoctrinate them with what he considered "the one true faith." So I had to think of a doctrine that all might accept.

My thoughts went to Graham Greene with whom I have always had a love-hate relationship. I loved the famous theme song of *The Third Man* and was almost addicted to playing it on the piano. In the preface to my translation of *Silence* I wrote that Shusaku Endo was the Japanese Graham Greene. Perhaps it was this that made Greene choose *Silence* as the novel of the year, making a roaring success of a book that had previously been a failure. In highlighting Endo, was he highlighting himself?

Greene described himself as a "Catholic agnostic." To me this was all right. I recall how at a pow-wow during dinner one Jesuit remarked, "Aren't we all Catholic agnostics?" He meant (and perhaps Greene meant) that we are all committed Catholics who are aware that God is the mystery of mysteries which (or whom) we cannot understand. And, in an interview with John Cornwell, Greene said something similar. He began to doubt his unbelief, as he put it, when he had "a slight mystical experience" during a Mass celebrated by the great mystic Padre Pio. The Mass seemed to last for only half an hour, but in fact it lasted for two hours. Graham Greene was overwhelmed by the mystery of Padre Pio. "I think...it's a mystery," he said. "There *is* a mystery. There is something inexplicable in life. And it's important.... It's a mystery that cannot be destroyed."

Seeing the mystery of life in this way, Greene was unwittingly hinting at what is common to all religions, as expressed many years later by the Second Vatican Council in its declaration on non-Christian religions. The council fathers, seeing the rapidity with which the world is coming together, tackled the problem of what all religions have in common. And their answer is that all religions attempt to solve the mystery of the universe and of life.

From the earliest times and even today, say the council fathers, men and women have asked, and continue to ask, about the tremendous mystery of human life, a mystery that deeply stirs our hearts. What is that ultimate and unutterable mystery which engulfs our being, from whence we come, and whither our journey leads us?

And there has always existed among different peoples a religious sense—a certain perception of that hidden power that hovers over the course of things and over the events of human life. At times there has been recognition of a supreme divinity. This, the council says, is the basic religious experience of humanity.

The Catholic Church, the council goes on to say, always remaining faithful to Jesus Christ and the Gospel, respects other religions and urges the faithful to dialogue with them and to promote their wisdom and goodness. In a later document the council insists on the right to religious freedom, holding that all men and women have an obligation to search for truth and to turn to the religion to which their conscience points.

I was made to think about all this many years later when I went to Dharamsala in northern India and met the Dalai Lama. This great Tibetan maintains that a variety of religions is good because each person becomes free to select the religion that suits his or her personality. The council does not use this terminology but it does insist on freedom to follow one's conscience, following St. Paul who says in the Epistle to the Romans that the Gentiles who do instinctively what the law requires are a law to themselves.

All this is far from the triumphalism of the past, which taught that outside the church there is no salvation, and even from the theology I learned in the 1950s. I did not ask my Sophia students to accept the council; I merely said that this is what the Catholic Church teaches today. I found that most of them, even agnostics, respected it.

Greene spoke of a tremendous mystery that will not go away. And to me it is interesting that he mentioned his own "slight mystical experience." I have always believed that mystics like Padre Pio are in the forefront of evolution and have the answers to our modern problems. Their lives speak very powerfully. Nor have I any difficulty in recognizing the mystics of Asia like Ramakrishna and Ramana Maharshi and Dogen and Hakuin. These may not use the word "God." They may speak of the Tao ("the Tao that can be named is not the great Tao") or the "big self" or whatever, but they are convinced of the existence of an inexplicable mystery that underlies the universe and human life. Their mystical experience, far from weakening my faith, strengthens it.

Having said all this, however, let me add that what I like most about Padre Pio is not his stigmata or his extraordinary experiences that shocked doctors and scientists and psychologists, but the fact that his mysticism was profoundly sacramental. He spent hours in the confessional—Graham Greene did not go to confession to Pio for fear of what he might be told—and the celebration of the Eucharist was his primary mystical experience. This has impressed me because the Eucharist is the center of my prayer and perhaps ultimately I gave up practicing pure Zen because I wanted to pray before the Eucharist.

MUCH MORE DIFFICULT than the existence of God was the divinity of Jesus Christ. Here again I had no intention of asking my students to believe; I simply wanted to explain what Catholics hold. This was particularly difficult for Muslims. I had just one Muslim in my class. A wonderful boy and extremely polite, he died tragically while he was still in his twenties.

In other parts of the university, however, I met Muslims whom I found equally friendly and polite. At Christmas Mass I first met a young Muslim brother and sister who had come from the Middle East to study in Japan. When I saw the woman's black headscarf I thought she might be a conservative Catholic nun. But no. She was a fervent Muslim. She and her brother told me that to be a Muslim one must believe in Jesus as a prophet. And as for Mary, the mother of Jesus, they had wonderful esteem for her. Every day they prayed, and since the Catholic chapel was the quietest place in the university, they prayed there.

I realized that we must reformulate our doctrine of the incarnation and the redemption and our way of speaking about Jesus Christ. The Councils of Chalcedon and Ephesus and Nicea were excellent in confronting the problems of their day, but we live in a different age, when dialogue between all religions is necessary for world peace. We must remember that to say that Jesus is Allah is the height of blasphemy for the Muslim.

I began to see that the expression "Jesus is God" is open to misunderstanding. It is true that the Fourth Gospel comes to a climax when

Thomas kneels before Jesus and says, "My Lord and my God," but the synoptic Gospels do not speak that language. And today, when we stress the humanity of Jesus, let us remember that the body of Jesus was not God, nor was his soul or his mind. Jesus was a Jew, educated in the Jewish tradition, thinking like a Jew, speaking like a Jew—and executed as a Jewish man. What we say is that his humanity was united with the Word in a very unique way which the early Greek Church called "the hypostatic union." That is to say, his person was the person of the Word.

Moreover (and this is an important message of St. Paul), Jesus was closely united with the whole human race, as Adam was. As all fell with Adam, so all are redeemed by Jesus. This means that Jesus is the firstborn of many, our elder brother, one with us. The difference is that he is son by nature, and we become sons and daughters by grace. The Second Vatican Council stresses the unity of the whole human race.

A student in my class (I'm pretty sure he was a baptized Christian) raised his hand and asked defiantly, "When will Christianity get rid of this 'hypostatic union' talk?"

I answered that Christian theologians are trying to express the mystery in a new language that will suit today's people. But this will take time. And, in my opinion, it will take mysticism. I suppose I could have gone into the Trinity, explaining that Jesus was the Second Person, the Word who was made flesh and dwelt amongst us. But I thought this would make the whole thing even more unintelligible, so I simply said it was mystery and that some theologians are now asking when—at what time in his life—Jesus came to know who he was.

It was during this period that I began to read the Canadian theologian, Bernard Lonergan. To me his great work *Insight* was double-Dutch and I gave up. Someone remarked to me that *Insight* will be one of "the great un-read." This makes sense to me.

More intelligible were Lonergan's *Method in Theology* and the collections of his talks, particularly *A Second Collection*. According to Lonergan, authentic theology is based on an experience, the experience of conversion. There are intellectual and moral conversions, but most significant for me was religious conversion, which means falling in love with God. Here Lonergan, usually so dry, uses the ecstatic language of the Song of Songs, speaking of the love of the bride and the bridegroom, the woman and the man.

When I met Lonergan in Boston, I told him that his understanding of religious conversion leading to being in love is in fact a way to mysticism. He was delighted and smiled, saying, "Yes, that's it!"

The great problem with the later Lonergan, however, is his emphasis on subjectivity, and his talk of "the neglected subject." In an essay in *A Second Collection*, which I have read umpteen times, he stresses the role of the mind in the grasp of truth. Truth, he tells us, can exist only in the mind—in the mind of God or in the mind of persons; this is in contrast to some neoscholastics who seem to think that truth is so objective that it can get along without minds. He then hints (if I understand him correctly) that one should not consider as adversaries followers of other religions who do not have this truth in their minds. Lonergan does not say this explicitly but this is how I understand him.

Now my old Irish friend and teacher Father John Hyde, who loved *Insight* immensely, was very critical of Lonergan's thesis of "the neglected subject." Lonergan, says Hyde, stresses the neglect of the subject so much that he neglects the object. In a review in the Irish periodical *Studies*, Hyde claims that Lonergan was influenced by a general movement in European philosophy from Descartes, through Kant, Fichte, and Hegel, a movement that was basically erroneous. And, Hyde claims, the neoscholastics who opposed this movement were basically correct.

I recall my philosophy days in Ireland when John Hyde, teaching theodicy, said that the great adversary to a true notion of God was Immanuel Kant. And in this review he pursues the same line. He agrees that the Second Vatican Council in *Gaudium et Spes* emphasizes the centrality of the human person and he agrees that Lonergan is trying to follow the council. But he asks if theology can be anything but a comment on God's revelation through Christ and principally about God. The movement started by Kant could make the theologian like a pilot traveling on a plane by night and unable to see anything except the dashboard.

Having said all this, Hyde admits that Lonergan is totally committed to the Christian faith and to the word of God. Hyde is questioning not Lonergan's faith but his explanation of the faith, an explanation which, having been produced by a human being, can be mistaken. He then advocates dialogue, presumably between the neoscholastics and the disciples of Lonergan, as a possible answer to the problem.

TEACHING STUDENTS and reading Lonergan, however, was not my real life. Deeper down were my meditation and my friendships.

In meditation I found that I had become restless. I would pace in my room repeating the Jesus Prayer or some aspiration while sometimes simultaneously turning over in my mind the next book I would write or translation I would do.

Then I discovered the lotus posture. This was a major breakthrough. I learned to sit in the half-lotus, aware of my breathing. "I will breathe in, I will breathe out." Buddhism taught me not to interfere with my breathing but just to breathe naturally, allowing the breath to become abdominal. I did this until one day I felt like shouting out, "I have it! This is it!" My breathing was rhythmical and abdominal. I could breathe this way while sitting in the *densha* (the electric train) and even when I was busy with other things. It was an achievement (yes, I call it an achievement) that has lasted all my life. Sometimes, of course, I forget the breathing and simply recite the Jesus Prayer, or I even remain deadly silent without breathing at all. Experts tell me I *am* breathing but I simply am not aware of it. I think this breathing later brought me into crisis—good crisis but painful—and I will write about that later.

But I also had friends. Pier Paolo was the expert on Buddhism and together we went to temples and ate Japanese *tempura* or *o-sushi,* always laughing at superiors and criticizing the establishment. Then there was Bill Everett whose room was beside mine. With his immense love for everyone, Bill was a constant confidant. Together we went to the mountains with students, and we fought vigorously because he was faithful to Sophia whereas I was a rebel and a supporter of the left wing. But Bill was critical of a lot of things. "I'm a coward," he used to say. "I don't say what I really think." There was also Dan McCoy who had come from New York but was of Irish descent. Dan was greatly loved by everyone. We sometimes went out for a walk in the evening, and we drank a cup of tea or a glass of wine and talked about everything.

And of course there was Amy. As our friendship deepened and grew, she changed her name from Amy to Aimée, "the loved one" in French. This caused some stir among her friends who asked, "Amy (or Aimée), what has happened?" But she kept her secret.

She was a great knitter. She knitted for me a warm red cardigan and two beautiful white sweaters that I still wear. "Love went into every stitch," she laughed. And I know that it did. I came to love her more and more.

But after many years I realized that friendship, while it is one of the greatest joys in life, has its suffering. Bill Everett had a stroke, and the last time I saw him he was unconscious and gasping for breath; then he died. Dan McCoy has lived into his nineties and is now in our province infirmary.

Pier Paolo eventually got sick. I last visited him at the Jesuit infirmary in Rome. He now had Alzheimer's and could speak no English. But looking into his eyes I saw the same old Pier Paolo, so I read him some English letters that I had brought from Japan. Then we walked to the elevator and he silently raised his hand to say good-bye. Here in Tokyo I still feel a pang when I look into the coffee shops where we spent so much time talking and laughing together.

Amy went to China to teach English. Eventually she went to Australia and we have exchanged oceans of letters which still continue.

Separation from someone we love is a great suffering, but it can also be a great blessing. Yves Raguin, who taught me about friendship, insisted that separation was essential for those who

My life-long friend, Italian Jesuit Pier Paolo Del Campana.

through friendship would go to God. My own experience has been that the tremendous pain of separation brings immense joy from the Holy Spirit. Now I wonder if Raguin taught mystical friendship. The love that Amy and I have shared has truly been a mystical experience for both of us.

22

The Coincidence of Opposites

In my classes, dialogue with Buddhism was of primary importance. Many of the foreign students were particularly interested in dialogue with Zen, which was becoming very popular throughout the world at that time. Some were searching for a type of meditation that would lead them to deep awareness and inner peace without the baggage of dogma, and they thought they might find this in Zen. I could not teach my students Zen but I could teach a Zen-influenced meditation that they could practice as Christians, Buddhists, or agnostics.

And so I proposed an optional course on meditation. Quite a large number of students turned up. I taught them to sit in the lotus or the half-lotus posture or to sit on a chair with their backs straight. Most important was breathing from the abdomen. "I will breathe in, I will breathe out," they would recite slowly and rhythmically.

Or I would give them a sacred word or mantra. Some could find their own words; others took the word I proposed. I found that a good phrase, suitable for anyone, was the Buddhist koan, "Every day is a good day." We all sat in silence, took a deep breath, and recited the koan again and again. Every day is a good day.

Of course, some students rebelled. "Every day is not a good day," they complained. "I flunked my exams! It's raining! I was rejected by my boyfriend or girlfriend! How can I say that every day is a good day?"

I tried to explain (as I try to explain all through this book) that there is a state of consciousness wherein we see the coincidence of opposites. That is to say, we see that every day is at the same time a good day and not a good day, just as man and woman are one and not one. Keep reciting the words "Every day is a good day" and you will come to that state of consciousness with great joy.

And many students did recite the words, not only in class but while sitting on the train or the bus or in the bustle of Shinjuku. And some broke through with joy. They found a level of consciousness at which they could laugh and say that every day is a good day. One student, I was told, slapped his thigh and said with glee, "It's true! It's true! Every day is a f--n good day!"

This koan, of course, was only one example. Some could take from the Bible, "God is love." Others would just use the word "Love." And, after a few weeks of ardent practice, some would wake up to a reality about which no scripture scholar could convince them. "Yes! God really is love." I myself, sitting with them, sometimes recited, "Come, Holy Spirit. Come, Holy Spirit. Come, Holy Spirit. Come, Holy Spirit." I felt that I needed the light of the Spirit to say and to do the right thing.

WHILE TEACHING THE STUDENTS I became more and more personally interested in what Buddhism could teach us Christians. I confess, however, that I was never tempted to leave Christianity to become a Buddhist. My love for the Gospel and for the Eucharist was too great for that. But I did talk (and argue) a lot with my Jesuit friend Tom Hand who practiced Zen

at Kamakura with Yamada Roshi. Together we went to Kyoto and admired the Buddhist statues which I loved. And Tom could tell me about the background and the history of anything Buddhist.

Quite different from Tom was my friend Pier Paolo who was teaching a course on Buddhism. "Oh! these kids are too young to understand Buddhism," he said with characteristic melancholy.

A Buddhist layman who influenced me was Professor Masao Abe of Nara. A devoted scholar, Abe was deeply interested in Christianity and took an active part in our dialogues. His wisdom came not just from study but also from meditation. I recall him

American Jesuit Tom Hand.

telling me that though he had been invited to lecture in the United States he would not go while his master Hisamatsu was still alive. In this he was a true Buddhist. After Hisamatsu's death Abe became one of the leaders of dialogue in America.

Abe loved the Epistle to the Philippians where Paul, perhaps quoting an ancient Christian hymn, tells Christians to have the same mind as Christ Jesus who, "though he was in the form of God, did not regard equality with God as something to be exploited, but emptied himself, taking the form of a slave, being born in human likeness. And being found in human form, he humbled himself and became obedient to the point of death—even death on a cross." This total self-emptying is the very key to the mysticism of the Christian apophatic mystics.

The self-emptying, known by the Greek word *kenosis* or the Latin *exinanitio*, is the way to the pinnacle of exaltation. For God highly exalted Jesus and, in the words of the hymn, "gave him a name that is above all names so that at the name of Jesus every knee should bend . . . on earth and under the earth, and every tongue should confess that Jesus Christ is Lord to the glory of God the Father." This text, showing the "all and nothing" or the *todo y nada* of the mystical life, is dear to the Christian apophatic mystics. Total renunciation brings exaltation and immense joy.

Now Professor Masao Abe says that this text is a beautiful expression of the Zen experience wherein one recites "*mu*" ("nothing") again and again and again, leaving everything and coming to utter emptiness (*ku* in Japanese or *sunyata* in Sanskrit) and to the immense joy of *satori*. In this way, Abe points to a remarkable similarity between Buddhist and Christian mysticism.

THIS INSIGHT IS SURELY BRILLIANT and precious for us Christians. It is not surprising that Abe received a Catholic prize in Rome for his work on dialogue. Yet it is necessary to point to the distinction between his understanding of the text of Philippians and that of the committed Christian. For Professor Abe, the text is symbolic. It could be told by any master who would lead his disciple to enlightenment.

For the committed Christian, on the other hand, the text is not only a powerful, symbolic story, it is a historical description of the real Jesus of Nazareth. It is the story of the Word made flesh, who died on the cross and ascended into heaven.

Does this make a difference to the meditator?

It makes a difference to me. When I reflect on this passage, I see the death and resurrection of Jesus not just as a symbol but as a great reality.

I see the redemption as a great event. I see the suffering Jesus of Nazareth as my Savior.

WITH MY SMALL GROUP of graduate students I read *Religion and Nothingness* by Keiji Nishitani and selections from the work of St. John of the Cross.

As we read Nishitani, I realized once again that the coincidence of opposites or non-dualism is the very core of Buddhism, as Aristotle's principle of contradiction is the basis of scholastic philosophy. But to understand the coincidence of opposites we must spend time in meditation and come to the realization that the human psyche is multilayered. Statements that seem ridiculous at the top level of consciousness make sense when one enters the deeper layers.

It is at the deeper layers that one realizes the saying of the *Heart Sutra* that "form is emptiness and emptiness is form." Or one realizes that every day is a good day and yet every day is not a good day. Or one realizes that yin and yang are one and not one. Nishitani quotes a Zen master who said, "Separated from one another by a hundred million *kalpas* [eons], yet not apart for a single moment; sitting face-to-face all day long, yet not opposed for an instant." I began to see that the aim of koan practice is to bring one to the deep level of awareness where we will see that things are one and not one.

In the West, the coincidence of opposites is associated with the fifteenth-century German theologian Nicholas of Cusa, who spoke of "learned ignorance." But I see it in all the mystics, and all through the Bible it is a principle necessary for Christian living. This seems to be what the archbishop of Osaka, Jun Ikenaga, was saying at the Asian Synod of 1998. He got some opposition when he criticized Western Christianity for its dualistic division between God and the universe. He went on to say that the West is very masculine whereas the East is feminine. Ikenaga told me afterwards that he was influenced by Shusaku Endo who constantly advocated non-dualism and the feminine dimension in God.

AND SO THE STUDENTS came to see that a man leaves his father and mother and cleaves to his wife, and the two are one, yet they are not one. Again, we are told to love and be one with our enemy, yet we are not one. And this is the very core of the Bible. I myself, praying before the Eucharist, experience Nishitani's "sitting face-to-face all day long, yet not opposed for an instant." Non-dualism is the very basis of my relationship with God.

I did not suggest to the students that we abandon the principle of contradiction, only that we complement it by the coincidence of opposites when we are faced with the terrible mystery of life and death, and the even more terrible mystery of God. Only with a deep level of awareness and a grasp of non-dualism will we get a glimpse into the mysteries of the Gospel. What a contribution Asia makes to the understanding of the Christian message!

Yet the dualism of the West and the non-dualism of the East stirred up some political controversy and discussion. One student attacked the "We are right and you are wrong. We are good and you are evil" attitude of Winston Churchill and Harry S. Truman. It was this hypocritical and ruthless stand that made the Allies demand unconditional surrender from the Germans and the Japanese. No dialogue. No talk. No mercy. No compromise. Wipe them out. Destroy the German cities! Annihilate Hiroshima and Nagasaki!

Even the Western Christian missionaries came in for criticism for their dualistic "We are right and you are wrong" attitude. Why were they unable to see good in other religions? One smiling Japanese Buddhist put the Buddhist position well when he said, "Let us be happy with our own religions."

I tried to explain that the old intolerant Christianity was dead and that now we were appreciating and learning from the Dalai Lama and Thich Nhat Hanh—and that as Christianity takes root in Asia the appreciation and learning would grow broader and deeper.

WHEN WE READ St. John of the Cross we were faced with the paradox of *todo y nada*. If you want to enjoy everything, enjoy nothing. In the light of Asian thought this began to make sense.

But the poetry of St. John of the Cross raised other problems. We read *The Living Flame of Love* and students interpreted the poem in their own way. When we came to the words, "Perfect me now, if it be thy will. Break through the web of this sweet encounter," one student understood this as a reference to sexual intercourse. "It's terribly erotic," he gasped.

In his commentary, St. John of the Cross himself keeps quoting the Song of Songs, and coming to the words that shocked my student he explains, "Perfect and consummate the spiritual marriage in me with the beatific vision of Thyself—for it is this that the soul beseeches." Is he, then, speaking of another kind of sexual intercourse? Is he speaking of a spiritual sexual intercourse? And, if so, what is its relationship to the sexual intercourse enacted by the physical body?

This problem was of the greatest importance for me, a celibate man, but I did not see the answer at that time. Now, however, I have some light on the matter. I realize that St. John of the Cross did not crush or repress his sexual energy as many celibate people do. As a result of his own mystical experience and his mystical interpretation of the Song of Songs, St. John of the Cross realized that as there are many layers of seeing, hearing, and touching, so there are many layers of sexuality and sexual intercourse. The deepest level is at "the center of the soul" which, the saint writes, is God. And here is enacted the beatific vision.

I believe that St. John of the Cross discovers a level of sexuality that is of the greatest significance for today's world and for both celibate and married people. It is important for married people because, as they grow older and sexual intercourse plays a smaller role in their lives, they may feel called to a spiritual or mystical sexual intercourse that does not crush their physical desire but goes beyond it. Surely this is the ideal of both married and celibate life.

IN 1978 MY JESUIT COLLEAGUE and friend Kakichi Kadowaki planned to conduct a tertianship in Japan for young Jesuits who wanted to be trained simultaneously in the spirit of St. Ignatius and the traditional spirituality of Japan. Kado (as we called him) had practiced Zen under the direction of a great Buddhist master who, he claimed, recognized the validity of his enlightenment. "I had it and I knew I had it!" Kado said to me triumphantly about his *satori*.

The tertianship was held at Lassalle's beautiful Zen center outside Tokyo. A river ran along the side of the wooden building and some tertians made their meditation by simply looking at the river and listening to its flow. We had about twenty-five young Jesuits from all over the world, but no Japanese Jesuit volunteered to join us.

I agreed to help with the Zen tertianship but I am not sure that I was a suitable person. Still in my early fifties, I was struggling with Buddhism, not sure about how I really felt. For one thing, I was deeply interested in "mindfulness" and scientific studies of how it influences the brain. Mindfulness, I saw, was quite similar to the quiet contemplation I was practicing and I was asking myself how this was affecting my body. On the other hand, my experience with Yamada Roshi in Kamakura had convinced me that Buddhist mindfulness is not the same as Christian contemplation, and I did not want to get confused or to confuse the tertians.

Almost twenty years had passed since I had met with Michel Ledrus in Rome. As I practiced contemplative prayer, my repressed unconscious (particularly my repressed sexuality) had come to the surface and I was still trying to integrate it. This caused a lot of turmoil. I had been greatly helped by friendship with women and, speaking to the tertians, I was very positive about such friendship. One time, after visiting Tokyo for a weekend, I told the tertians that I had spent some time at a coffee shop chatting with a woman friend. They were amused and pleased.

Then there was the Second Vatican Council. As a young Jesuit I had learned the maxim, "Keep the rule and the rule will keep you." But the council does not say this. It stresses conscience. According to conscience we will be judged. And so we live in a world that stresses not fidelity to rules but fidelity to one's true self, that is to say, integrity. In our choice of religion and in our moral life, the first thing is fidelity to the inner light or the inner voice. What will bring men and women together and lead to a world community? Not belief in the same things, but fidelity to conscience.

But how are we to become aware of the voice of conscience?

Here I stressed prayer—specifically contemplative prayer. When one of the tertians asked me what the aim of the tertianship was, I answered that the aim was that the tertians should learn how to pray and to discern the action of the Spirit. And so I stressed Zen-like prayer and the repetition of an ejaculation.

In this I think our Zen tertianship was different from the traditional tertianship that stressed obedience as the path to finding God's will. Of course, I spoke of spiritual direction as a necessary part of discernment, but the director does not tell us what to do but helps us to discern the movement of the spirits. I believe that in 1978 we foresaw the direction in which the world and the church were moving.

It was a good tertianship, an experiment in inculturation. We sat cross-legged as we went through the Spiritual Exercises. Many entered into the silence of contemplative prayer. Together we celebrated the Eucharist on the massive rock in the meditation hall. We walked outside and admired the brown foliage of the autumn leaves and listened to the flow of the river. Of our tertians, several became Jesuit provincials in their own provinces; others left the Society of Jesus to get married.

After the final summing up, Father Pedro Arrupe, who was now superior general of the Society and had given permission for this experiment, decided that we had not yet reached the point where the practice of Zen could be integrated into Jesuit training. Dialogue, he said, was essential, but tertians could *practice* after having done tertianship in the traditional way.

DURING THE TERTIANSHIP I got sad news of the death of my eldest brother Tom. He and his family had been living in Newcastle on Tyne. His wife Anne, a wonderful person who had stood by him through thick and thin, had died of cancer in June and Tom had died of a stroke in September. Tom was a bit ambivalent about his Catholic faith. A brilliant musician, he loved to play the piano, and I once heard him say that he should have been a Methodist where the piety was all musical. But in the end our brother Kevin had brought Tom back to Belfast and he had died with the sacraments.

Some months earlier I had visited the family in Newcastle. At that time Anne was dying and Tom's health was not good. I recall how his little daughter, Anne Junior, seeing the tragic situation, stamped her foot on the ground and said tearfully, "It's not fair!" I was amazed that this child of ten or eleven could see so clearly the basic problem of human life: it is not fair.

I made no comment. It was only much later that I realized that life is fair and not fair. We always come down to non-dualism, the coincidence of opposites. This is the paradox at the heart of existence.

23
Oxford and All That

IN THE AUTUMN OF 1980 I was invited to Oxford to give the D'Arcy lectures. My books were becoming recognized and I was seen as a suitable person to lecture about mysticism East and West. From my childhood, Oxford had been surrounded for me by an aura of wisdom, and my ambitious mother had wanted me to study there—a desire that was frustrated by the war. Now was my opportunity to fill a prestigious chair in this center of learning. How wonderful!

It sounded great, but I had my critics among the Jesuit brethren. I was becoming more than ever a globe-trotter, restless and unable to stay in one place. In accepting the invitation from Oxford, I knew I would be criticized for packing my bags and traveling once again. A man's enemies are those of his own household.

I now see my problem in the context of the whole Society of Jesus. On the one hand I was committed to obedience, and on the other hand I had to be true to my self. This was the doctrine of the Second Vatican Council as I saw it, and for me its teaching was reinforced by Buddhism. My ongoing discernment had made it increasingly clear that I had a vocation to pray and to teach prayer. And this I wanted to do. But what if my superiors wanted me to teach English?

Back in 1958 my beloved Jesuit director in Rome, Michel Ledrus, had warned me that fidelity to an institution could be a snare. Ignatius of Loyola, he saw, did not want his sons to be tied to an institution or throttled by rules. He wanted them to be free to travel to any part of the world (*quavis mundi plaga*) where there was "hope of God's glory and the good of souls." About the Jesuits who were teaching language in Sophia Ledrus had quietly said, "They know that is not what they should be doing."

So the challenge of the Jesuits was to reconcile fidelity to their conscience with obedience to the church. I see that this was the problem of the whole Society under the leadership of Pedro Arrupe, who clashed with Popes Paul VI and John Paul II, and it was the problem of many individual Jesuits like Teilhard de Chardin.

In 1980 Sophia University, influenced by the council, was not a bureaucratic institution. Joseph Pittau, whom I have mentioned earlier, was successively president and rector of Sophia and provincial of the Japanese province. Intelligent and prayerful, besides being an astute Italian diplomat, he had a good sense of humor. Beppe, as we called him with his Italian name, listened to what I said and together we looked for God's will. He knew, of course, that I was a restless Irishman, but he was able to see at a deeper level and realized that I was not running around the world to enjoy myself but was trying to follow a deeper call. And so, laughing at the criticism, he encouraged me to go to Oxford and to travel.

AFTER ARRIVING IN OXFORD I took up residence in the Jesuit house called Campion Hall. This was the Oxford I associated with the names of Martin D'Arcy (who died in London in 1976) and Frederick Copleston and Philip Caraman. These and their fellow Jesuits were open to deep friendship with the intellectual and artistic elite of Oxford at their time. As one reads their biographies one comes across the names of C. S. Lewis, Ronald Knox, Evelyn Waugh, Graham Greene, Dame Edith Sitwell, T. S. Eliot, Alec Guinness, and a host of other eminent people. Martin D'Arcy knew them all; he spoke of Winston Churchill as the greatest man of his generation.

D'Arcy's books are difficult to read, but he was a brilliant conversationalist. He had gone to Japan in 1953 to speak about philosophy and visited the language school where I was studying Japanese. I recall his sparkling conversation and his magic presence, but I was a bit surprised at his negative comments about Zen. Did he know enough to speak as he did?

I HAVE BEEN SPEAKING of Oxford in the middle of the twentieth century. When I arrived, this Oxford was dead. The galaxy of Jesuits who had influenced intellectual life there had done their work. Decimated by the Second Vatican Council, which many could not accept, they had passed on, and no one had taken their place. How to explain what had happened?

Before Pedro Arrupe left Japan to attend the Congregation that was to elect him superior general, he had said to his friend Father Tony Evangelista, "What we need is another John of the Cross and Teresa of Avila."

Pedro Arrupe, provincial of the Jesuits in Japan and later general of the whole Society of Jesus. Here he is praying in Japanese style.

Evangelista told me this story and then, sadly shaking his head, he went on, "But Arrupe changed!"

Another Spanish Jesuit, hearing this story, said, "Yes. He changed. He was converted!"

Arrupe was a mystic. As a young Jesuit he had sponsored the translation of St. John of the Cross into Japanese. When the atomic bomb fell on Hiroshima, he immediately turned his novitiate into a hospital for wounded refugees. Later, visiting Latin America, he was shocked by the dire poverty and the cruel injustice, and perhaps (as the Spanish Jesuit had said) he *was* converted—this time, to a love for world justice.

Together with the Jesuit Congregation, Arrupe wanted to lead the whole Society to the search for justice in the world. And this, along with the Congregation's wish that the vow of special obedience to the pope be rethought, brought him into conflict with Paul VI, who wanted no change. As mentioned earlier, Arrupe and his consultors thought that, in accordance with the teaching of Ignatius of Loyola, they had a right to make a representation. At this the pope became angry, gave Arrupe a dressing-down for disobedience, and made known his displeasure with the way the Society was heading. I have been told that when Arrupe emerged from his meeting with the pope, his eyes were filled with tears.

This, as well as other gigantic changes in the world and in the church, reduced the Jesuits vastly in numbers and in influence.

The old Oxford Society of Jesus died.

NEVERTHELESS, my lectures were well attended and greatly appreciated. I suppose they were a breath of fresh air in Oxford. I spoke about Zen and Christian mysticism from a Christian perspective. One knows a religion, I said, only if one is committed to it and practices it. I could not speak authoritatively about Buddhism, but as a Christian I could speak about the wonderful things I had learned in Asia.

Following the great old Zen master Uchiyama Kosho who lived near Kyoto, I started with the problem of death, dividing old age into three stages.

The first stage, from sixty to seventy, is not burdensome. One is still able to travel and to enjoy oneself.

The second stage, from seventy to eighty, is more painful. One loses one's teeth and one's hearing. One's friends get sick or die. One becomes lonely.

Most painful of all is the third stage, after the age of eighty. Now you spend your days at home. You may become depressed and senile. All you can do is wait for death, the inevitable end.

What a pity, says Uchiyama Roshi, to fall into depression in this third stage! For this is the time to meditate, the time to deepen your faith and devotion. Above all it is the time to come to the realization that life and death are not two things but one. In other words, it is the time to realize the coincidence of opposites.

Again the coincidence of opposites! As every day is a good day but not a good day, as life is fair but not fair, as all is one but not one—so too life and death are one and not one. This is the mystical enlightenment that is now coming to the whole world. It is associated with the Hindu *advaita*, the Buddhist emptiness, and the words of the *Heart Sutra* that "form is emptiness and emptiness is form." It is the core of *The Cloud of Unknowing* and the writing of St. John of the Cross. Is not this at the center of all mysticism?

It is clear that this enlightenment cannot come from the top level of consciousness. The Oxford dons (with the possible exception of T. S. Eliot) were working from the top, intellectual level. That is why Martin D'Arcy could not understand Zen and adored Winston Churchill. But the enlightened Zen man or woman (like the enlightened mystics of all religions) experience life from a deeper level of consciousness.

And so the great challenge for me was to find, or re-find, a Christianity that would carry me down, down to the depth of my being where I would find God who is love. I had to realize that the kingdom of God is within. I had to cry out with Paul, "I live, now not I, but Christ lives in me." I had to resonate with Augustine who searched for God outside but found Him within. Above all, I had to find in the Eucharist the presence of the Risen Jesus at the center of my being.

To enter deeply into this inner kingdom I had to let go of all attachment and clinging. "Let go! Let go! Let go!" is the advice of masters and mystics. We are like a man standing on the electric train and holding a briefcase. When the train lurches he must let go of his precious briefcase and grasp the bar. In the same way I had to let go of my precious briefcase. Concretely that meant letting go of my selfish clinging to Amy, to Japan, to my books, to my mother, and to everything. All attachments had to go if I was to find God within myself and within all beings. This is the *mu* of Buddhism, the *todo y nada* of St. John of the Cross, the true love of the Gospel.

In my lectures I taught the class how to sit in the lotus posture, how to breathe, how to cultivate inner silence, how to come face to face with the koan, how to pray with the body. All this I have found in dialogue with Buddhism. It is quite different from the methods of the Spiritual Exercises in which I was trained. I outline my Oxford lectures in two books, *The Inner Eye of Love* and *The Mirror Mind*.

I came to realize more and more that although this spirituality is different from that of the the Spiritual Exercises, it is not so different from traditional Christian mysticism. As I gave my lectures, it became increasingly clear to me that Buddhism at its height, like Christianity, Judaism, Islam, Hinduism and all the religions, is profoundly mystical. And it is toward mysticism that we must go if we are to dialogue with Asia and save the world of the third millennium. "This kind is driven out only by prayer."

From this time, finding a new mystical theology has been my principal concern in life. I see that only in collaboration with other religions can this be done. We Catholics must get rid of our suspicion of mysticism and interpret in a new and broader way the thesis of the old theologians that there is a universal vocation to mysticism. Only recently did I get insight into the inner life of the Christian *sanyasi*, Swami Abhishiktananda, who found the peak point of mysticism in the "I am" of Jesus. Not "I am the Messiah" or "I am he" but simply "I am" (*ego eimi*). And Abhishiktananda follows this back to Moses who, having asked Yahweh his name, received the answer, "I am who I am." This, the Swami claims, is the key to all mystical experience. We are all called to say, "I am." And is not this an experience beyond reasoning and thinking, beyond space and time?

I HAVE SAID THAT Uchiyama Kosho focuses our attention on death. He himself came close to death and, entering into a deep level of consciousness, got a realization of the non-dualistic truth that life and death are not two things but one. No doubt his spiritual experience was beyond reasoning and thinking, outside space and time.

As a small boy I took it for granted that death was the passage into another country where I would get reward or punishment. I recall my mother, who was deeply interested in astronomy, asking a visiting priest if life after death could be on another planet. The priest answered, "Oh! That is most heretical!"

But he did not say what or where life after death was.

Now I think that Uchiyama points in the right direction. I do not mean that he solves the problem—he does not—but he tells us that he got into a very deep realm of his psyche, and there he saw a dimension of reality that ordinarily is hidden. I cannot help thinking that Paul says something rather similar. Speaking to those who ask about the risen body he first says, "Fool!" as if to say, "Don't ask foolish questions!" Then he goes on to say that after death a seed remains and God gives to each the kind of body He wishes, a spiritual body that is unimaginable. Just as Uchiyama is liberated from the fear of death, so Paul can cry out, "O death, where is thy victory? O grave, where is thy sting?"

WHILE IN OXFORD I went once to a sauna in the suburbs. For a while I was alone and then I found that the sauna had been rented out to a naturist group. The men and women who entered the sauna were friendly and invited me to stay. I enjoyed their company, but afterwards I felt a deep sense of guilt. Had I committed a serious sin? And what would my audience at Campion Hall think if they knew?

Then I came to realize that the sexual education I had received in school in Liverpool and in Belfast, together with unconscious fears from childhood, had injured me greatly. I had learned—also in theology in Tokyo—that there was no parvity of matter (*parvitas materiae*) in questions of sexuality. This meant that all sexual sins, even in thought, were mortal sins and merited eternal damnation. It seems to me that theologians may well say that masturbation or looking at an "impure picture" are not good things to do, but where is the evidence for making these things mortal sins deserving eternal punishment?

I began to ask myself if sexuality had a role in the celibate life and if there is a relationship between sexual energy and spiritual energy. Is not this an area in which further understanding of St. John of the Cross and his love for the Song of Songs can still help us? Then too dialogue with Asian religions may give us light.

FROM OXFORD I WENT straight to Israel. Having toiled so hard in dialogue with Buddhism I wanted to find my Christian roots and to see what was distinctive about our own mysticism. I had been in Jerusalem before and found that it reminds me of my native Belfast. The same atmosphere of strife and religion! The Jews and the Muslims are like the Protestants and the Catholics. Will it ever end?

In Oxford I had been lonely. I had made no intimate friends there. But Israel was different. I stayed with the Grail sisters in Bethlehem and my friend Amy joined us from Japan. Rachel Donders drove us around to all the famous places. I went back in time to the Gospel and I prayed before the Eucharist. I found the apophatic roots of St. John of the Cross and *The Cloud of Unknowing*, particularly in the transfiguration of Jesus, when the disciples were terrified as they entered the cloud. I feel that Abhishiktananda and others would be less upset by their love for Asian mysticism if they had really seen the Christian equivalent.

About Israel I wrote a fast-moving book with a San Juanian title, *The Wounded Stag*. One reviewer wrote that the author of this book was desperately trying to find himself. This was true.

Who am I? Belfast, I saw, was in my blood. As Abhishiktananda in India had found that he was "terribly, terribly French," so I discovered that I was terribly, terribly Irish. The Belfast "troubles" I drank in with my mother's milk. To some extent I got them out while writing that book, but something remains. I still turn to God and try to pray with the psalmist, "Yet it was you who took me from the womb; you kept me safe on my mother's breast."

24
To the Philippines

I LEARNED A LOT in the Philippines.

The Society of Jesus, under the direction of Pedro Arrupe, had made a radical option for the poor. Impressed by the frightening poverty of Latin America, the injustice of the rich, the threat to world peace and even to world survival, Arrupe had gone all out for the poor. This was a tremendous change for the Jesuits who had always hobnobbed with the rich from the time that Francis Xavier, seeing that poverty did not help his mission, dressed in regalia to meet the emperor of Japan. Subsequent Jesuits, always anxious to influence the influential, were confessors to princes and kings. In Oxford I saw how Martin D'Arcy and the rest were in cahoots with the famous and powerful. This was their apostolate.

Now I was in the Philippines and for the first time in my life I saw the value of poverty. The Filipinos were cheerful and good-humored. They were able to laugh. Their poverty did not make them depressed. "Blessed are the poor!" I saw that money does not make people happy; it can sometimes make them miserable. The poor in the Philippines were smiling, but the rich (and I, alas, belonged to that class) were afraid of losing their money or their reputation or their what-not. Blessed are the poor!

I do not mean by this that we should stop working to alleviate the suffering of the poor. On the contrary, we should. We must. The imbalance in today's world where the rich drive around in Cadillacs while the poor cannot survive is one of our greatest evils—it is one cause of the terrorism that threatens the very existence of the human race. But how are we to reconcile our love for poverty with our war against poverty? What is the right attitude toward poverty? That is the question.

I myself, at this point in my life, can see poverty only in the light of the coincidence of opposites. Poverty is good and not good, just as everything is one and not one, just as life is fair and not fair. In other words "Blessed are the poor" is an enormous koan. We see that poverty makes us blessed, yet we must fight tooth and nail to banish abject poverty from the face of the earth. What a koan!

We active people often see our personal poverty as motivated by a love for the poor, a desire to be one with people who have nothing. "We will share their lot! How can I eat a hamburger when people are starving?"

This is very good. It is the way in which many saintly people have embraced poverty.

But I have found that the wisdom of Buddhists, like the wisdom of the Christian apophatic mystics, goes deeper and is greatly in accord with the Gospel. It sees an intrinsic value in the poverty that Buddhists call emptiness. It sees in *total emptiness* the *total fullness* that makes human beings truly blessed. That is why serious Buddhists share Professor Masao Abe's love for that text of the Epistle to the Philippians where Paul writes that Jesus emptied himself, taking the form of a slave, and was raised up to have a name that is above all names. Here we have the emptiness (total poverty) and the fullness (authentic richness) coming together in Jesus. By total emptiness Jesus is raised up and saves the world. This is a koan that cannot be understood by scholastic metaphysics but only by enlightenment.

Again, Paul composes an extraordinary koan in the Second Epistle to the Corinthians when he speaks of "the generous act of our Lord Jesus Christ, that though he was rich, yet for your sakes he became poor, so that by his poverty you might become rich." Does Paul describe our true attitude toward the poor? That by our poverty they may become rich? What a koan!

I have seen Buddhists face this koan. It is particularly challenging for those Buddhists who meditate reciting *mu, mu, mu* and enter into the great emptiness where nothing, the most abject poverty, is everything. They can then embrace poverty while fighting against it.

We Christians see the answer in St. Paul and in the Christian tradition. Dialogue with Buddhism has given me a new understanding of the Epistle to the Philippians. Blessed are the poor! Woe to you who are rich! Lazarus is happy in Abraham's bosom while Dives begs for a drop of

water to cool his tongue. And the answer to people who cannot understand this is in the prophets: "They have Moses and the prophets."

THE GOSPEL IS ALIVE in the Philippines and explains the joy of the people in suffering. I found the Gospel in the jeepny drivers who rush joy-
fully through the crowded streets of Manila, their cars full of pious
symbols. I saw it in the hearts of those who pray silently before the Eucharist. I know that someone will say, "But what about the robberies?
Watch your wallet in that jeepny or even in that church!" Yes, that is
good advice. But who can deny that the Filipinos put into practice the
most important teaching of the Gospel, love one another? In any airport
or station, as in any church in Tokyo, you will find Filipinos gathered together, talking, laughing, and joking. And they help one another. Is not
this the Gospel?

In fact, living in the Philippines has taught me that the Gospel is for
the whole world. I could never accept the diaspora theory of learned theologians who say that the Gospel is for a privileged few, a *diaspora*, called
to preserve the word for future generations. This is nonsense. The Gospel
is vitally necessary for the masses of people in China and India and Africa.
Not that the masses will be baptized and enter an institutional church,
not that they will abandon their Buddhism or Islam of Hinduism. They
may well keep these religions, but through dialogue they will learn to live
the Gospel, and they will try to observe the most important commandment of Jesus, to love one another. This is the hope of the world. The
Philippines has given me optimism about the future of the Gospel and the
future of the world.

BUT LET ME GET TO my reason for being in the Philippines.

The Jesuits there had organized an international tertianship, much
like the one we had had in Japan, for young Jesuits from all over the
world. I was asked to take part as a director, assisting Tom O'Gorman,
who was in charge. We—young tertians, younger novices, and ancient directors (I was in my middle fifties and Tom was a bit younger)—lived outside Manila in the little village of Novaliches. Our life was quite austere.
We did, however, have a swimming pool, though one visiting Jesuit who
was a doctor remarked after a swim, "That pool is full of urine!" The food
was adequate. The climate was hot and oppressive. One time I fainted
during Mass and had to be carried to my bed by burly novices.

All this took place in the early 1980s, which was a stormy time in the
Catholic Church. Sexual abuse by priests was coming to the surface and

we priests were fast losing credibility. Pope John Paul, ruling with a rod of iron, made it clear that he would tolerate no opposition and make no concessions either to celibate or married people. In 1981, he went to Japan and visited Sophia University. Unfortunately I missed his visit, but I heard that the Jesuits, under strict orders from the provincial, put aside their neckties and greeted the pope wearing black suits and Roman collars. That was in February of 1981, and in May of the same year the pope was shot by a Turkish dissident.

The attempted assassination was on May 13, the anniversary of the Fatima revelation which took place on May 13, 1917. Convinced that his life had been spared through the intercession of Our Lady of Fatima, the pope went to the shrine in Portugal and put there the bullet that was meant to kill him. From that time Fatima secrets and the advice of Sister Lucia were crucial in the ruling of the Catholic Church.

This background history could not but influence our tertians. All the more so when, a couple of years later, Pedro Arrupe, returning to Rome from the Philippines, had a massive stroke. Pope John Paul, departing from the ordinary procedure of the Society of Jesus, personally appointed Fathers Paolo Dezza and Joseph Pittau as new superiors. We were told that the pope had toyed with the idea of appointing a non-Jesuit as superior but changed his mind.

This was a tremendous blow to the Society. The prestigious Karl Rahner protested vigorously. But, strange to say, I was not bothered. I don't think I even spoke about these problems to the tertians. I had more important things to say.

I saw that if the tertians were to survive as priests in today's world they must first learn how to pray. Moreover it would not be enough to go through the Spiritual Exercises of St. Ignatius at the top level of consciousness. They must go deeper; they must go to the contemplative level of consciousness which I had found in *The Cloud of Unknowing* and St. John of the Cross. This contemplative prayer was becoming more and more common in the West with the growing popularity of Meister Eckhart and the mystics and with the Asian dialogue of Thomas Merton, John Main, Thomas Keating, and many others. How would this fit into the spirituality of the Society of Jesus?

I found that most of the tertians were open to contemplative prayer. Some were already practicing it. Some were doing yoga, regulating their breathing, sitting cross-legged. They could well understand the "letting go" that I spoke about. Some liked to recite the Jesus Prayer again and again, or they said, "Come, Holy Spirit" or "Abba, Father."

As for the Spiritual Exercises of St. Ignatius, I explained that one can go through these meditations and exercises in a horizontal or in a vertical way. It was the latter way that I encouraged, telling the tertians to continue with their mantra, going down, down down, breaking through superficial levels of awareness until they came to what the Buddhists call the true self and what St. John of the Cross calls the center of the soul.

Some tertians wanted to give up all thinking and to enter into the great wordless silence. I encouraged them, suggesting that they read the text of the Exercises outside the time of prayer, just as the Zen Buddhists chant the sutras and then enter into silence. Above all, I told them—as I tell all Christians who enter into silent prayer—to read sacred scripture as a jumping off ground for contemplation.

My way of direction was well accepted and I heard no significant criticism. Some, I was told, said that my way was more Carmelite than Jesuit but this was not said bitterly. "Bill, you taught them to pray," said one older Jesuit at the end of the tertianship. This made me happy.

THE TRUTH IS THAT I was teaching the tertians my own spirituality, with its strong points and its defects. A number four in the enneagram, I am the tragic romantic who likes to be alone, who is a misfit in community, who has little interest in liturgy (though I do love the Eucharist), and who is strongly drawn to apophatic mysticism.

At this time I was sitting and breathing in the presence of God, who I knew was dwelling at the center of my being. And, as always happens in such prayer, my unconscious was coming to the surface. I saw this as what Jung calls the shadow that appears on the road to individuation or, in more Christian terms, as the dark night that we must pass through on the way to God. Within me there arose fears and anxieties and panic that made me all the more a misfit. Above all, my long repressed sexuality now rose up with incredible strength. I do not think I committed a serious sin, but I was anxious and fearful and scrupulous.

Looking back, I see this as an important stage in my spiritual journey. An extraordinary energy was arising from within. I say "extraordinary," but it is an inexplicable force found in all mystics and even in some artists and athletes. I later saw it as what Hindus and Buddhists call *kundalini*, "the serpent power," and what Christian mystics call the fire of love, the *incendium amoris*. St. John of the Cross experienced this as "the living flame of love" and in his beautiful poem with this title he wrote, "Since thou art no longer oppressive," indicating that at one stage this exquisite flame of love caused great depression and anxiety.

I myself later experienced this flame in a frightening way—I shall speak about it anon—but now it was not recognizable as love. It was a powerful force that caused fear and anxiety, making me cry, "What on earth is happening to me?"

THE TERTIANSHIP LASTED for only six months and for the other six months of the year I was free to stay in the Philippines or to go abroad. At this time I was invited to give a retreat to the Carmelite sisters in Zamboanga. This was a wonderful opportunity to go from the Catholic atmosphere of Manila to what I had heard was the Christian-Muslim culture of Mindanao. I was warned that there might be danger and terrorism, but the sisters met me at the plane and assured me that they had good relations with the Muslims and there would be no problem.

Indeed, I found there a real effort at dialogue. There was a Jesuit university in Zamboanga and the bishops were anxious to talk to the Muslims. Sister Mary, a Carmelite out-sister, had close Muslim friends to whom she introduced me, bringing me even to the island of Jolo. I see now that the very existence of the human race may depend on dialogue between Muslims and Jews and Christians, with those Buddhists who, like the Dalai Lama, are friendly with everyone serving as go-betweens.

The plane that would return me to Manila was delayed for many hours and I spent the time talking to Sister Mary in the parlor. We talked not only about Muslims but also about prayer, contemplative prayer, in which we were both interested. Praying and teaching prayer was what we both wanted to do. Indeed, teaching prayer not only to laypeople but also to priests and even to bishops became the calling of Sister Mary. Convinced that the future of the Philippines will depend on the prayer of the people, particularly of the priests and bishops, Sister Mary has written small books that have been read by thousands.

Back in Manila, Sister Mary introduced me to the secular Carmelites. Virgil and Thelma Antonio became good friends. They welcomed me into their family where I stayed overnight, and later they both attended a retreat I gave in Hong Kong. Sister Mary also brought me to Cebu where I met her family, her mother and her brother and her charming nieces, Babette and Chona. Swimming in the sea with all these people was good for me. It brought me into a different world from the austere tertianship of Novaliches. We sometimes went to the movies, and, of course, we enjoyed the good Filipino food with its halo-halo and all the rest.

As Mary and I became more and more friendly I thought about Amy and whether this friendship might look like infidelity. It is true that friendship is different from marriage and there is no obligation to exclusivity, but I had read about how Teilhard de Chardin caused great suffering to his celibate friends and to himself by having several close relationships. Moreover, something happened that made me think.

One time when I returned to Tokyo from the Philippines, Amy met me at Narita airport and we went together for a meal. As we were eating, she fixed on me a somewhat unusually stony look and said, "Who is 'my dearest Mary'?" I knew immediately what had happened. The letters had got mixed up. I asked for the letter and, after looking it over, I said, "But there is nothing here. What's all the fuss about?" Amy answered quietly, "I made no fuss. You made the fuss." And that was that.

Nevertheless, I realized that there is a great responsibility in friendship. I saw that for me, friendship with a woman had to be founded on God and on prayer. Besides being an important opportunity for tremendous joy and support, such friendship is also an opportunity for growth and purification. The challenge is to love without clinging, to let go of the other, to let her have other friends while I have other friends. For me this has been a lifelong struggle.

I also see that all my relationships are built on my relationship with my father and mother and their relationship with one another. The same is true of my brothers. Psychologists who point to the first five or six years of life as being decisive are not foolish.

25
Serpent Power or Inner Fire?

As I HAVE SAID, tertianship in the Philippines lasted for only six months, and for the other six months I was free to give seminars or retreats wherever I was invited. My Indian friend Tony Coelho asked me to give retreats and talks in Bombay and Calcutta. Tony had helped us run the tertianship in Japan and during that time he and I had taken long walks through the beautiful mountains. Sometimes I wept on Tony's shoulder, but he did not take seriously my Shakespearian "alarums and excursions." And our friendship blossomed.

I had already been in India where an Irish Columban sister had arranged for me to go north and meet the Dalai Lama. On that trip I had made my way to Dharamsala and seen the little village with its Tibetan huts and working monks. I think I took part in their liturgy, and then I came face to face with the great man. He was cheerful and kind, even charming, but our meeting was quite uneventful.

So this time I went south to the ashram of Bede Griffiths, who impressed me tremendously. Tall and stately, with brown hair and a brown beard and dressed in saffron robes, he greeted me courteously and each morning after breakfast I visited his little hut where we talked about many things. Bede had a remarkable grasp of what was happening in the church and in the world and he had a sense of humor. After a while, he noticed that I did not attend his liturgy (I mean his recitation of the divine office— I did attend his Eucharist and I loved it) and he asked me to come. I suppose he was a true Benedictine and I was a true Jesuit.

Some people have said that Bede was naive, attracting weirdos from all over the world. This may be true. But he lived the Gospel. I enjoyed very much my stay in his ashram.

But let me get back to Tony Coelho.

After a week or two in Bombay we, a group of five or six, took the train for Calcutta. When we stopped off at a station on the way, we placed all our luggage in front of us on the platform. I had a beautiful little black briefcase that I treasured immensely and (what a naive fool I was!) I put into that case all my important possessions—passport, money, plane ticket, notes, and the rest. Going to the toilet I pointed to the briefcase (again, what a naive fool I was!) and said to one of our group, "Keep an eye on that briefcase!" Then I went away, and when I returned the briefcase was gone.

The fellow who stole my briefcase was a genius. He took it like a flash. No one saw him. I said afterwards that he deserved a Nobel Prize.

But everything important was gone and I could not continue my journey. Tony and I went to the local church where the pastor and his young curate received us kindly. I went to the police who promised to search for the precious bag.

However, a Catholic soldier from Kerala who came frequently to the church said to me with a smile, "Father, the police know very well who has your bag. But they are getting their cut!"

This gave me some insight into an India where not everyone was like Ramakrishna and Aurobindo. The Japanese would not act that way, I reflected. Or would they?

Anytime I lost something in Japan (and I lost quite a lot) it came back to me either through the police or from an individual. One time I left my wallet on the counter in a post office and when I returned an hour later it was still there. On another occasion I dropped my wallet on the street, and I got a card from the police telling me to come and pick it up. There is a basic honesty in the Japanese.

On the other hand, I have heard that Japan has one of the highest rates of organized crime in the world. The so-called *yakuza,* in cahoots with similar groups throughout Asia, are selling women, selling drugs, blackmailing, and making stupendous money in crimes that make the stealing of my little bag look like child's play. It seems that the *yakuza* have an understanding with the police. And, of course, they do good things, taking care of victims of earthquakes and *tsunami* and other disasters. But they present a tremendous problem of justice that has not yet been faced.

TONY WENT ON TO CALCUTTA after a few days and left me alone with the two priests. I was depressed. This was a real experience of emptiness and nothingness—*mu* and *ku*. I had followed St. John of the Cross and *The Cloud of Unknowing* in dialogue with Zen. I had prayed "nothing, nothing, nothing." And now God had answered my prayer with a vengeance. I was stranded in an Indian village with nothing.

Nor was my nothingness complete with the loss of my briefcase. I wanted to go to Calcutta for my seminar, but the police did not allow me to do this. I could not travel without a passport. They insisted that I go back to Delhi—to the Irish Embassy for a new passport and to the Indian authorities for a new visa. And all this, I was warned, would take time. Alas, the priests and sisters waiting in Calcutta did not understand my predicament. They thought I was simply depressed and unwilling to travel. Tony told me later that when he heard I was not coming, he broke down in tears. I felt (rightly or wrongly) that besides losing all my possessions I had lost my reputation.

Now I see that Our Lord was preparing me for the even bigger crash which was to come later. *I had to lose everything; I had to be attached to nothing.* That is the way of the mystics, of St. John of the Cross and Ramakrishna and Dogen and the rest. It is the way that Jesus outlines for his disciples, telling them to take no gold, no silver, no copper in their belts, no bag for their journey, no two tunics, no extra pair of sandals, and no staff. But my nothingness in India was only the beginning.

I arrived in Delhi and was greeted by the Indian Jesuits who kindly brought me to the Irish Embassy and the relevant Indian office. The Irish consul, a graduate of a Jesuit school in Ireland, was very courteous and when I explained my situation he said, "Ordinarily, in these circumstances, we give only a year's passport so that the person involved can get back to Ireland. However, Father, your circumstances are different...." I saw that our Jesuit schools in Ireland brought some advantages!

The Indian visa was more problematic and could have brought considerable difficulties with red tape and the rest. But the Jesuit who looked after me, the Australian assistant to the provincial, was applying for Indian citizenship and spoke fluent Hindi. He was friendly with the authorities, and I got my new visa in next-to-no time. This, together with the Indian dinner to which my Australian friend brought me, made me feel that after all Our Lord was looking after me.

Looking back on the whole situation, I do not know whether to laugh or to cry. I think I can laugh. The fellows who took my bag did me a tremendous favor. They prepared me for the experience of *mu* that was to come.

BACK IN THE PHILIPPINES for the next tertianship I found that I was in charge. Previously I had been assistant to Tom O'Gorman, who had now received a new assignment. I was his successor and had a couple of Jesuits assisting me. Elated at first, I soon found that this was to be another experience of nothingness and emptiness. When Tom was in charge, the tertians complained to me about their problems and I could show compassion and understanding with a smile. But now I was the target, and the tertians went to my assistants with their gripes. This was not so pleasant.

When a group of celibate men in their middle thirties are cut off from the world to live in a big house in the countryside, any commonsensical person knows that problems and squabbles will arise. So it was with us. And I was caught in the middle. One tertian told me wisely that I was not an institutional man and that I should be working as a freelancer. Another told me angrily that in trying to fix up a problem I had acted like a child. Yet another asked defiantly what the tertianship was all about. What was its aim, what were we there for, what were we trying to accomplish? This was more serious.

I said that, in my opinion, the aim of these silent six months was that the tertians should learn how to pray. Before going into a secular and busy world they should find their way to union with God. Otherwise they would quickly go down the drain.

And I tried to make the tertianship a place of prayer. Just that. Every day we all sat cross-legged (though those who preferred a chair could use one) for an hour before the Blessed Sacrament. I did not—I could not—teach pure Zen, but I was influenced by Kakichi Kadowaki and our tertianship in Japan. I realized that with Thomas Merton, Bede Griffiths, Abhishiktananda, Hugo Enomiya Lassalle, and the rest a new Asian mysticism was evolving in the Catholic Church. And we Jesuits could not neglect it.

And so I encouraged the tertians to repeat the mantra or ejaculation of their choice, or to use a koan from the Bible, and to enter into a contemplative and unitive silence. And most of them liked doing this.

At the end of the tertianship most of the tertians realized that they had prayed and learned something about prayer. And I think they realized that prayer is the most important thing in today's world.

However, I felt the tension. One time during Mass I felt weak and went out of the chapel, only to collapse in the corridor. When I came to, I found myself in bed with five or six novices grimly standing around me. They thought I had had a heart attack. But the hospital, after keeping me for a few days, said it was only stress or tension and recommended good food.

I had to get out of that atmosphere sometimes. I had to relax. My friends Virgil and Thelma Antonio were only too glad to show me the glories of Manila and to invite me for dinner with their five children, and I had other Filipino friends who took care of me.

Then my Carmelite friend Sister Mary came north from Zamboanga to teach prayer at the center for secular Carmelites where Thelma Antonio was a big-wig. Sister Mary and I sometimes went out for a good meal and we went quietly to movies on a couple of occasions. We enjoyed one another's company.

It became increasingly clear that for me celibate friendship with the opposite sex was a *sine qua non* for emotional balance and mental health. Not only that—it was also part of my way to God, and I believe it brought to God the persons I loved. This is not to say that it was easy, nor is it to say that I made no mistakes. It was in fact a great struggle.

As the tertianship came to an end, it became clear to superiors (how I dislike that word!) that I was not the man for this job and I began to prepare for a future elsewhere.

AND THEN AGAIN CAME TRAGEDY. Or was it comedy?

At the end of the tertianship we all went to Baguio in the mountains to make a retreat and to reflect on what had happened during those six months. One night, when I was in a deep sleep, something within, like a spring of water, came sizzling up inside me. It seemed to come from my belly (I prefer the Japanese words *hara* or *tanden*) to the surface of my consciousness and I woke in fear and trembling. What had happened to me? This swish! And I could not go back to sleep. I lay awake for the rest of the night.

We were in a Jesuit retreat house and the next morning I went in great distress to the Jesuit in charge and I gasped, "I can't sleep! I'm lying awake in anxiety and I don't know what I'm anxious about!" He listened carefully and said, "I don't know either. We'll have to wait and find out." That was not very helpful, but it was honest.

On reflection I saw that I had felt something of this inner energy for quite a while, but I was able to repress it in my waking hours. When I was fast asleep it could uninhibitedly come to the surface. But what was it? And why was I filled with anxiety?

Some Jesuits I talked to thought it was very good; others thought I was sick. To me it was like Gethsemane, and I wanted it to go away. My friend Tom Hand, who was deeply interested in Oriental spirituality, said it was a powerful energy that sounded to him like *kundalini*, or the serpent power of Hinduism and Buddhism. It was part of my journey, he said, and he wondered if it had something to do with my interest in breathing. I felt that he really understood.

Another Jesuit whom I met in Ireland saw it as something very valuable. "Throw away your sleeping pills and even your rosary," he said, "and attend to this inner fire." I could not throw away my sleeping pills immediately, but I appreciated this Jesuit and he became my director for some time.

I now think of the beginning of John's Gospel where Jesus speaks of a force that is greater than that in the conscious mind. "The wind blows where it chooses and you hear the sound of it, but you do not know where it comes from or where it goes." And Jesus adds, "So it is with everyone who is born of the Spirit." Was I born of the Spirit? And was this energy coming from an awakening of the indwelling Spirit, from something deeper than "me," pushing up more unconscious elements that needed to be healed?

These reflections, however, came much later when I saw how many religions speak of the awakening of a transcendent power that leads to mystical experience and a new life. "A man's spiritual consciousness is not awakened," said Sri Ramakrishna, "unless his *kundalini* is aroused." I wondered if my experience was something like the arousal of my *kundalini*. Or was it like the fire of love, the *incendium amoris* that some Christian mystics speak about?

THE TERTIANSHIP came to an end. I said good-bye to my friends in Manila and left for Hong Kong where I had agreed to give a couple of retreats.

And I carried my insomnia and anxiety with me.

26
The Song of Songs

I ARRIVED IN HONG KONG at the beginning of 1985. Little did I realize that the awakening in Baguio was the beginning of a crisis that would last on-and-off for five years.

Yes, it was an awakening, a frightening awakening, that I later associated with the Song of Songs when the bride, asleep in bed, hears the knocking on the door. "I slept but my heart was awake." I, like the bride, slept, but something deep in me was awake. "Behold, my beloved is knocking." The knocking on the door! This was a constant theme in my dreams. "Open to me, my sister, my love, my dove, my perfect one . . . ."

Who was knocking? I could not get out of bed to answer. Yet he persisted (yes, it was a man), "Open to me, my love. . . . for my head is wet with dew, my locks with the drops of the night." At last I opened the door, but the one who had knocked was gone. "I opened to my beloved, but my beloved had turned and was gone." Where was he? Why did he not come in?

I went out in search of him. "Have you seen him whom my soul loves?" The sentinels found me. "They beat me; they stripped me; they wounded me, those sentinels of the walls." But at last "I found him whom my soul loves. I found him and would not let him go."

Whom did I find after those five years in the darkness? Did I find my true self? Or was I like Mary Magdalene who, after her many tears, found Jesus who said, "Mary!" and she answered, "Rabouni!" And Jesus said, "Do not cling to me!"

He did not want to come in because he wanted me to go out. He wanted me to go out into the cold night where I would be stripped naked and beaten until I fell in the dust. Only then could I find him and not let him go.

AFTER A FEW DAYS with the Jesuits in Kowloon I crossed by ferry to the Island of Chung Chow to give a retreat in the beautiful Jesuit retreat house, high in the mountains, with its magnificent view of the blue sea in the sparkling sun. After being greeted by a group of priests, sisters, and laypeople, I began to conduct my contemplative retreat. I followed the Gospels in accord with the pattern of the Exercises of St. Ignatius, but I encouraged the people to become aware of their breathing, to recite the mantra of their choice, and to enter into unitive silence.

Among the retreatants was a Chinese sister who had studied psychology. And (wow!) had she acute psychological insight! She came to me for direction, but soon it became clear that she was directing me rather than I her. I spoke about my dreams and my fears, and she, a good counselor, understood me as Michel Ledrus had understood me in Rome, decades before. We talked and talked. She was always optimistic and encouraging. And at the end of the retreat I refused to accept her stipend, since she had done all the directing, helping me a lot. And like a good Chinese she accepted my proposal.

I had recurring dreams that terrified me. One concerned the knocking on the door. A tough man, a German with crew-cut hair, smashed down my door and drove me out to where a group of Chinese or Japanese were waiting. On another occasion I was asleep in bed and on the veranda outside I heard slow measured steps like those of a very strong man. "Knock! Knock!"

I shouted, "Come in!" and the steps reversed. The man who had been knocking went off into the night. I woke up, asking myself in terror, "Why did he not come in?"

In another dream I was jogging around the mountain, and I fell into a deep hole. That, too, was terrifying.

Another frightening symbol was the bell. The sound of any bell, whether a church bell or an alarm clock bell, would send shivers down my spine. Once I went to Macau and spent the night with the Jesuits. Outside the door of my room was a big clock that chimed every fifteen minutes. I spent a terrible sleepless night plagued by anxiety. In the morning I was desperate. It was not just the loss of physical sleep that upset me. Something more was going on.

Then during a retreat I began to turn over in my mind the words of Jesus in the Gospel, "I am." Suddenly I was overwhelmed by fear. What was it all about? I had thought that the words "I am" would lead me to the tremendous joy of enlightenment, but they filled me with terror. They left me shattered.

I tried to say these things to an Irish Jesuit friend who was a missionary in Kowloon. He was kind and tried to understand, but he thought I was sick. Many years later, I asked him if he remembered those days. "You were lucky to get out of that!" he said.

The Chinese sister was different. With her help I began to ask, very tentatively at first, if my troubles were a period of transition. Was the bell wakening an even deeper level of my unconscious self that was reluctant to be awakened, that wanted to remain asleep? Was the big self knocking on the door? Was this big self driving out the small self that had to die? Jogging around the mountain and falling into a hole in the ground! Was I falling into the emptiness of *mu* or *ku* that was pointing the way to enlightenment? Perhaps, after all, I was not sick but on a path of growth.

My problem was sleep. I could not sleep! The sizzling energy that had awakened me in Baguio, spiraling to the surface of my consciousness during deep sleep, grew and continued to irritate me. It was like a buzzing in my head. Eventually it irritated my whole body. Call it *kundalini*, the serpent power. Call it the fire of love. Call it the life force. Call it what you will. Whatever it was, it kept me frightened and awake and I kept swallowing sleeping pills.

Much later, an acupuncture doctor in Japan told me I did not need sleeping pills. I should be able to sleep without them. Or if I wished, I could take a tiny pill at night to allay my fears. In Ireland, my wise psychiatrist Eamonn Ryan asked me to describe this energy vibrating in my head, and then he said, "That's only the blood in your head. It won't do you any harm!" And when I kept asking him what caused this irritating vibration, he said with a smile, "That's the Western question. Why can't you just accept it as it is?"

I told this to Tom Hand, who remarked, "That shows he doesn't know what it is!"

Tom was right. In Hong Kong I did not know what this buzzing was. And I think my Chinese sister counselor did not know either. She understood very well my unconscious going back to my mother's womb. But now I see that in mystical experience there arises an extraordinary energy, sometimes causing depression and at other times bringing joy. Psychologists and scientists do not understand this. We need dialogue. Psychologists can help us trace our inner lives from the time we emerged from our mother's womb, but this alone will never explain the extraordinary energy of the mystical life. At first this extraordinary energy is frightening and even oppressive but later it becomes a living flame of love and brings the joy of ecstasy or enlightenment.

Be that as it may, experience of this energy brought a great change in my lifestyle. My friendships, my homilies, my retreats, my writing, and above all my prayer became better. Even my writing entered a new phase, and I believe that all the books I wrote after that time were deeper.

MY SIX WEEKS in Hong Kong were valuable, thanks to the wisdom of the Chinese sister and to the time I spent in prayer.

My next stop was Tokyo.

The Japanese provincial was not someone I could talk to, but he felt that a holiday in Ireland would do me good. I started the trip by flying from Tokyo to San Francisco and south to Salinas where I stayed with my old friend and cousin Brian Finegan, his wife Carol, and their daughter Coleen. I also met another Irish cousin, Harry, a doctor, who lived in northern California with his large family. Harry had some understanding for my problems. "Talk to some of your own men when you get to Ireland," he said. "Don't go to a psychiatrist!"

I stayed for a few days with my wonderful friends, the Carmelite sisters in Reno, and then took the plane to New York and on to Dublin. My sixtieth birthday, July 30, 1985, I celebrated in Cushendall, with my brother Kevin and his wife Eileen and their children, looking at the entrancing Scottish coast and drinking good Irish beer. From my letters they had thought that I was in really bad shape, and now they were pleasantly amazed to see me so perky. After a pleasant stay with them, I moved south to meet the Jesuits.

The Irish Jesuits gave me a great welcome. I suppose I was like the prodigal son who had left the Irish Province for more attractive things. A group of Jesuits was going on vacation to the South of Ireland (I think it was to Limerick) and I went with them. I am one hundred percent a northerner and I had never been south of Dublin. It was a new experience to see the world of "Angela's ashes."

Every day we went swimming in the blue Atlantic. The Irish provincial, a man in his late forties, was with us, and he loved to run along the beach and practice his yoga. One time a little boy was sobbing and refusing to go into the sea. His mother coaxed him, pointing to the provincial and saying, "Look at that old man! He's not afraid!" We had a great laugh at that. One of our Jesuits would point his finger at the provincial and say, "Look at that old man!"

I might add here that while the provincial was happy to welcome us "old missionaries" to Ireland for a holiday, he did not want us to stay. I heard that he said to one missionary, "If you are coming back, come back before the age of fifty-five." And about the missionaries from Hong Kong and Africa he said quite bluntly, "We don't want them here. And the general knows that!" This did not upset me. I didn't want to stay in Ireland anyway."

IN IRELAND, as in Japan and the Philippines, I needed friends. I needed people to talk to, one to one. While large groups are not quite my cup of tea, I have always found it necessary to pour out my soul to individuals whom I trust. And so (in spite of the advice of my cousin Harry) I went to see a psychiatrist, Eamonn Ryan, not precisely as a friend but as someone I could talk to about my inner struggles, confident that what I said would remain a secret between us.

Eamonn lived a short distance from the Jesuit theologate where I was staying, and I walked to his house a couple of times each week. He would always open the door personally, greet me cordially, and bring me to his small study upstairs. He was a tall man with fair hair and I thought he must be a couple of years younger than I.

Eamonn was extremely non-directive. He just listened to everything I said and made me feel unconditionally accepted. He had, moreover, a good sense of humor and I could tell him anything. In fact he was a good successor to Michel Ledrus to whom I had opened my soul in Rome more than thirty years before. Eamonn saw that my problems were intimately connected with my life of prayer. So, apart from sleeping pills, he gave me no medication. And when I said something about going to the hospital he reacted quite strongly, "There's no question of your going to the hospital! No question!" Just talking to him relieved my anxieties.

Another friend I could talk to—though not about my inner struggles—was an Irish Jesuit whom I shall call Noel. Nervous and something of an insomniac, Noel had a car and we drove around Ireland, visiting our old novitiate at Emo and reminiscing about our old master of novices. We had had similar experiences and could laugh. We visited other parts of Ireland, and since Noel had friends everywhere, we never stayed in a hotel.

We visited Tullabeg where I had studied philosophy from 1948 to 1951, and I recalled the old days with Frank Besses, Joe O'Meara, and John Hyde. I turned over in my mind the sentimental poem my mother loved to quote, "All, all are gone, the old familiar faces!"

But now in Tullabeg I had one of the most terrible yet most significant experiences of my whole life.

One night I was lying awake in bed. I could not sleep. I was looking up at the ceiling, when suddenly a column of smoke came down from the ceiling and struck my breast very violently with the tremendous clang of a bell. It was not just a symbolic experience; I felt deep physical pain and I shouted out, "Oh! Oh! Oh!" Then I lay awake. What was happening?

The next morning I went to Noel's room in my pajamas and tried to explain what had happened. Noel was in bed. He laughed. "You've a wonderful imagination, Bill," he said. "Now I'll tell you what to do. Take two of these pills" (and he gave me a small bottle of sleeping pills) "and start reading this book" (and he gave me a detective novel) "and you'll be asleep before you know where you are."

"He doesn't understand," I reflected. But I took his book and his sleeping pills.

I don't usually draw diagrams of my experiences, but this time I drew something like this:

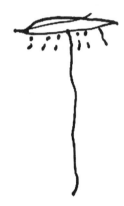

The drawing is crude, but it depicts the smoke pouring down and smashing my self open with the clang of the bell.

Later I spoke to Eamonn Ryan, who listened attentively. However, I don't think he was very impressed. He simply asked me, "Was it a dream?" But it was not a dream. I was wide awake.

Without explanation from Noel or from Eamonn Ryan I was left to my own resources. And after some years I came to see this incident as an awakening of my true self which, hard and brittle, had to be broken open violently with the crash and the clang of the bell. The smoke, I now see, came from a fire that came to burn within me. The smoke seemed to come down from above but perhaps it was like the serpent power rising up from below. The fire came to burn gradually. Only after some time could I call it a fire. Eventually, however, it became very strong and moved from my breast to my head and back again to my whole body. It kept me awake. It was not at all pleasant.

Was this the fire of love, the *incendium amoris*, experienced by many Christian mystics? In fact, I have met several people who have had this kind of experience, with shivering and trembling in their whole body. They have been prayerful people. One was an English woman who suffered very much. Another was a Chinese nun who, together with this type of experience, had out-of-the-body experiences and found herself unexpectedly in the chapel without actually going there. Again, the Catholic mystic, St. Philip Neri, experienced heat all over his body and laughed at the young men who were afraid of the cold. And St. John of the Cross, the mystic with whom I am most familiar, writes poetically of "the living flame of love that tenderly wounds my soul in its deepest center." When he writes this poem, the living flame of love is a tender and beautiful fire, but he hearkens back to an earlier time when the flame was oppressive.

I now see that this energy is awakened in people of all religions, and I believe it will have a special role in the dialogue between religions that lies ahead.

I SPENT MORE THAN SIX MONTHS in Ireland. And powerful months they were. Yet I was glad to get back to Japan, even though I was not completely liberated. And I knew nothing about what lay ahead.

The sad thing about friendship is that friends die. Noel died while swimming in Spain. Tony Coelho died in a bus crash in India. He had given his seat to a woman who had a child. Tony died in the crash; the woman and child lived. Eamonn Ryan died, but I have not heard how or when. I will die too.

"All, all are gone, the old familiar faces."

27
O Guiding Night!

My reading of St. John of the Cross and my study of *The Cloud of Unknowing* had introduced me to the dark night of the senses and the dark night of the soul. However, as I read Jung, talked to Michel Ledrus, and contacted Buddhism, I began to see the dark night as less mysterious than I had first thought. I began to see that it is nothing less than the purification of the unconscious that the Western world discovered only in the nineteenth century. Jung drew my attention not only to the personal unconscious but also to the collective unconscious and the archetypes and a whole world that lies beneath the surface of our daily, busy lives. This world I now see as the key to understanding meditation and mysticism. It was the key to understanding what was happening in my life.

My dark night entered a new phase in India when I lost my baggage and even my reputation. It continued in Manila when I seemed to mess up the tertianship. And then the smoke descending from the ceiling and my wild dreams were all part of the process of purification. In Jung, as I understand him, an archetype that demands purification in men is the feminine dimension or *anima*. This Michel Ledrus had pointed out to me, without explicitly referring to Jung, when he had said that my principal problem was my mother fixation. Jung held (and I wonder if he was speaking about himself) that for some men the integration of the *anima* is a life's work.

In fact I wonder if my whole dark night was rooted in my father and mother and the violence in Belfast, with the British soldiers questioning innocent people and searching them in the streets. When I was already in my sixties and returned to Belfast as a Jesuit, I saw British soldiers walking backwards down the Falls Road with guns pointing toward the ground, and I am still amazed at the unconscious rage that surged up within me and the tendency (which, of course, I resisted) to sympathize with the IRA, no matter what they did.

Perhaps the process of purification goes back even further to the collective unconscious. That is how I understand the agony and the dark night of Jesus in Gethsemane when he took on himself the sin of the world and faced up to all evil. In the garden he prayed, "Father, if it be possible, let this chalice pass from me. Yet not my will but thine be done." And I, like Jesus, though in my own little way, had to face up to purification through painful prayer in which my unconscious came to the surface and the trauma of my past claimed to be accepted. Only then could I forgive everyone in my whole life, not only my parents and teachers but even the British soldiers who walked backwards down the Falls Road with guns pointing toward the ground.

WHEN I RETURNED TO TOKYO from Ireland, I learned that Amy had accepted a post to teach English at a university in China. She, too, had her unconscious and she told me that in going to China she was living out the unconscious desire of her Chinese father who, born in Singapore, had always wanted to visit the country of his ancestors but never got much farther than British-occupied Hong Kong.

The departure of Amy was painful for me. My suffering in Ireland had made me deeply attached to her. Without her I felt lost. In fact, I wept, and I talked at length to my Irish friend Gerry Bourke as we walked through the mountains of Hakone. Amy and I exchanged letters (Amy was a powerful letter writer) and I became more and more interested in China, which was then in an early state of development.

In fact, however, Amy's going to China was a grace both for me and for her. Yves Raguin insisted that in the development of celibate friendship separation is quite necessary. He quoted the Gospel of John where the disciples were sad because Jesus had said he was going away, and Jesus said, "It is expedient for you that I go, because if I do not go the Holy Spirit will not come. But if I go I will send him." Raguin claimed that the early church fathers used these words in connection with the separation that inevitably comes in human friendship. Whether or not this is true of the fathers, I do not know. Quite certainly, it was true of Amy and myself. We came to a certain detachment that eventually brought the deep joy of celibate love, a true gift of the Holy Spirit. But that took time.

Anyhow, I saw Amy off at the airport and settled in to write my next book. The title of this book, *Being in Love,* I took from Bernard Lonergan who speaks of religious conversion as taking place when "my being becomes being-in-love." Here there is no object. I do not love anybody or anything. I transcend subject and object and become love. I found this in a masterly chapter in *Method in Theology* where Lonergan outlines the mystical experience *par excellence,* without using the word "mysticism." Here I found some similarity with Zen which, following the mystical tradition of Asia, goes beyond all dualism, saying that life and death are not two things but one. The fact is that all authentic mysticism goes beyond subject and object. I become one with the object but not one. This is, once again, the coincidence of opposites.

Some people have said that *Being in Love* was a new start for me, my best book until that time. I think it was. The dark night (or the beginning of the dark night) that I had been through gave me an extraordinary energy, which appears in this and in subsequent books. The energy rose from my belly—my *hara* or *tanden.* Was it *kundalini?* Was it the serpent power? At that time, I did not think of it in these terms, but now I do. Writing in the tradition of Timothy to Dionysius or the author of *The Cloud* to his dear disciple, I wrote to a fictitious character whom I called Thomas. The letter, however, was finally written to myself and about myself. It was autobiographical, an outline of the development of my own prayer. *Being in Love* was influenced by my life in Asia, but the reader will realize immediately that it does not teach Zen.

For this reason I think it was foolish on my part to accept the "Zen retreat" I was asked to give in Korea, just at that time. This was in 1986 when the church was beginning its admirable dialogue with Asian religions. I loved the dialogue, but I did not yet realize how different was my commitment and my culture from that of Zen Buddhists. I got the retreatants—mainly foreign priests and sisters—to sit cross-legged on the floor, to become aware of their breathing, to recite the Jesus Prayer or some other Christian mantra, and to enter into deep, contemplative silence. This teaching I do even today, but now I make no claim to be a Zen master, simply calling myself a teacher of Christian contemplation in dialogue with Zen and other Asian forms of prayer.

From Korea I went to the Philippines where I had agreed to give a couple of retreats, and on my way back I stopped off at Hong Kong to meet my Irish brethren. Then I went north to meet Amy, who was teaching English at the university in Jinzhou.

Amy was waiting at the airport in Beijing when I arrived and we had a great reunion. But what pell-mell was there! Mao, it is true, was no longer in control, but the airport was primitive, masses of people surged through the streets, while shoals and shoals of bikes flowed on and on. We took the night train to Jinzhou—I slept pretty well —and we reached our destination early in the morning.

I got a warm welcome at the university and was given a simply furnished room. The head of the English Department, who spoke fluent English, invited Amy and me to his home for tea. In accordance with government regulations, he had only one child but he invited all kinds of relatives and friends and we had a hilarious time. He also drove us to the Great Wall of China and I could throw my mind back through millennia of Chinese history. Amy told me she always attended Mass at the little government-supported church, but now I had brought wine and hosts so we could celebrate Mass together in my little room and talk about the Gospel of the day. Little did I realize that after a decade Christianity would be the religion of millions of Chinese and that, as Xavier saw so well, the key to the conversion of Japan was China.

After a few days I said good-bye to Amy and to all my new friends. One woman, whom I met again in Tokyo, presented me with a beautiful Chinese walking stick covered with designs. What a treasure it was! And what a tragedy when I lost it in Tokyo!

I took the train alone to Beijing, and soon I was back home in Tokyo.

FOR ME TOKYO IS ALWAYS HOME, but this time I entered the most strange and painful period of my life. My prayer went on, and I gave retreats, but a new area of my psyche seemed to have opened up. Perhaps it was a continuation of my prayer, a continuation of that experience when the smoke came down from the ceiling and broke open my inner self. I recall how, giving a retreat at Kiriyu high in the mountains, I lay awake all night, night after night. And this experience (I cannot find a word to describe it) at the very depths of my being went on. I could not sleep and I could not take sleeping pills. It was as though my being rejected sleeping pills and told me that I must remain awake.

A new dimension of energy or a new level of consciousness seemed to awaken, yet I did not toss around in bed. I lay in utter and deep silence. It was an experience of nothingness, a dark nothingness at the depths of my being. I was terrified at the thought of getting no sleep.

On that retreat was a sister I could talk to. She was kind and helpful, even though she could not understand what on earth was happening to me. Each day I went to a nearby convent. The sisters gave me a room where I could take some kind of siesta and drink a cup of tea.

The retreat over, I returned to Tokyo and talked to my good friend Al Nebreda. He was a cheerful optimist who laughed, told me I was okay and urged me to have the prostate operation that the doctor at Keio Hospital had recommended. This I did, but I became more and more upset. What was wrong with me? The fact that I could not sleep was very terrifying. Yet my inner being continued to say, "You *must* be awake! Do not sleep! Do not take those sleeping pills!"

Amy came back from China for her summer vacation, expecting a great welcome from me, but it was obvious that I was broken down. She was very distressed. Likewise, my Jesuit brethren concluded that I was sick. A young Irish Jesuit whose room was close to mine urged me to go back to Ireland. So I wrote to the Japanese provincial under the seal of privacy asking to go back to Ireland for a rest, and he immediately agreed.

WHAT WAS HAPPENING TO ME? That was my problem. Was this a Christian experience? Or was it a Buddhist experience? Or was it just a human experience? Or was I sick?

Let me say that all this took place in the 1980s when I was in my sixties. Only now in the third millennium can I look back on it all and smile.

In fact there was no "solution." I simply had to let the process take place. This was the advice I had received from the Chinese sister in Hong Kong at the beginning of my crisis. "Let the process take place," she had said. "Let God act! Don't fight against God!" And this was wonderful advice. Gradually, over a period of years (altogether it was five years), I began to sleep, at first with sleeping pills and then quite naturally. All the time I kept praying either with my mantra or my breathing or in silence. I celebrated the Eucharist each morning, either with my community or alone. And I recovered.

As I talked to men and women in difficulties I saw that my experience was not exceptional. I found holy and prayerful people who had vibrations or pains in their head and in their whole body and who suffered from insomnia, and these people were assured by doctors that nothing serious was wrong. I found some Jesuits who were branded as "sick," and the misunderstanding of ignorant superiors was an important part of their journey. In fact it has helped them to become mystics.

Needless to say, I got help from many people. During the summer, while taking the place of a priest in a northern island of Japan close to Russia, I talked to a Japanese sister about my insomnia. She laughed and said, "I am going to give you some homework. Don't sleep tonight! You must not sleep! Stay awake!" I followed her advice and it was good.

The Jesuit who understood me best was Tom Hand. I will never forget how he paused and said to me slowly, "Something very deep is going on in there!" And he was right. Something very deep was going on, and I had to let it happen. Tom and I talked a lot and we had a powerful mutual understanding. That was friendship!

I can now get a glimpse of what God was doing. I see that I was, and still am, on a mystical journey that is found in all religions with different symbols and in slightly different ways. This has enabled me to help others who walk with me on this path and to understand their suffering. Moreover, it helps me appreciate dialogue with the mysticism of other religions, getting rid of the narrow-minded triumphalism that I picked up earlier in my life. Hinduism, Buddhism, Islam, Judaism—all have much to teach us about the practical path of mysticism.

In terms of my own personal path, the first thing was, and still is, the following of Jesus to the cross and resurrection. Jesus is condemned to death by Pilate and I also am condemned to death. Jesus is made to carry his cross and I am made to carry mine. Jesus stumbles and falls and I do too. Jesus meets his mother and I meet mine. Veronica wipes the face of Jesus and a tender and loving Veronica wipes mine. Jesus is stripped of his garments and I too am stripped naked. Jesus dies on the cross and I will die on my cross. Jesus rises from the dead and I hope to join him in my resurrection.

AND I HAVE BEEN GREATLY helped by the Hindu description of this journey. Of special importance is the story of Gopi Krishna who finds at the base of his spine the serpent power known as *kundalini*. This rises up, suddenly or gradually, with enormous energy that knocks one for a loop and fills one's whole being. This is cosmic energy that fills the universe and moves the stars.

I have been helped by Buddhism. I have already spoken of the *Heart Sutra* and its doctrine of *mu* or nothingness or emptiness that resembles the Epistle to the Philippians where Jesus empties himself, taking the form of a slave. I have also been helped by the Buddhist search for the Ox, which is the true self. "Who do people say that I am?" said Jesus. And who am I? I tame the Ox. I ride the Ox. But then the Ox disappears. And I myself disappear in what is known as "the great death." This is the loss of the small self but the wonderful finding of the true self. And this doctrine helped me in my sleepless nights and anguished days.

Finally, I have been influenced by *The Cloud of Unknowing* and St. John of the Cross who led me into silence and into the dark night of the senses and the dark night of the soul. Is this doctrine influenced by neo-Platonism? It resembles the *mu* of Buddhism: all and nothing, *todo y nada.*

And so I can cry, "O Guiding Night! O Night more lovely than the dawn!" This was the night that guided me more surely than the noonday sun to where he waited for me, him whom I knew so well, in a place where no one else appeared.

28
Toward an Asian Spirituality

LET ME RETURN TO 1988 when I went back to Ireland. I thought I was a broken man, but what precisely was wrong with me I could not, and cannot, say. When I returned to Japan two years later the Japanese provincial, who was a psychologist and former master of novices, asked me if this kind of breakdown had happened before. I said, "Yes! It happened in my noviceship." I am now surprised at my own insight, but it was spontaneous and probably true. The provincial gasped in astonishment. "In your noviceship!" he said.

Anyhow, I returned to Ireland and was warmly greeted by the new provincial Phil Harnett who gladly opened the doors to returning missionaries. The enthusiasm with which he greeted me was in itself healing.

I stayed in the theologate at Milltown Park and once again went to my old psychiatrist, Eamonn Ryan, who had not changed. I felt he understood me really well and my recovery went on.

The Jesuits in the community thought I was a bit tired, but no one said I was broken down. And so I set to work on my next book, *Letters to Contemplatives,* which I think was pretty good. Like *Being in Love,* it was written in the light of what I had gone through. Most of the letters were in fact written to myself or about myself, even though I put other people's names on them. Particularly important is the letter to Robert, a great old contemplative, who had had a rough experience, something like mine. *Letters to Contemplatives* is now in a new edition from Fordham University Press, with a different title, *Letters to Friends.* The old reference to contemplatives put off people who did not aspire to deep prayer.

I spent a good deal of time in Northern Ireland with Kevin and Eamon and their families. Then came the question of whether or not I should go to the University of Santa Clara where I had been invited to lecture on mysticism East and West. Eamonn Ryan, as always, was non-directive, but I sensed that he thought I should go. So I packed my bags and headed for the United States.

I taught at the University of Santa Clara and the students received my lectures pretty well, particularly as we read *The Cocktail Party* by T. S. Eliot. This play has a romantic dimension that the students liked, but I also see the heroine Celia as a mystic who finally dies a martyr's death. Eliot does not use the word "God" even once. In this he was appealing to a modern audience but he was also influenced by the apophatic tradition of *The Cloud of Unknowing,* which he loved. Here God is the mystery of mysteries that no human word can express.

The students were enthusiastic about Eliot and *The Cocktail Party* and we had some good discussions, but I did not spend enough time with them. I still had my own problems and I wanted to talk to Tom Hand, who was really a friend in need.

Tom, like myself, had spent many years in Japan and, like myself, he had returned to his own country broken down. After some years, however, he studied theology at Berkeley and recovered completely. Then he settled into a retreat house called Mercy Center in Burlingame where he gave retreats and seminars while continuing his study of Zen and Asian thought. Tom, who had done Zen under Yamada Koun in Kamakura, was keen to bring Buddhist philosophy into the Christian message without in any way compromising on the essentials of the Gospel.

Tom and I had already been good friends in Japan, but we fought a lot. I was conservative and afraid of Zen, while Tom was enthusiastic, particularly about Yamada Koun, for whom he had immense admiration. Yamada recognized Tom's *kensho* (i.e., his first step on the road to enlightenment) and then Tom gave up his practice in the temple, though he continued to practice privately.

It was great to meet Tom in California. I told him my whole story, not omitting anything about my insomnia and my dreams. Unlike Eamonn Ryan, Tom knew about *kundalini*, though he preferred to use just the word "energy." He also knew about Zen and Christian apophatic contemplation. And his suffering had taught him both positive and negative things about the Society of Jesus. In one of his books he calls himself "a marginal man," and in calling myself a misfit I thought we had something in common.

We traveled around California by car, driving high into the mountains, always talking about mysticism East and West. I confess I could not fathom Tom's efforts to explain the Trinity in the language of the *Heart Sutra*, but anyone interested in this can find Tom's doctrine in his little book, *Always a Pilgrim*, which was published some years later. What helped me was his quiet and practical advice. I will never forget that.

Later, when he came to Japan, Tom listened to a homily given at Mass by a Spaniard in our St. Ignatius Church. "It was a brilliant homily," he said. "But exactly the same homily could have been given in Barcelona or New York! There was nothing Japanese in it." This comment was typical of Tom, who had a great love for Japan and a fantastic understanding of Japanese culture.

THIS WAS IN 1989 when the student riots broke out in Tiananmen Square. Television coverage was excellent. Tom and I spent hours watching the reports, our eyes glued to one of the most incredible dramas in human history. Surely that was an eruption of the collective unconscious of students who had been repressed for decades. It reminded me of the Japanese students in 1960 who had made Eisenhower cancel his visit to Japan, and again of the Japanese student uprising in the late 1960s, protesting against the renewal of the Security Treaty with the United States.

Now, in Beijing, Deng Xiaoping called in the military and the tanks rolled into Tiananmen Square. "What country would permit such a thing?" said a Chinese spokesman. But to Tom and me, the demonstrators looked like courageous youngsters calling for democracy and respect for human rights. The demonstration was brutally quelled—much more brutally than the corresponding demonstrations in Tokyo—and we saw on television courageous students forced to apologize for what they had done.

Amy was teaching in China at this time and I was worried for her, fearing that the demonstrations might spread to the whole country. So I phoned her sister in Hong Kong. Eric, her sister's husband, answered the phone and was very laid back about the whole thing. "No problem!" he said. So my mind was set at ease.

SANTA CLARA WAS RESTFUL for me, and I am still grateful to Tom for his companionship. The university did not invite me to return—I had neglected my work with the students—and I went back to Ireland. The Irish provincial, seeing that I was in good shape, agreed that it was best for me to return to Japan. So back I went.

I decided to return via Hong Kong and again meet the Irish Jesuits with whom I had studied decades before. From Hong Kong I took the plane to Qingdao where Amy was waiting at the airport. In the university car we held hands and she said, "So you're here!" Perhaps she thought we would never meet again, but God has his own ways. Somehow I take this meeting with Amy as the conclusion of a dark night that had lasted for five years—from 1985 to 1990, when I turned sixty-five. Not that I had no more problems. But one cycle was over.

Amy introduced me to an American family (a husband and wife with two children) who were teaching English at the university. We also walked around the parks of Qingdao where simple old people relaxed. It was a quiet city, giving no indications of the ruthless persecution of Christians, the appalling suffering of the Cultural Revolution, and the courageous bravado of Tiananmen Square. But it was a good place to rest, and after a few days we left for Beijing.

The train was packed. We were traveling with the cheapest tickets. The passengers, filled with curiosity, kept asking Amy in Chinese about this strange foreigner and what he was doing in China. In Beijing, Amy had booked two rooms in a little hotel where there were mainly Chinese but also a few foreigners. It never occurred to me that it might be dangerous, and in fact it was not.

We spent a good deal of time in Tiananmen Square with its huge picture of Mao Zedong. This man, responsible for the death of millions, is still (or so it seemed to me) hailed as the great leader of China and the one who had brought freedom. "The Chinese people, one quarter of the human race, have stood up . . . no one will ever humiliate us again," Mao had said in 1949. And, in spite of his merciless slaughter, millions of Chinese revere him as one who gave them self-confidence and self-respect, pointing to China as the future leader of the world.

With Amy Lim at Tiananmen Square in Beijing.

We visited a church and talked to the priest, who was very kind. However, I preferred to offer Mass in my little room in the hotel, and after a few days I left for Tokyo and Amy went back to Qingdao.

I was glad to get back to Tokyo, but I was not sure that I would be able to persevere. The upheaval of my dark night (if it was a dark night) had left me shaken and uncertain. Sometimes I wanted to return to Ireland, always with the understanding that I could come back to Japan if I wanted to. The American rector of Sophia, Father Gerry Barry, was very sympathetic. He agreed with my proposal. "Don't make any decision now," he said. And that was good advice. Gradually my old love for Japan emerged, and now in the third millennium I would not go back to Ireland for all the tea in China.

BACK IN JAPAN I continued to teach in Sophia, but because I was sixty-five my class load was reduced. I became more and more interested in the creation of an Asian spirituality. Speculative theology did not interest me much. Prayer and mystical theology were what I wanted to study.

Shusaku Endo had written in *Silence* about his need for a *Japanese* Christianity, but in his last novel *Deep River* (and the deep river, be it noted, is the Ganges) he is searching for an *Asian* Christianity, which he finds in India. The hero, a Japanese Catholic priest named Otsu (as always in Endo a holy misfit in the church), goes with several other Japanese to India in search of "something" that will give meaning to their lives. All find something in their own way. Otsu finds the mystical roots of Christianity and dies a martyr, carrying lepers to the river.

This novel became a movie which I enjoyed very much. It portrays Otsu praying in our chapel at Sophia University and brings out his celibate relationship with a Japanese woman who, after his death, weeps and weeps in a boat on the Ganges. When I visited Endo in the hospital just before his death he said in his weak voice that such a movie was unique in Japan.

I have become increasingly convinced that Christianity is deeply rooted in Japan and in China. In both countries Christians have undergone excruciating suffering with their eyes fixed on the crucified Jesus. The Japanese, it is true, do not lightly receive baptism. But many Japanese men are now married to Filipino women. They do not receive baptism but at heart they become profoundly Christian.

THE FACT IS THAT we Western missionaries made appalling blunders in our preaching of the Gospel. The first was that we tried to spread a European Gospel. The theology I learned in Tokyo was built on Plato and Aristotle and Augustine and scholasticism, complete with Thomas, the angelic doctor. We heard about Matteo Ricci but I had no idea of what he taught. Our theology was just the same as that taught in Milltown Park in Dublin.

The second blunder was our belief that in order to implant Christianity we had to destroy the Asian religions and ignore their wonderful tradition of meditation and mysticism. Asian culture, too, was "infected" by these religions and was studied by only a few mavericks.

The third blunder was that we cooperated one hundred percent with the colonial powers. The Irish Jesuit superior in Hong Kong was known for his constant, "The Governor and I . . . ." The colonials were the superior people. Wise men and women imitated them and spoke their languages—English, French, Spanish, or Portuguese. This was humiliating for the local people. Hence the appeal of Mao Zedong: "Never again will we be humiliated!"

But now the world has changed. Colonialism is over. A short time ago, when China and India began to talk, an Italian Jesuit remarked to me, "If these two countries get together we can forget about Europe!" I laughed at this. My friend was Italian, like Matteo Ricci and Robert de Nobili.

I have always thought that, even if these giants do not get together, the world of the coming century will be dominated by Asia. This means that the religions, including Christianity, must adapt to Asian culture and tradition. It means that we Christians, with feet firmly planted in the New Testament, must continue our dialogue with Buddhism, Hinduism, Islam, and with all the riches of this huge continent.

It was during this time that I wrote my two most important books, *Mystical Theology* and *"Arise, My Love . . ."* I wrote them with the conviction that only in mysticism can Western Christianity dialogue with Asia and with the belief that mysticism is the way of the future. That is why I put great emphasis on the 1986 Assisi meeting in which Pope John Paul II invited religious leaders of the world to come together to pray for peace. I see Assisi as the beginning of a new era in which dialogue is conducted not through philosophical reasoning but through prayer and mysticism. This surely is the way of the future.

A GOOD FRIEND OF MINE, a Japanese businessman, who was going to China with his wife, partly on business and partly on vacation, invited me to come along. We went first to Beijing and Sister Theresa Chu, a Chinese nun, came to our hotel (alas, it was a plush Japanese hotel!) and brought me to the seminary to give a talk to the Chinese seminarians. Sister translated my English into Chinese. I spoke about prayer to a large group of young men who listened attentively. After this, we went to Shanghai and visited the Cathedral of St. Ignatius, the old Jesuit church, where we attended Mass and met the priests. It was an exciting experience.

Back in Tokyo I heard a lecture by Bishop Tong of Hong Kong. Thoroughly Christian and thoroughly Chinese, the bishop had visited mainland China many times, speaking in friendly terms to government officials and to Chinese Christians. His aim in China was to talk to the Communist government and to create unity within the church. It would be wrong, he insisted, to think of the priests and bishops who work with the government as renegades or traitors. Many of them are heroic men who have suffered much for their faith. Thanks to their efforts, Chinese Christians are growing in numbers, even though their millions are a tiny fraction of the enormous population of China. The bishop said that Confucius and Mencius, properly understood, would play an important role in Chinese theology of the future.

I HAVE SAID THAT Shusaku Endo moved from his search for a Japanese Christianity to a search for an Asian Christianity. I myself saw something of this Asian Christianity when I stayed with Bede Griffiths at Shantivanam in south India. Bede's ashram was deeply Indian and deeply Christian.

In my book *"Arise, My Love..."* I refer to Jun Ikenaga, the Japanese archbishop of Osaka who, as I mentioned earlier, criticizes Western Christianity as being extremely dualistic, distinguishing between God and the universe, heaven and hell, good and bad, right and wrong, ending up with two worlds set one against the other. A Western Christianity, the archbishop notes, is extremely masculine. Eastern thought, on the other hand, is "monistic" and feminine. It is maternal and all-embracing. He appeals for a more Asian, more maternal mode of expression that will be acceptable to Asian people.

In fact there is a lot of this "monistic" or feminine spirituality in the Christian mystical tradition of the West. It is found in the coincidence of opposites that I keep referring to as the very core of mystical experience East and West. That is why I propose for the future a theology based on the mystical traditions of East and West, a theology that will enable us to see that all religions are good and that the religions can cooperate to bring peace to the world.

29
The Struggle in the Cloud

As I came out of my traumatic crisis, I existentially realized more and more that there are many layers of awareness in my psyche and that new layers, ordinarily dormant, had been awakened.

I had experienced incredible fear. I had not been able to sleep night after night. I had been terrified by the sound of a bell, and a knocking on the door had disturbed my dreams. I had been further terrified by the buzzing in my head.

Speaking of the transfiguration of Jesus I have often quoted St. Luke who says that the disciples "were afraid as they entered the cloud." And then I have asked, "What were they afraid of?" And I have answered my own question by saying, "They were stricken with fear by the cloud of unknowing into which they had entered." Now I began to wonder if that was what had happened to me. I had entered the cloud—or more correctly I had been drawn into the cloud—and I had been filled with paralyzing fear.

A new level of my psyche was opened in my noviceship. This was because in my prayer I repeated a mantra—the Jesus Prayer or "Come, Holy Spirit" or some words from the Gospel—that led me into deep silence. In this way I swept clean the upper layers of my psyche and allowed something of my repressed unconscious to emerge, but my noviceship crisis was also caused by the trauma of leaving home with all its securities and entering the lonely and frightening cloud of unknowing.

As my silence deepened, I kept going down to the depths of my being, particularly when I went to Japan (again leaving all security), entering the cloud of unknowing in the language school. And the climax came when the column of smoke descended from the ceiling and struck me forcefully on the breast, again opening up a frightening new world.

But eventually there came great joy and energy when I transcended the fear and found the one I loved waiting for me in a place where no one else appeared. Then I had a new energy that led me to write better books, to love men and women in a contemplative way, and to pray for hours before the Blessed Sacrament.

I sometimes think of Jesus in Gethsemane. So terrible was his agony that he even asked his Father to remove his chalice! Only secondarily did he add, "But not my will but thine be done!" And when he came out of the garden and was faced with the terrible suffering of crucifixion—only then, filled with the joy and energy, could he reprimand his disciple, "Put away your sword! The chalice my Father has given me, shall I not drink it?" It is as though he were now saying, "Let me drink the chalice. It is the gift of my Father. I want to drink it." What extraordinary energy was here!

And so I appreciate again Tom Hand's comment to me, "Something very deep is going on in there!" The deep thing was purification. Jesus went through purification for the sins of the world. I, in my little way, went through purification for my own sins and the sins of my ancestors. Can I dare to hope that, like St. Paul, I was also making up for what is wanting in the suffering of Christ for his body which is the church?

In my spiritual path, then, I experienced a very great energy that terrified me at first and made me suffer, but then purified me and led to joy and creativity.

This energy, I have said, is well known in the Christian neoplatonic tradition and is often associated with Bishop Nicholas of Cusa in the fifteenth century. Nicholas emphasized the unknowability of God, thus earning himself the name "Doctor of Ignorance." But Nicholas was no atheist. He was one of the main spokesmen for the *coincidentia oppositorum* whereby opposites come together so that we can at the same time know God and not know God, who is the mystery of mysteries. This way of speaking was carried into Eckhart, Tauler, *The Cloud of Unknowing*, St. John of the Cross, and the whole Christian apophatic mystical tradition.

I myself was educated in scholastic philosophy and theology, which had little interest in energy or mysticism. I read, it is true, the mystical theology of the Jesuits Auguste Poulain and Joseph de Guibert and their disputes with the Dominican Garrigou Lagrange, but these writers had little to say about my theological studies, and even in my prayer I was encouraged to follow the Exercises of St. Ignatius at the top level of consciousness. Mysticism was not even spoken about.

Then I discovered *The Cloud of Unknowing* and saw there the kind of prayer I wanted. While the Second Vatican Council was in session, I wrote my doctoral thesis, showing that the anonymous English author of this treatise, like St. John of the Cross, was completely loyal to the scriptures and to church teaching. This study was of immense value to me personally, letting me see that many of my problems stemmed from the fact that I was in the cloud of unknowing.

My study of the *Cloud* took place before and during the Second Vatican Council when the Catholic attitude towards other religions was negative. Hugo Enomiya Lassalle, it is true, was practicing Zen, but he was highly suspect and letters of protest were pouring into Rome.

The council, however, opened the Catholic Church to dialogue with other religions. In Orthodox spirituality, little influenced by scholasticism, I found great emphasis on energy, particularly in Symeon the New Theologian and his followers. But going farther East I found the *kundalini* of Gopi Krishna and others who speak of psychic energy in art and poetry and music and dancing. What psychic energy must have flowed through the veins of Shakespeare and Mozart and Beethoven!

I once read (I cannot remember where) that Jung, in a conversation with Einstein, asked if there might be nuclear energy dormant in the human person. Einstein was open to such a possibility. And, of course, in China and Japan energy (in Japanese *ki* and in Chinese *chi*) is central to human life. I need not say that energy is central to the lives of the Christian mystics—think of Padre Pio!—if only we have eyes to see. All this led me to see that energy in its various forms is a universal phenomenon.

A powerful way of tapping into that energy is through meditation, a moving beyond the top level of consciousness to a deeper level of awareness. Sometimes the top level goes wild (Teresa of Avila calls it "the fool of the house"), but that is irrelevant. One simply sits and breathes, reciting a mantra, entering into unitive silence, and opening one's being to the rise of energy. As will be clear, I am speaking here of the silent prayer of the *Cloud*. This prayer is found also in St. Paul who tells us in Romans that there are times when we do not know how to pray and then the Spirit teaches us to pray in wordless sighs. And the Christian mystical tradition puts great stress on the deep, deep silence that goes beyond all words.

Silent meditation of this type is also found in Asian religions. In Zen, for example, one enters into the depths of one's being where one finds the true self. When this happens one pays no attention to the upper levels of the psyche in order to remain in silent peace with the new self.

This makes dialogue between Buddhism and Christianity very fruitful. But it raises the question: Is the silence of the Buddhist and the silence of the Christian mystic exactly the same? Some Christians, after considerable experience in Asian meditation, have said that at this level of silence there is no difference between the Buddhist and the Christian. They hold that the *nada* of St. John of the Cross and the *mu* of the Buddhist are the same.

I was made to think of this whole problem when an Italian Jesuit cardinal gave a retreat to us Jesuits here in Tokyo. At question time I asked about "silent prayer." The cardinal said, "Silent prayer! Silent prayer! Yes, it is good. But if it is not based on the Bible I would be suspicious." Of course he was talking to Christians.

What the cardinal said struck me deeply. It fits with my experience. I enter into silence with a Christian mantra and from the silence I sometimes return to my mantra, be it the Jesus Prayer or a phrase from the scriptures. It seems to me that the Christian silence is penetrated with the explicit message of Jesus, the Buddhist silence is penetrated with the sutras (which the monks recite again and again and again) or with the koan.

While I love the *nada* of St. John of the Cross, I see it penetrated with the love of one who cries, "O living flame of love..." and "Upon my flowering breast which I held for him alone." This is not to deny that the Buddhist silence is filled with compassion. In neither case does "nothing" mean "no thing is there." In both cases there is content. The scriptures and the sutras are vitally important.

Perhaps it was for this reason that I could not continue my practice of Zen in a Buddhist context. I sensed that my experience was different from that of the Buddhist. And this may be something that Buddhists also recognize. I think of Hugo Enomiya-Lassalle who, as I noted earlier, may have been inwardly split or "divided." Although he practiced for many years under Buddhist masters, he was not greatly appreciated by the Buddhists. Yamada Koun, somewhat reluctantly, finally agreed that Lassalle's hours and hours of silent sitting in the lotus had led to something, but in Japan Lassalle was never recognized as a Zen master.

Each of us must retain our own basic identity and commitment. The Jesuit Kakichi Kadowaki, author of *Zen and the Bible*, asked about "double belonging," first made clear his Christian identity. The Dominican Shigeto Oshida guided the retreat known as *sesshin* and knew the Buddhist language, but he never said that he practiced Zen. Likewise the Carmelite Ichiro Okumura and the Jesuit Tom Hand.

IN 1995 AT THE AGE OF SEVENTY I decided to make another thirty-day retreat. Now I would go to north Wales where I had spent six months as an evacuee during the war. On one of my so-called repose days I went to Mia Hall where I had stayed with Joey Woodlock and so many friends. Where were they now? Old memories came to the surface of my consciousness.

I made the retreat in my own way. That is to say, I repeated my mantra—the Jesus Prayer or "Come, Holy Spirit"—and entered into contemplative silence, while the general themes of the Exercises hovered in the background. Each day I met my director, the well-known English Jesuit Michael Ivens, and I found him understanding and encouraging.

The big experience at that time, however, was not the Exercises themselves but my meeting with a young priest, also making the long retreat, who had gone through a traumatic experience very similar to mine. I was amazed when he told me of the inner fire he had experienced, his sleepless nights, his terrible fears, including a fear of not sleeping, his thinking he was going insane, his talk about going to hell, his seeming breakdown and consultations with doctors. He had had no contact with Asian religions except that he had read an article on *kundalini* which had fascinated him. He had read some of my books and was impressed by my advice, "Let the process take place!" and "Don't fight against God!"

I began to see again that deep religious experience—can I call it mystical experience?—is quite similar in Buddhism, Hinduism, and Christianity. In each case one breaks through the ordinary consciousness to a deeper consciousness. And this is frightening! Forces that were previously dormant are now awakened.

I also saw that Eastern medicine is of great value in these circumstances. I mean acupuncture, acupressure, breathing, massage, and the various ways of controlling the *ki* or *chi*.

Some years later I got a letter from this priest. He had just completed an eight-day retreat, a powerful experience, in which he spent the whole time with the same passage from John's Gospel. One word was enough.

This experience reconfirmed me in my conviction that we Christians must bring to life our mystical tradition if we would enter into dialogue with the spirituality of Asia.

30
The Mystical Way

AFTER RETIRING FROM THE UNIVERSITY I realized that my vocation for the few remaining years would be to pray and to teach prayer. This, in fact, had been my vocation from the first day of the noviceship but I had not always seen it so clearly. Now I knew without a doubt what I was called to do.

In the university I began by teaching English literature and then I moved to religious studies in the Department of Comparative Culture, the only part of the university where classes were taught in English for Japanese and for people from all over the world. Here, among other things, I taught an elective course on meditation for students of any religion or no religion. We sat with our backs straight, regulated our breathing and used a mantra, with each student choosing his or her own. I sometimes suggested a Zen koan that would be of universal validity.

Teaching this class I saw clearly the difference between religion and spirituality. Students who rejected all religion and called themselves agnostics wanted to meditate. Many were interested in Zen. I began to see why the spirituality of Buddhism is making such progress in Europe.

The world has changed radically since that fateful day in 1943 when my father gave me his blessing in Dublin and I took the bus to Emo in the center of Ireland to join the Jesuits. At that time we Jesuits, thirty-six thousand in number, had immense power in the whole world through schools and universities and magazines and retreat houses, and we had influential theologians who spoke authoritatively to the world.

Now in the third millennium we are faced with a different scenario. We live in a completely different world. No one knows when a crazy idiot in Iran or London, in North Korea or Washington will decide to press a button that will destroy our civilization. What can we do about that?

The threat of an atomic explosion is of special significance in Japan. This is the first (and until now the last) country with direct experience of horrific atomic explosions which in a second annihilated tens of thousands of civilians. And what was the result? When I came to Japan in 1951 I saw a whole country united in a "religion" of peace. "No more Hiroshimas! No more Nagasakis!" could be heard from one end of the country to the other. The Japanese felt that they, the first people to experience the bomb, had a duty or a mission to tell the world that this must never happen again.

One leader in this movement was a doctor who had lost his wife and his everything in Nagasaki. Takashi Nagai, whom I have already mentioned, pleaded to the world for peace. His book *The Bells of Nagasaki* and the song with the same title echoed through the country to which I arrived. Nagai was an artist and, as he lay dying of leukemia, he wrote his cry for peace in beautiful characters that he gave to thousands:

Nagai's formula for peace was simple. "Love your neighbor as you love yourself." This will change the world.

Nagai was a mystic of peace. His life and death have more significance for our future than the achievements and the speeches of Douglas McArthur, Winston Churchill, and Pope Pius XII. I realize that for America and China and Britain and France and the other great powers Nagai's plea to give up all nuclear weapons will sound like an impossible ideal. "We cannot do this," they will say. "The so-called rogue countries must abandon their quest for nuclear weapons but we need these weapons to maintain our security."

The Japanese said something similar about their war machine in the 1940s, and they were forced to eat their words. And the so-called great countries today will undergo an even worse fate than the Japanese if they

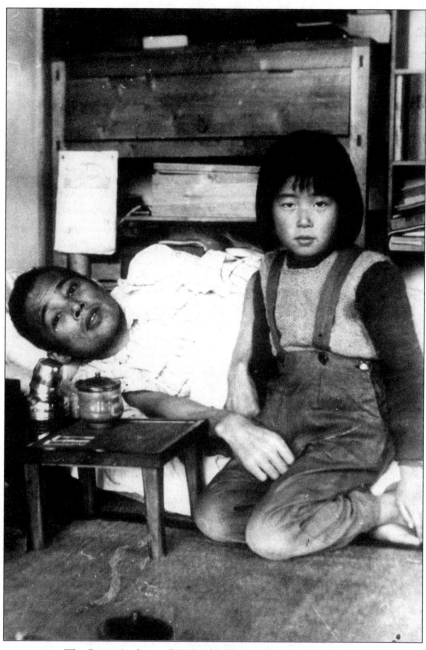

The "atomic doctor," Takashi Nagai, dying of leukemia,
here with his daughter Kayano.
(COURTESY OF THE NAGAI CENTER, NAGASAKI)

do not give up their nuclear weapons voluntarily, realizing that peace will come only through dialogue and prayer to God.

I am reminded of the disciples saying to Jesus, "Look at these wonderful stones!" And Jesus warned them, "Not a stone will be left on a stone. All will be destroyed!" Yet the message of Jesus was optimistic. The coming destruction was no more than birth pangs, the preparation for something very wonderful. And will the destruction of our civilization be like that? Will it be the preparation for something wonderful?

Takashi Nagai, a convert, got to the very heart of Christianity. He talked and wrote not just for Christians but for everyone, making a desperate plea that we all love one another and avoid world suicide.

I myself, having been criticized for my translation of Shusaku Endo's critical novel *Silence*, decided to make amends by translating into English *The Bells of Nagasaki*. It is the work of a sincere Christian who sees the essence of his religion in love of God and love of neighbor. My translation has been widely read, but amid all the talk of his beatification under Pope John Paul II, Nagai (alas, alas) has been overlooked.

Yet a somewhat similar plea for peace has been made by a Swiss theologian who came to Tokyo to receive the Niwano Peace Prize from the Buddhist religious sect, Rissho Koseikai. Hans Küng, seeing that peace cannot come from the efforts of one religion working alone, calls for a global ethic that will win the support of all the religions. Now his efforts, it is said, may lead to the promulgation of a global ethic by the United Nations. *The Japan Times*, commenting on Küng's visit to Tokyo, said that his work for ethical unity "may be one of the most significant events in the course of human history."

And if a global ethic is possible, what about a *global meditation?*

Today there are prayer meetings throughout the world. The charismatic prayer meetings are clearly ecumenical. Then there is the World Meditation Group founded by John Main and now carried on by Laurence Freeman, and there is the centering prayer of Thomas Keating and a group of Cistercians. These groups have been greatly influenced by Asia and most of their leaders have met the Dalai Lama. They are less interested in discursive prayer than in the repetition of a mantra, leading to contemplative prayer at the level of the true self. I see these prayer groups, together with the interest in Zen and in Transcendental Meditation, as significant steps forward in the onward thrust of the evolution of consciousness in today's world.

I have asked myself if we can do something like this in Tokyo. Actually, the fact is that we already are doing it in our little prayer group. When the group began, its leader was Nobuo Maruyama, who is a devout Christian, but soon he shared the leadership with Toshie Araki, a fervent Buddhist, who sits splendidly in the lotus posture and who eventually asked for baptism. (Alas, my days for sitting in the lotus are over and I now use a chair!). At first we called our meditation "Zen" and then it became just "Meditation."

A key characteristic of our little group is that it is interreligious. Even though we pray before the Blessed Sacrament, our group consists of Catholics, Protestants, Buddhists, and agnostics, and the non-Christians receive a blessing during the ensuing Mass. Finally, we are all closely united as we drink tea and eat Japanese cakes.

Looking back over the years, I recall two of my leading meditators, neither of whom was Catholic. One was a Buddhist who sat in the lotus posture with back straight and eyes half open. While the others received Holy Communion during Mass, she came forward for a blessing. Once, when I had to be absent, I asked a fellow Jesuit to take my place and he said to me afterwards that the Buddhist was ready for baptism. I was horrified! She was following her conscience, I told him, and that is enough. However, the surprise came. Quite unexpectedly the Buddhist lady asked for baptism. She had come to see that she could be a good Christian without abandoning her Buddhist heritage.

Another meditator was a Lutheran, loyal to her church and following her conscience. I realized that my approach to evangelization in Japan had changed. At first, like Xavier, I wanted everyone to be baptized; then I became more like St. Paul who said, "Christ did not send me to baptize but to preach the Gospel."

Let me say that I have baptized many Japanese and I am glad that I did so. They are happy in their faith. But I also see that millions of people throughout Asia and throughout the world will live the Gospel without baptism. Nor do I join my respected and beloved Karl Rahner in calling these people anonymous Christians (Buddhists find this terminology frightfully patronizing) but leave them to their own terminology. To these people, together with baptized Christians, I would like to teach meditation so that we may all work together for peace. This is what I mean by "global meditation."

Now, you may ask, what exactly does our little group do for peace?

To this I would answer that we are a tiny part of a world-wide meditation movement—consisting of Christians, Buddhists, Hindus, and agnostics—that addresses the very core of today's problems. We see the chief problem in our world today as being a craving for money and power and oil. I say "craving" or "attachment" because I believe that money and oil and power are necessary. But we are addicted. How can we be liberated from addiction?

This is where meditation enters in. I believe that the core of all meditation is "nothing." In the Christian tradition, we must slowly lose our attachment to everything. The Gospel tells us to take nothing on our journey. Unless we renounce all that we possess we cannot be the disciples of Jesus.

And Buddhism has a similar doctrine of nothingness or emptiness. Key words in Zen are *mu*, meaning nothing, and *ku*, meaning emptiness, represented by the powerful ideographs:

Both of these ideographs are translations of the Sanskrit *sunyata*. My friend, the top-flight Buddhist scholar Pier Paolo, used to say that *ku* meaning emptiness is the best translation, but *mu* being more mellifluous is repeated by the Zen meditator.

Moreover, Buddhism places the greatest emphasis on compassion, as Christianity puts its emphasis on love. This means that both religions, with different founders and different motivation, aim at liberating us from attachment to money and power and all things so that we can devote ourselves to the search for justice, to helping the poor and suffering.

Nor is this program of meditation just for the top dogs who rule the world. I myself have always sympathized with the underdog since childhood when I admired the IRA. But now I have renounced my sympathy for terrorism. I see that terrorists who use violent means are no less addicted than the rich. We must strive for justice by peaceful means. "The one who takes the sword will perish by the sword."

IN THE EARLY 1990s Amy returned from China and, after a brief stay in Japan, went to Australia to exchange her Hong Kong passport for an Australian one. We met a few times in Tokyo and then I saw her off at Narita as she took the plane south to stay with the Sacred Heart sisters near Sydney.

And then came the tragedy.

While walking in Tokyo, Amy once paused and said she felt she was losing her balance. I helped her to stand. And now from Australia she wrote that she had a brain hemorrhage and would have to undergo surgery. She had found a young Chinese Australian doctor who understood her case very well. He warned her, however, that after the surgery her face would be disfigured. Amy was seventy years of age and she sent me some photographs taken shortly before the operation, which would change her appearance for life. She still looked young and beautiful.

This news was a shock to me. While talking to a sister who taught at Sophia I broke down and wept. The sister was amazed at the intensity of my reaction. "They don't know you!" she said. And by "they," I suppose she meant the Jesuits. Anyhow, I kept in touch with Amy and with her superior in Japan and I learned that the surgery had gone well.

AT THAT TIME Laurence Freeman, director of the World Community of Christian Meditation, invited me to lead his seminar in Canada. I had known Laurence for some time. He had always joked that I went to Japan the year he was born. This made me feel ancient.

I enjoyed the Canadian seminar very much. Most of the participants were laypeople who already had a life of prayer and were anxious to learn about Oriental meditation. They were cheerful and enthusiastic. It became clear to me that the future of the Catholic Church is in the hands of the laity. The laity will, of course, consult the hierarchy and the priests, but they will make their own decisions through discernment.

At the seminar I met an Australian woman who invited me to give a series of lectures in Australia on prayer. So, a few months later, after all the preparations had been made, I found myself in Australia.

Amy, together with an Australian nun, met me at the airport in Sydney. Her surgery had been a great success, but, as she had foreseen, her face was disfigured. At first this was a shock to me but soon I realized that our love was much deeper than anything external. Her surgery and its effects only deepened our relationship and made it more contemplative.

I stayed with the Sacred Heart sisters for a few days. Then Amy and I went to a Jesuit retreat house to make an eight-day retreat together.

Each morning we prayed separately and in the afternoon we got together to talk about our prayer experience. This was good. Yet Amy, reflecting on the experience afterwards, felt that she had thought too much about me and not enough about Our Lord and she did not want another retreat like this. So that was that.

My lecture tour went well, even though I had periods of anxiety and sleeplessness. This was in the 1990s and the Australian church was going through the same crisis as the church elsewhere. Priests were leaving to get married. The Jesuit master of novices left the priesthood. Priests were accused of sexual harassment. What was the answer?

One thing was clear to me. If there was a crisis, I was part of it. I was a celibate priest in this turbulent world. I felt all the struggle and all the suffering that my fellow priests were going through. And the crisis was affecting not only priests but also sisters and brothers and laity.

My first response was prayer. I had learned to pray in my noviceship and had remained faithful to my hour of prayer each morning. My prayer had developed in Asia and become contemplative. This meant that I had a sense of God's presence at the depth of my being and at the depth of the universe. I prayed constantly to the Holy Spirit for light. And even though I committed plenty of sins and made umpteen mistakes, I was aware that God was with me. I was, to use a term that Michel Ledrus had used many years before to describe me, "cyclothemic." That is to say, I plunged into something like despair before rising up to hilarious good-humor. All this I tried to share with the people who came to my lectures.

In the area of chastity I felt (and still feel) deeply grateful to Yves Raguin. I recall those cool evenings when we walked in the garden of the Jesuit house in Taiwan and Yves spoke movingly about the beauty of friendship with women. Yves was a mystic and I began to see that the friendship he recommended was contemplative. He did not deny the power of physical sexuality but said that we celibate people must go beyond it. This was a great struggle but a happy one. I have experienced the joy he speaks of not only in my friendship with women but also in friendship with my fellow Jesuits.

I love the Second Vatican Council's statement that companionship between man and woman is "the primary form of interpersonal communion." The word "communion" appeals to me. I have not been seeking for cooperation—even though this is of great value—but for communion like that which I experience while kneeling before the Blessed Sacrament in the chapel. To come to this communion in friendship takes prayer and time, and it may involve failures, but I believe it is the acme of chastity for celibate and married alike.

BACK HOME I WAS ASKED TO GIVE a retreat to some sisters at a retreat house near Tokyo. I gave my first talk with something like élan, but to the surprise of the community I did not show up to celebrate the Eucharist. The sisters were concerned and went in search of me. They found me lying unconscious on the floor of my room. It seems that they put me in an ambulance and drove me to the hospital. I say "seems" because I remember nothing. I can recall only that I woke up in bed and found my Jesuit superior and the infirmarian sitting beside me smiling. The hospital had apparently done all kinds of tests on me, but I had been unconscious and remember nothing. After two days the doctors told me there was nothing wrong with me and they saw no reason for me to stay in the hospital. So I went home.

The whole thing was a mystery. I phoned across the Pacific to Tom Hand, who at that time was in the Jesuit infirmary in California. When he heard my story, Tom said immediately, "Bill, that was a spiritual experience!" As usual Tom understood me best and I am grateful to him.

This kind of thing has happened to me so often that I have been forced to look again into the whole question of what in India is called *kundalini* and in Christianity the inner fire of love. I have discovered this energy all through the Bible. In the New Testament power and energy go out from Jesus. I see a tremendous energy in the destruction of Jerusalem and in the death of Jesus—when the veil of the temple is torn in two from top to bottom.

But to understand this extraordinary power I now see that we must read the Bible with the eyes of the mystic rather than with those of the scholar.

31
From Ego to Self

AND SO MY STORY comes to an end. I have called it a mystical journey and that is what it is. In this book I have written about the major problems in my life and my attempts to solve them. It has not been my intention to give solutions that will suit everyone. I am quite sure that many of my readers will not agree with what I have said and done. But I have tried to be authentic and to tell the truth. Not the whole truth—since I trust my reader to understand that I have a right to my secrets—but the truth that stands out in my mind and may interest others who struggle with the baffling mystery of life.

A short time ago some representatives of BBC television came to Japan to make a video about Christianity in Japan. We spoke at length about this country and finally we touched on Ireland. I must have given myself away, because my interviewer asked, "Is the North of Ireland still in you?" I answered, "Yes!"

"After fifty years in Japan!" he gasped.

I began this book by saying that I was born in the midst of terror. I really was. And when I returned to Ireland after seven or eight years in Japan I smiled, seeing in huge letters on the gables of the houses in the Falls

In Belfast, the house where I was born, as it is today.

Road, "BRITS OUT." This reminded me of my childhood and of my ego that was now dying or being transformed. For the big thing in my life of meditation has been the death of the ego and the birth of the true self. In childhood my ego cried for a united Ireland and I admired the gunmen who sacrificed their lives for this noble cause. Now my ego was dying—or was it being transformed?

My big self, almost unconsciously, still wanted a united Ireland. Now it was willing to work for this through dialogue with people of different ideas, with peace and joy and love. And I cannot help feeling that throughout the North of Ireland many people, like me, are losing their little ego and finding their true self. My brother Kevin, who visited the prisons in Belfast, found some political prisoners looking for a non-violent solution. Surely our hope for the future is in people like these.

My experience of Northern Ireland gives me sympathy for terrorists in the Middle East and the whole world. It is not that I sympathize with violence—far from it!—but I see many people suffering from very terrible injustice, destroyed by nations that talk about freedom in their search for oil. The great task of the religions—Islam, Buddhism, Judaism, Hinduism, Christianity—is to collaborate in teaching the world, particularly these suffering people, about justice and peace through dialogue.

My brother Eamon at the Johnston grave in Belfast.

All the great religions have a powerful mystical tradition which, I believe, can save the world and civilization. In my own experience I have found the distinction between the ego and the true self both in Asian religions and in the Christian mystical tradition and I was fascinated to find it also in Jung. Human consciousness is multilayered. The ego is at the top level of consciousness and it is here that most people lead their lives, often tortured by the craving for money and power. But there are deeper levels, ordinarily unconscious, into which we can enter. Vertical meditation provides a way of entering into these deeper levels, of going down and down to the awakening of the true self.

In this book I have described how I was led from the ego to the self. I began in the Jesuit noviceship with a rational meditation, using the so-called three powers of the soul—the memory, the understanding, and the will. I thought about the truths of the Gospels and the truths of the Spiritual Exercises of St. Ignatius and I spoke to Our Lord.

As time went on, however, my prayer became more simple as I repeated one ejaculation like "Lord Jesus, Son of the Living God, have mercy on me a sinner," or "Come, Holy Spirit." These aspirations entered so deeply into my consciousness that I found myself repeating them not only in time of prayer but even when I was engaged in other activities. A new level of consciousness was awakened and I found that I had a strong sense of presence.

When I came to Japan I quickly realized that this kind of meditation exists in other religions and is called "mantra meditation," mantra being the word for ejaculation or aspiration. I have learned a lot from these religions, especially about sitting with back straight and reciting my aspiration, or remaining silent with deep breathing. For me, the breath is a symbol of the Holy Spirit and I have spent many hours in silent abdominal breathing. "I will breathe in, I will breathe out." In this way I believe I am filled with the Holy Spirit. I also began to practice some kind of yoga, training my body for silent meditation.

I entered a new phase when I entered into deeper areas of awareness and my unconscious surfaced. This period I now see as my dark night of the soul. I was overwhelmed by fear. I could not sleep. The sound of a bell shocked me terribly. (Since then I have learned that in some Asian traditions the sound of the bell is the sound of the very origin of the universe). Then came the knocking on my door both in dreams and in conscious life. Finally there was within me a frightening movement which I now call a ray of darkness. This I could not understand. It was oppressive and frightening.

In this book I have related how I spoke to various people who helped me. Most important was the Dublin Jesuit who said categorically, "Throw away your sleeping pills and even your rosary! Attend to this inner fire!" How right he was. For the dark night was my way to mysticism and the torturing ray of darkness eventually became a ray of light, the raging fire that St. John of the Cross calls a living flame of love.

I have spoken about my dark night in the earlier pages of this book. I bring it up again because I begin to ask if this darkness is not only in myself but in the whole church and the whole world. As I see the terrorism and the earthquakes, the scourge of AIDS and the scandal of pedophilia, the storms and the wars, I ask myself if we are in the midst of a great religious crisis, leading us to something good. Are the great religions being called to open themselves to the mysticism which is their authentic heritage, the mysticism that will eventually save the world? Are the religions being called to work together to move the world away from its little ego that is playing with nuclear weapons to the true self that really wants love and peace?

Collaboration between the religions is already under way. When I came to Japan in the 1950s Hugo Enomiya-Lassalle had already seen the beauty of Zen and was practicing in Buddhist monasteries. In India Abhishiktananda and Bede Griffiths had felt the appeal of Hindu forms of prayer. Later the Indian government gave a state funeral to Mother Teresa—what other country would have done that? And in Europe Christians of various denominations were gathering with love and understanding to pray together.

With the Second Vatican Council we Catholics were reminded that what matters is that each person follow his or her conscience. We were told to appreciate and even to promote the good in non-Christian religions. Dialogue became popular.

All this was very important for me, as I was studying theology and teaching religion in Japan. I was particularly impressed by the prayer meeting in Assisi in October 1986. This, significantly enough, was not held in the Vatican and was not organized by the Roman Curia. It was held in Assisi, the home of the much loved *Poverello*, and put together by the lay community of Sant' Egidio. The charismatic Pope John Paul II insisted that it was not a theological congress but a meeting of prayer. In holding this meeting, Pope John Paul II opened a great future for communion between religions. The pope emphasized peace. He wanted the world to see that there is another way to peace, that is, the way of prayer in common.

Needless to say, there were objections. The pope, I have been told, insisted that he was following the Second Vatican Council. I encountered some questioning in the BBC interview about which I spoke at the beginning of this chapter. My interviewer, who was a fervent Christian, said with some perplexity that he had met in Japan people (probably Buddhists) who had no sense of God but only of the universe. I saw immediately that he was up against the old distinction between Buddhists and Christians, namely that Christians were dualistic (they see God and the universe as separate) and Buddhists were monistic because they see only the universe. And in fact I now see that this problem can be solved only by the coincidence of opposites whereby we see that God and the universe are one and not one, just as man and woman are one and not one, life and death are one and not one, all religions are one and not one.

Those who gathered in Assisi were not there to engage in discussion of philosophical or theological issues. The participants were there to pray. First there was a long period of silence. Then the participants went to various parts of Assisi to pray according to their orthodox traditions. In my opinion, both of these forms of prayer were essential. In their traditional prayer Catholics knelt before the Eucharist (how happy I was to see this!) while Buddhists recited the sutras and Muslims used the Koran. It is clear that Muslims will not sacrifice the Koran, as Christians and Jews will not sacrifice the Bible and Buddhists will not sacrifice the sutras.

Assisi of 1986 was no more than a beginning, but enthusiasm for interreligious prayer is growing fast. As I see meetings like Assisi, where God is so clearly in the hearts of all the participants, I know that God is very pleased and will continue to pour grace and love and light into such meetings. If we continue to develop this communal prayer, God will surely bless our crazy human family with peace and justice and love.

Acknowledgments

Many people helped me to write this book. Some of them, like Pier Paolo Del Campana, Bill Everett, and Tom Hand, have already gone to God. Of the living I am particularly grateful to Dermot Brangan, who read each chapter as it was written and made valuable comments. Dermot does not necessarily agree with all that I have said but he is a loyal friend. And how can I express my gratitude to Gerry Barry who worked assiduously on his computer to help me? Then there is Amy Lim who gave me marvelous inspiration, and Matt Shimamoto and SuJa Ra who gave me constant help and encouragement. Then there is Nobuo Maruyama and all those who join me in meditation, particularly Hiroko Goto and Toshie Araki.

For anyone who would like to know more about my story, I have left letters and photographs with my good friend Caroline Carney who lives in Northern Ireland in Dumdrum. Caroline's mother, one of my oldest friends, toddled with me to the kindergarten of the Dominican Convent on the Falls Road. She has carefully read these pages, making her comments and expressing her appreciation.

I hope and pray that what I have written will give my reader reasons for living and hoping.

Index

Numbers in italics indicate photographs.

Abe, Masao, 152–53, 167
Abelard, Peter, 51
Abhishiktananda (Swami), 94, 163,
     165, 176, 218–19
Akijiro, Aki, 70
Alcoholics Anonymous, 75
all and nothing, 52. See also *todo y
     nada*
Always a Pilgrim (Hand), 196
America, decline of, beginning with
     Hiroshima bombing, 56
Amy. *See* Lim, Amy
Angela's Ashes (McCourt), 91
anger, as problem of terrorists, 19
anima, integration of, 187
Antonio, Thelma, 171, 177
Antonio, Virgil, 171, 177
Aquaviva, Claudio, 126
Aquinas, Thomas, 77
Araki, Toshie, 210
archetypes, 93
"Arise, My Love . . ." (Johnston), 199,
     200
Aristotle, 53
Arrowsmith, Bob, 120
Arrupe, Pedro, 68–69, 70, 78, 79,
     80, 82, 90, 95, 101, 123, 128,
     142, 157, 160–61, *161*, 166, 169
Art of Good Writing (Couch), 23
Asia, acceptance of Catholicism in, 61

Assisi, prayer meeting in, ix—x, 83,
     99, 199, 219–20
Association for Contemplatives, 124
atomic explosion, threat of, 206–9
Australia, 142–43

Barrett, Boyd, 80
Barry, Gerry, 198
Being in Love (Johnston), 189
Belfast, 22, 56–57, *215*
The Bells of Nagasaki (Nagai), 207,
     209
Berchmans, John, 37
Bernard of Clairvaux, 51
Bertagnolio, Luciano, 72
Besses, François (Frank), 54, 55, 56
Bitter, Bruno, 65, 68
Bosch, Franz, 67–68, 82
Bourke, Gerry, 57, 61, 64, 67, 70,
     188
Boxer, Charles, 66, 106
Brennan, Jack, 89
The Bridge on the River Kwai, 82–83
Brooke, Basil, 1
Buddhism, 14, 26; dialogue with,
     151; monastic vows of, 34;
     St. John of the Cross resembling,
     52. *See also Zen entries*
Buddhist-Christian dialogue. *See*
     Christian-Buddhist dialogue

Burns, Flavion, 104
Byrne, Tommy, 47, 48, 55, 82

Call My Brother Back (McLaverty),
    57
Cap (priest at the Bog), 51
Capra, Fritjof, 74
Caraman, Philip, 160
Carlson, Clayton, 124
Carmelites, 123–25
catechism, teaching, 14
Catholic Church, future of, in hands
    of laity, 212
celibacy, 213
Celibacy for Our Times (Raguin),
    130
celibate friendship, 128
celibate love, 87
centering prayer, 138, 209
chastity, 36, 130, 213
cheerfulness, virtue of, 35
China: Christianity in, 61, 198;
    church in, challenge confronting,
    61; persecutions in, 59–60
Chinmoku (Endo). See *Silence*
Christian-Buddhist dialogue, 76,
    137–38, 152, 153, 204
The Christian Century in Japan
    (Boxer), 66
Christianity: deeply rooted in China
    and Japan, 198; essence of,
    38–39; meditation movements
    within, 94
Christian moral theology, 27
Christian-Muslim culture, 171
Christian Zen (Johnston), 114, 118,
    137
Churchill, Winston, 19, 21, 22, 37,
    155, 160
Clearkin, Thomas ("Pa") (author's
    grandfather), 3–4, 15, 17
Clearkin, Winnie (author's mother),
    2, 4, 6–7, 8, 9–10, 11–12, 16,
    17–19, 21, 22, 24, 26, 33, 35,
    37, 44, 47, *54*, 56–57, 86, 89

Close, Leo, 2
Close to Jesus, 11
Cloud of Unknowing, x, 50, 53, 73,
    101–2, 126, 142, 162, 193, 203
The Cocktail Party (Eliot), 195
Coelho, Tony, 173, 174, 175, 186
coincidence of opposites, 50, 52,
    115, 151–52, 154–55, 158, 162,
    167, 189, 200, 219
collective unconscious, 74, 88, 93,
    187, 188
Collins, Lady, 124
Come Back, Come Rope (Benson), 24
Communion, 20
confession, 20
consciousness, top level of, 51, 87,
    92, 114, 141, 203
contemplation, call to, 52, 126
contemplative prayer, 157, 169;
    effects of, 72; Ignatian introduc-
    tion to, 125
contemplative retreats, author lead-
    ing, 138
Conway, Bill, 23, 24
Conway, Joe, 89
Copleston, Frederick, 160
Craig, James (artist), 3
Craig, James (Lord Craigavon)
    (member of Parliament), 1
Cromwell, Oliver, 7
Cullen, Francis, 22, 43
Cumman na mBan, 2

Dalai Lama, 39, 75, 145, 155, 173
Daly, Cahal, 53
D'Arcy, Martin, 160, 162, 166
dark night, 73, 87–88, 170, 187–89,
    193, 218
de Caussade, Jean-Pierre, 31–32, 126
Deep River (Endo), 80, 111, 198
de Guibert, Joseph, 95, 126, 202
Del Campana, Pier Paolo, 64, 65,
    66, 67, 69, 71–72, 79, 80, 85,
    101, 114, 129, 133, 143,
    149–50, *150*, 152, 211

de Mello, Tony, 94
Deng Xiaoping, 196
de Nobili, Robert, 60
Denzinger, Heinrich, 71, 77
de Valera, Eamon, 9–10
Devane, Dicky, 25
Dezza, Paolo, 79, 169
discernment, 95
discipline, the, 43–44
Dōgen, 34, 104, 146
Doi, Cardinal, 80
Donders, Rachel, 165
Donnelly, Don, 58
double belonging, 118, 133–34, 204
Doyle, Charles, 11
Doyle, Willie, 11
dreams, 92, 93, 140, 142, 181
Dublin, 46
Dumoulin, Heinrich, 92, 99, 102–3, 104, 116, 118, 137

Eastern medicine, 205
Eckhart, Meister, x, 27, 50, 104
ego, 25–26
Eiko High School, 66
Einstein, Albert, 203
election, 139–40
Eliade, Mircea, 129
Eliot, T. S., 162, 195
Elworthy, Priscilla, 8
Endo, Junko, 111
Endo, Shusaku, 80, 107–12, *108*, 144, 154, 198, 200
enneagram, 170
Erlinghagen, Helmut, 99–100
Evangelista, Tony, 101–2, 160–61
Everett, Bill, 149
examen, 42
examinations, 77–78

fainting, author's predisposition to, 79–80
Fatima, secrets of, 169
Ferreira, Christopher, 107
fidelity, 159

Finegan, Brian, 183
Finegan, Carol, 183
Finegan, Coleen, 183
forbidden books, 71, 85
forgiveness, as only method of healing, for terrorism, 19–20
Forster, John S., 65–66
Fox, James, 103
Francis of Assisi, 136
Freeman, Laurence, 209, 212
Freud, Sigmund, 86, 92
friendships, particular, 43

Gandhi, Mahatma, 75
Gaudium et Spes, 93, 148
Glenravel (Northern Ireland), 15–16
global ethic, 209
global meditation, x, 209–11
Glynn, Mortimer, 44
God: being in love with, 11; presence of, 42, 57, 72
Gonzales, Emmanuel, 78
Gopi Krishna, 192, 203
Grace, "Putty," 14
Graham, Aelred, 103
Green, Elmer, 124, 125
Greene, Graham, 110–11, 144–45
Gregorian University (Rome), 49
Gregory, St., 20
Grey Eminence (Huxley), 35, 126
Griffiths, Bede, x, 74, 92, 94, 173, 176, 200, 219

Hakuin, 34, 146
Hall, Willie, 43
Hand, Tom, 134, 152, *152*, 178, 182, 192, 195–96, 202, 205, 214
Harnett, Phil, 194
Hearn, Lafcadio, 56
Heart Sutra, 154, 162, 192, 196
Hermoso, Francisco, 63
Herzog, Peter, 80–82, 109
Hinduism, 14
Hirai, Tomio, 124
Hitler, Adolf, 16

Hogan, Arnie, 89
homosexuality, 132
Hong Kong, 58–59, 179–83
Hongo, way of life in, 113–14
Humani Generis (Pius XII), 50
Huxley, Aldous, 35, 126
Hyde, John, 39, 49, 51–55, 53, 102, 148

Ignatius of Loyola, 20, 35–36, 39, 73, 74, 77, 95, 120, 126, 142, 159
Ikenaga, Jun, 154, 200
The Imitation of Christ, 45
incendium amoris, 170
India, 173–75
infused contemplation, 51, 72, 125–26
The Inner Eye of Love (Johnston), 163
Insight (Lonergan), 49, 147, 148
insomnia, author's, 32, 43, 64, 181–82, 190–92
interpersonal communion, 213–14
interpersonal relations, 131–32
Ireland, 183–84, 215–16. *See also* Dublin, Northern Ireland
Ivens, Michael, 205
I Would Like to Be a Japanese, 101

Jaffe, Aniela, 93
Janssens, Arnold Baptist, 54–55, 64, 65, 128
Japan: anti-American feelings in, 100; author's arrival in, 56, 63–64; author's exposure to, effect on prayer, 137; bombing of, in World War II, 65, 66; changes in, 112; Christianity banished in, 106–7; Christianity rooted in, 60; martyrs of, 106–7; peace as religion in, ix; student problems in, 105–6
Jenkins, Paul, 89
Jesuits. *See* Society of Jesus
Jesus Christ, divinity of, 146–47
Jesus Prayer, 31, 32, 139

Jogues, St. Isaac, 37
John of the Cross, St., x, 27, 39–40, 50, 51–52, 73, 88, 95, 127, 135, 142, 155–56, 162, 170, 193
John Paul II, ix–x, 79, 160, 169, 199, 219
Johnson, Tom, 67, 68, 69
Johnston, Anne (author's sister-in-law), 88, 158
Johnston, Anne Junior (author's niece), 158
Johnston, Eamon (author's brother), 5, *5*, 10, 11, 12, 15–16, 18, 22, 23, 37, 44, *54*, 57, 88, *216*
Johnston, Eamon (author's nephew), 88
Johnston, Eileen (author's sister-in-law), 183
Johnston, Kevin (author's brother), 4–5, *5*, 10, 11, 17, 18, 22, 44, *54*, 57, 63, 89, 158, 183, 216
Johnston, Mary (author's aunt), 4, 15, 16
Johnston, Thomas (author's brother), 4, *5*, 10, 11, 17–18, 19, 21, *54*, 57, 158
Johnston, William (author), photographs, *5, 13, 27, 54, 58, 132, 141, 180, 218*
Johnston, William (author's father), *2*, 4, 5, 6, 7, 9, 10–11, 12, 15, 16, 17, 18–19, 21, 22, 23, *27*, *54*, 89
Jokiel, Heinrich, 71
journaling, 46
Joyce, James, 91
Julian of Norwich, 74
Jung, Carl, 26, 46, 92–93, 130, 142–43, 187, 203, 217

Kadowaki, Kakichi, *118*, 118–19, 130, 137, 156, 176, 204
Kant, Immanuel, 49, 148
Kapleau, Philip, 134

Keating, Jim, 24
Keating, Thomas, 209
Kelly, Bob, 43, 89
Kelly, Hugh ("Hugo"), 42, 45–46,
    47, 49, 89, 91
kenosis, 153
Kerr, Hugh, 15
Kitagawa, Joseph, 129
Knowles, David, 104
koan practice, 154
Koseikai, Rissho, 209
ku, 99, 153, 174–75, 211
kundalini, 170, 178, 182, 192
Küng, Hans, x, 209

Lagrange, Garrigou, 134
Lallement, Louis, 126
Lassalle, Hugo M. Enomiya, x, 54,
    64, *75*, 75–76, 104, 115–16,
    117–18, 129, 133–34, 136, 137,
    176, 203, 204, 218
learned ignorance, 154
Ledrus, Michel, 72–73, 85–88,
    89–90, 92, 128, 159, 187
Letters to Contemplatives (*Letters to
    Friends*) (Johnston), 73, 194
Lewis, C. S., 35
Lim, Amy, 131, *132*, 133, 149, 150,
    165, 172, 188–91, 196–98, *197*,
    212–13
Liverpool, 10–11, 15
The Living Flame of Love (St. John of
    the Cross), 155
Lonergan, Bernard, 11, 38, 49, 85,
    88, 96, 136, 147–48, 189
Lost Horizon, 12
lotus posture, author discovering, 149
Luhmer, Klaus, 102
Lumen Vitae, 90, 91

MacArthur, Douglas, 56, 65, 66
MacErlean, Mary (author's grand-
    mother), 4
Mackey, Ernest, 45
MacMahon, John R., 25

Maguire, Mairead Corrigan, 8
Maharishi Mahesh Yogi, 94
Maharshi, Ramana, 146
Main, John, 94, 138, 141–42, 209
mantra meditation, 94, 217
Mao Zedong, 56, 59, 197
Marella, Cardinal, 137
Marmion, Joe, 52, 89
Martin, Malachi, 43
Martini, Father Provincial, 108
Maruyama, Nobuo, 210
Masao, Tsuchida, 70, 82, 84
Mathy, Frank, 67, 105, 107
McCourt, Frank, 91
McCoy, Dan, 81, 149
McDermott, Billy (author's uncle), 15
McDonald ("Pa Mac"), Father,
    31–32, 37
McErlean, John (author's cousin),
    4, 5
McKelvey, Hugh, 2
McLaverty, Michael, 57
McMullan, John ("Jakie"), 23, 24,
    32, 57
meditation: Asian tradition of, 114;
    faith as core of, 119; true self
    awakening in, 26. *See also* global
    meditation, mantra meditation,
    Transcendental Meditation
Merry in God (Doyle), 11
Merton, Thomas, x, 39, 76, 94,
    102–4, *103*, 118, 132, 137, 176
Method in Theology (Lonergan), 147,
    189
Michiko, Kamba, 100
Milward, Peter, 91, 101, 105
mind, multilayered nature of, 93
mindfulness, 156
The Mirror Mind (Johnston), 130, 163
missionaries, as conquering force, 59
monasticism, Christian-Buddhist
    similarities, 34
Moore, Brian, 23
morality, as fidelity to one's true self,
    96

Mother Monica, 11
Mother Teresa of Calcutta, 75
Mott, Michael, 104
Mount Fuji, *62*, 63
mu, 88, 135, 163, 175, 193, 211
Muggeridge, Malcolm, 73
Mulhall (Muller), Father, 45–46
mystical experience, 205
mystical life, energy of, 182
Mystical Theology (Johnston), 199
mysticism, 32, 39, 75, 77; desire
    for, 95–97; dialogue with
    science, 124; types of, 104;
    universal vocation to, 163
*The Mysticism of "The Cloud of Un-
    knowing"* (Johnston), 104, 123

Nagai, Kayano, *207*
Nagai, Takashi, 66, 207, *207*, 209
Nash, Robert, 24–25
Neary, John, 29, 32–33, 45
Nebreda, Al, 191
Neri, Philip, 186
Newman, John Henry, 50
Nhat Hanh, Thich, 155
Nicholas of Cusa, 50, 154, 202
Nishitani, Keiji, 154
non-dualism, 154–55
non-violence, author's conversion
    to, 7–8
Norena, Carlos, 64, 67, 68, 69
Northern Ireland, conflict in, ix,
    1–5, 7, 9–11, 15, 19, 23
North Wales, 9–10
novitiate, author's time in, 29–33,
    35–40

obedience, 36–37
O'Brien, Joe, 80
O'Connell, Dennis, 30
O'Conor, Charles ("Charlie"), 41,
    42, 44–45, 47
O'Flaherty, Vince, 138–41
Ogon mo Kuni (*The Golden
    Country*) (Endo), 107

O'Gorman, Tom, 168, 176
O'Grady, Luigi, 82, 89
O-Hige Sama, 67
Okumura, Ichiro, 118, 137, 205
O'Meara, John, 50
O'Neill, Barney, 30, 52–53
option for the poor, 166
O'Rahilly, Alfred, 11
Oshida, Shigeto, 104, 116–17, *117*,
    136, 137, 204–5
Oxford University, 159, 160–64

Padre Pio, 104, 144, 145–46
Pannikkar, Raimon, 137
Paul, St., 31, 73, 145, 147, 153,
    162–63, 164, 167, 203, 210
Paul VI, 78, 137, 160, 161
Pearse, Patrick, 18
Peeters, Hubert, 82
personified Evil, 73–74
Petitjean, Père, 107
Pfister, Paul, 68
Philippines, 166–72, 176–78
Pittau, Joseph (Giuseppe), 79, 113,
    123, 127, 160, 169
Pius X, 67
Pius XI, 71
Pius XII, 37, 50, 58
pope, obedience to, 78–79
Poulain, Auguste, 202
poverty, 35–36, 166–67
prayer: abandoning Jesuit practice
    of, 93–94; author's attraction to,
    24–25; horizontal vs. vertical,
    87, 92; ordinary vs. extraordi-
    nary, 125; regulated at Rathfarn-
    ham, 44–45
probabilism, 20
purification, 187–88, 202

Raguin, Yves, 87, 128, 129, 130,
    130, 132–33, 150, 188, 213
Rahner, Karl, 132, 169, 210
Ramakrishna, 104, 146, 178
Rathfarhham Castle, 41, 43, 44–45

religion, distinguished from spirituality, 206

Religion and Nothingness (Nishitani), 154

religions, dialogue among, 34, 61, 71, 118, 119, 121–24, 129, 134, 137–38, 146, 189

renunciation, 34

Rhyl County School, 19–21

Ricci, Matteo, 60, 64

Roberts, Tommy, 12–13

Rome, author's return to, for study, 84–90

Roothaan, John, 95

Russel, Johnny, 89

Ryan, Eamonn, 182, 184, 185, 186, 194–95

sacrament of the present moment, 31–32

Saint Francis Xavier's (Jesuit college), 11, 12–15, 19–21

Sambokyodan, 133, 134

scholasticism, 49, 50–51, 77

Scots Presbyterians, 5

scruples, 18, 20, 25, 45–46

A Second Collection (Lonergan), 147, 148

Second Vatican Council, 38, 50, 71, 73, 74, 93, 98, 127, 131, 137, 145, 147, 148, 203, 213, 219

self, moving to, from ego, 217

sex, author's struggles with, 85–87, 89–90, 92, 127, 156–57, 164–65, 170

sexual abuse, by priests, 168–69

sexual intercourse, 155–56

Shakujii, 70–76

Shaw, George Bernard, 91

Shinmeikutsu, 116, *116*

Shogo, Hayashi, 70

silence: accepting call to, 94; author drawn to, 31–32; author's attraction to, 51; call for, x

Silence (Endo), 13, 80, 106–9, 111, 144, 198, 209

Silent Music (Johnston), 124

Sister Laureen, 123–24

Sister Mary (Carmelite out-sister), 171–72, 177

Sister Mary Pius, 6

Sister Theresa Chu, 199–200

Slater, Jack, 63

Society of Jesus: approach of, to contemplation, 126; approach to Asia, 59–60; as aristocracy of Catholic Church, 27–28; author's entering, 25, 27, 29–30; author's questioning of vocation in, 140–41; author's time in novitiate, 29–33, 35–40; changes in, 78–79; forbidden topics among, 43; importance to, of Society's name, 128; reconciling fidelity to their conscience with obedience to church, 159–60; positions in, 77–78; reduced influence of, 161; spiritual marriage of, 39; spirituality of, reconciling with Carmelite spirituality, 52; survival of, 142

Song of Songs, 88, 136, 147, 155–56, 179

Sophia University (Tokyo), 54–55, 67–68, 98, 99–100, 101, 105–6, 123, 143–44, 160, 169, 198

Sophocles, 86

The Spiritual Exercises (Ignatius of Loyola), 20, 31, 35–36, 51, 75, 87, 95, 125, 127, 138–39, 141–42, 169–70

spiritual marriage, 39

Steere, Douglas, 118, 119, 137

The Still Point: Reflections on Zen and Christian Mysticism (Johnston), 120, 121, 133

St. Malachy's College, 10, 23–24

Suarez, Francis, 37

Suzuki, Daisetsu, 76, 102
Suzuki, Shunryu, 122
Symeon the New Theologian, 203

Teilhard de Chardin, Pierre, 79, 92,
    126, 132, 172
terrorism, caused by anger, healed by
    forgiveness, 19
tertianships, 41, 82, 89–90, 156–57,
    168, 176
Theophane the Recluse, 73
Thérèse of Lisieux, 25
third eye, 49–50
The Three Pillars of Zen (Kapleau),
    134
three powers of the soul, 31
Tiananmen Square, 196
todo y nada, 88, 95, 109, 125, 153,
    163, 193
Tong (bishop of Hong Kong), 200
Transcendental Meditation, 94
true self, 25–27
Tullabeg ("the Bog"), 46, 48–55
Tyrrell, George, 71

Uchiyama Kosho, 50, 162, 164
ultimate reality, confrontation with,
    20
unconscious, purification of, x
United States, author drawn to
    (1970), 119–20
universal Christianity, 61
University College (Dublin), 42,
    46–47
University of San Francisco, 120,
    121–22
upper community, at Rathfarnham,
    45–46

Valignano, Alessandro, 60, 100
vertical theology, 36–37

vocation, mystery of, 25–27
Voss, Gustav, 66, 78

Walsh, James, 102
Werbalowsky, Zvi, 119
West, materialism taking over, 74
Western missionaries, blunders of,
    198–99
Western nations, imposing culture in
    Asia, 58–59
The White Man (Shiroi Hito) (Endo),
    110
Williams, Tommy, 23
Wilson, Des, 24
Woodlock, Joe, 13, 13–14, 15,
    19–20
World Community of Christian
    Meditation, 212
World Meditation Group, 209
World War II, 17–19, 21, 22, 37
The Wounded Stag (Johnston),
    165

Xavier, St. Francis, 43–44, 56

Yamada Koun Roshi, 117, 129,
    133–36, 156, 195, 204
Yoshinari, Kono, 70, 71

Zaballa, Al, 120, 122l, 133
Zamboanga, 171
Zen, 26, 27, 50, 75–76, 118
Zen and the Birds of Appetite (Mer-
    ton and Suzuki), 102
Zen Center (San Francisco), 122
Zen-Christian dialogue, 115–19,
    122, 129–30
Zengakuren, 105
Zen Mind, Beginners Mind (Suzuki),
    122
Zen tertianship, 156–57